Ethical Dimensions of
Political Communication

PRAEGER SERIES IN POLITICAL COMMUNICATION
Robert E. Denton, Jr., *General Editor*

Ethical
Dimensions of
Political Communication

Edited by
Robert E. Denton, Jr.

Praeger Series in Political Communication

New York
Westport, Connecticut
London

Library of Congress Cataloging-in-Publication Data

Ethical dimensions of political communication / edited by Robert E.
   Denton, Jr.
        p.   cm.—(Praeger series in political communication)
      Includes bibliographical references and index.
      ISBN 0–275–93550–7 (hb. : alk. paper)—ISBN 0–275–93551–5 (pbk. :
   alk. paper)
      1. Communication in politics—Moral and ethical aspects.
   2. Political ethics.   I. Denton, Robert E., Jr.   II. Series.
   JA79.E8185   1991
   172—dc20   91–3552

British Library Cataloguing in Publication Data is available.

Library of Congress Catalog Card Number: 91–3552
ISBN: 0–275–93550–7 (hb.)
      0–275–93551–5 (pbk.)

First published in 1991

Praeger Publishers, One Madison Avenue, New York, NY 10010
An imprint of Greenwood Publishing Group, Inc.

Printed in the United States of America

The paper used in this book complies with the
Permanent Paper Standard issued by the National
Information Standards Organization (Z39.48–1984).

10 9 8 7 6 5 4 3 2 1

This book is dedicated to my sons,
Robert E. Denton III and Donald Christopher Denton,
with love and the hope
that they grow in the ethical dimensions of life.

Contents

About the Series

Those of us from the discipline of communication studies have long believed that communication is prior to all other fields of inquiry. In several other forums I have argued that the essence of politics is "talk" or human interaction.[1] Such interaction may be formal or informal, verbal or nonverbal, public or private, but always persuasive, forcing us consciously or subconsciously to interpret, to evaluate, and to act. Communication is the vehicle for human action.

From this perspective, it is not surprising that Aristotle recognized the natural kinship of politics and communication in his writings *Politics* and *Rhetoric*. In the former, he establishes that humans are "political beings [who] alone of the animals [are] furnished with the faculty of language."[2] And in the latter, he begins his systematic analysis of discourse by proclaiming that "rhetorical study, in its strict sense, is concerned with the modes of persuasion."[3] Thus, it was recognized over two thousand years ago that politics and communication go hand in hand because they are essential parts of human nature.

Back in 1981, Dan Nimmo and Keith Sanders proclaimed that political communication was an emerging field.[4] Although its origin, as noted, dates back centuries, a "self-consciously cross-disciplinary" focus began in the late 1950s. Thousands of books and articles later, colleges and universities offer a variety of graduate and undergraduate courses in the area in such diverse departments as communication, mass communication, journalism, political science, and sociology.[5] In Nimmo and Sanders's early assessment, the "key areas of inquiry" included rhetorical analysis, propaganda analysis, attitude change studies, voting studies, government and the news media, functional and systems analyses, technological changes, media technologies, campaign techniques, and research techniques.[6] In a survey of the state of the field in 1983 by the same authors and Lynda Kaid, they found additional, more specific areas of concern, such as the presidency, political polls, public opinion, debates, and advertising, to name only a few.[7] Since the first study, they also noted a shift away from the rather strict behavioral approach.

Today, Dan Nimmo and David Swanson assert that "political communication has developed some identity as a more or less distinct domain of scholarly work."[8] The scope and concerns of the area have further expanded to include critical theories and cultural studies. While there is no precise definition, method, or disciplinary home of the area of inquiry, its primary domain is the role, processes, and effects of communication within the context of politics broadly defined.

In 1985, the editors of *Political Communication Yearbook: 1984* noted that "more things are happening in the study, teaching, and practice of political communication than can be captured within the space limitations of the relatively few publications available."[9] In addition, they argued that the backgrounds of "those involved in the field [are] so varied and plurist in outlook and approach, . . . it [is] a mistake to adhere slavishly to any set format in shaping the content."[10] And more recently, Swanson and Nimmo called for "ways of overcoming the unhappy consequences of fragmentation within a framework that respects, encourages, and benefits from diverse scholarly commitments, agendas, and approaches."[11]

In agreement with these assessments of the area and with gentle encouragement, Praeger in 1988 established the Praeger Series in Political Communication. The series is open to all qualitative and quantitative methodologies as well as to contemporary and historical studies. The key to characterizing the studies in the series is the focus on communication variables or activities within a political context or dimension. Scholars from the disciplines of communication, history, political science, and sociology have participated in the series.

I am, without shame or modesty, a fan of the series. The joy of serving as its editor is in participating in the dialogue of the field of political communication and in reading the contributors' works. I invite you to join me.

Robert E. Denton, Jr.

NOTES

1. See Robert E. Denton, Jr., *The Symbolic Dimensions of the American Presidency* (Prospect Heights, IL: Waveland Press, 1982); Robert E. Denton, Jr., and Gary

C. Woodward, *Political Communication in America* (New York: Praeger, 1985; 2nd ed., 1990); Robert E. Denton, Jr., and Dan Hahn, *Presidential Communication* (New York: Praeger, 1986); and Robert E. Denton, Jr., *The Primetime Presidency of Ronald Reagan* (New York: Praeger, 1988).

2. Aristotle, *The Politics of Aristotle*, trans. Ernest Barker (New York: Oxford University Press, 1970), p. 5.

3. Aristotle, *Rhetoric*, trans. Rhys Roberts (New York: Modern Library, 1954), p. 22.

4. Dan Nimmo and Keith Sanders, "Introduction: The Emergence of Political Communication as a Field," in *Handbook of Political Communication*, Dan Nimmo and Keith Sanders, eds. (Beverly Hills, CA: Sage, 1981), pp. 11–36.

5. Ibid., p. 15.

6. Ibid., pp. 17–27.

7. Keith Sanders, Lynda Kaid, and Dan Nimmo, eds. *Political Communication Yearbook: 1984* (Carbondale: Southern Illinois University Press, 1985), pp. 283–308.

8. Dan Nimmo and David Swanson, "The Field of Political Communication: Beyond the Voter Persuasion Paradigm," in *New Directions in Political Communication*, David Swanson and Dan Nimmo, eds. (Beverly Hills, CA: Sage, 1990), p. 8.

9. Sanders, Kaid, and Nimmo, *Political Communication Yearbook*, p. xiv.

10. Ibid.

11. Nimmo and Swanson, "The Field of Political Communication," p. 11.

Foreword

For over 2,000 years, political writers have linked the practice of politics with human ethics. Plato's *Republic* is essentially a work of political ethics, as is, of course, Aristotle's *Nicomachean Ethics*. For Plato and Aristotle, politics was the "master science" because they could not conceive of anyone living outside of and apart from a political community. In addition, for both Plato and Aristotle, the good "man" was identical with the good citizen in the right polis. The concept of civic virtue implies a citizenry that is informed, active, and enlightened (i.e., selfless) and that seeks justice. Politics was conceived as a process of issue development, public deliberation, and social resolution.

In the ancient classics, the search was for the best life and the best polis. Today, we have largely abandoned that search. Our quest follows more the thoughts and philosophies of Thomas Hobbes, John Locke, John Stuart Mill, and Sigmund Freud: self-preservation, self-actualization, comfort, convenience, property, and ultimately the pursuit of happiness. It seems that our concept of government endorses only the last element of Lincoln's eloquent conclusion of his Gettysburg Address: a government "of the people, by the people, for the people."

Yet after nearly every contemporary presidential campaign, there are cries of unethical behavior, motives, and practices. The 1988 presidential campaign renewed public outrage at the current state of electoral politics. Paul Taylor reports that 61 percent of the electorate believe that there is something morally wrong in America and 80 percent do not trust our leaders as much as they used to (1990, 226). If not a pervasive malaise, there is at least a pervasive cynicism all over the world about government and politics. Are politicians less moral and ethical, or have the processes of electoral politics and governing deteriorated?

The discipline of rhetoric and communication studies has long been interested in the subject of ethics. There is universal agreement that human communication demands concern for ethics. Renewed interest in the area is demonstrated by the formation in 1985 of the Commission on Communication Ethics within the Speech Communication Association and a special issue of *Communication Quarterly* on communication ethics. Such concerns, however, have not reached undergraduate or graduate education. Vivi McEuen and her colleagues report that of 46 doctoral programs surveyed, not one offered a course devoted entirely to communication ethics (1990, 286). In addition, ethical issues are discussed 15 percent or less of the total course time, and only 6 percent of the respondents had taken a graduate course devoted to research ethics (1990, 288–89). And less than 25 percent of undergraduates will take a course substantially devoted to ethical considerations (1990, 281).

Although one can find books on communication ethics, political ethics, media ethics, and so on, there has not been a specific book written on *political communication* ethics. *Ethical Dimensions of Political Communication* is an attempt to address ethical concerns related to traditional areas of political communication. In this volume, ethical issues are addressed in the areas of political culture, campaigns, media, advertising, ghostwriting, discourse, politicians, and new technologies.

Dealing with ethics is a difficult and perhaps even a dangerous business. All the contributors, upon completion of their chapter, expressed a certain uneasiness at tackling their topic. Clearly the authors struggled with the implications of their subject matter. This struggle, of course, is good.

The central theme that emerges from the essays is that we cannot depend upon the politicians, their handlers, or even the media or the press to correct real or perceived problems of ethics in American politics. The task is ours. Only as citizens can we alter or affect the quality of the polity.

I hope that colleagues, scholars, students, and interested citizens will find the essays stimulating, disturbing, and yet hopeful. More questions are raised in the chapters than are answered.But throughout the book one finds various methods, criteria, and issues for exploring and addressing ethical concerns. While certainly not a conversion experience, I know that as a result of reading this volume, my approach to and teaching of political communication will change. Simply stated, more time, effort, and content will be devoted to addressing ethical dimensions of political communication and the related concept of civic virture.

Robert E. Denton, Jr.

REFERENCES

Aristotle. 1954. *Nicomachean Ethics*. W. Rhys Roberts, trans. New York: Modern Library.

McEuen, Vivi S., et al. 1990. A Survey of Doctoral Education in Communication Research Ethics. *Communication Quarterly* 38:281–90.

Plato. 1968. *The Republic of Plato*. Allan Bloom, trans. New York: Basic Books.

Taylor, Paul. 1990. *See How They Run: Electing the President in an Age of Mediaocracy*. New York: Alfred Knopf.

Acknowledgments

Editing a book is either an enjoyable experience or a horrible one. Luckily for me, the contributors made this experience a most exciting, rewarding, and pleasurable endeavor. Over the years I have learned from their work and shared insights. I appreciate their participation in this volume and their wonderful contributions.

I also want to thank my colleagues in the Department of Communication Studies at Virginia Polytechnic Institute and State University who encourage me to continue to pursue projects of interest and protect me, as department head, from sinking in a bureaucratic sea of paper and minutiae.

The folks at Praeger, from the top to the bottom, are outstanding. With a relationship that spans over seven years and several projects, they have always been sensitive, interested, and professional. A special thanks to Alison Bricken, Anne Davidson, and Ron Chambers.

And, of course, I want to thank Paula, Bobby, and Chris for their love, encouragement, and support. They provide the basis of my hope for the future, my joy of the present, and the purpose of all my endeavors.

Ethical Dimensions of
Political Communication

Chapter One

Political Communication Ethics: An Oxymoron?

Robert E. Denton, Jr.

Several years ago, much younger and less wise, I attempted to interest two colleagues in writing a book on political communication ethics. Gary Woodward laughed. Richard Johannesen was not sure such a thing was possible. I am thankful that they both at least agreed to contribute to this volume.

Indeed, we live at a time when we expect not only politicians but also just about everyone else to lie, or at least not to tell the "whole truth and nothing but the truth." At this writing, Milli Vanilli is just one more recent example of public fraud. For those of you less attuned to pop culture, they won the 1990 Grammy for a song they never sang. Other examples abound. A few years ago Beech-Nut received a $2 million fine for distributing sugar water labeled as apple juice. Janet Cooke won the 1981 Pulitzer Prize for a fictitious story of an eight-year-old heroin addict. Rosie Ruiz slipped out of the crowd near the finish line to win the 1980 Boston Marathon. Museums and galleries are full of fakes. Now we even question whether Shakespeare wrote the plays bearing his name as author and Martin Luther King, Jr., parts of his dissertation.

Examples of public fraud within our "culture of lying" are too numerous to identify here. However, for over a decade, countless columnists, scholars, and writers have noted the rise of public and private deception.[1] Many express alarm at the growing attitude of "everyone does it" and the general acceptance of deceit as a means to attain ends.

Historically, it seems we have always been skeptical about politics and politicians. We accept the fact that they seldom espouse their own words and must make promises to garner support and votes. Politicians, as a group, often rank below car salespeople as the most dishonest profession. The epitome of this perception in the 1970s was best expressed by the poster consisting of a picture of Richard Nixon with the sarcastic question "Would you buy a used car from this man?"

The 1988 presidential campaign sparked a renewed interest in ethics and politics. Gary Hart spoiled his chances of receiving the Democratic presidential nomination with allegations of sexual indiscretions. Democractic Senator Joseph Biden withdrew from the race as a result of charges of plagiarism and deception. Even television evangelist Pat Robertson was accused of exaggerated and misleading statements about himself on his résumé. Of course, the negative tone and demeanor of the general campaign has led many observers to conclude that the quality of American electoral politics is at an all-time low.

Bush's flip-flop on taxes illustrates the dilemmas of campaigning versus governing, as well as the general level of public cynicism. In the 1988 presidential campaign, George Bush's pledge to not raise taxes was the central plank of his platform and of the ultimate sound bite, "Read my lips—no new taxes!" After only six months in office, Bush recanted his pledge amid cries of willful deception and outright lying. Yet, according to a *Washington Post*/ABC News poll taken only a week after the election, seven out of every ten voters did not believe Bush's pledge to not raise taxes (Taylor 1990, 7). Isn't it ironic that Americans thought Bush was lying but voted for him anyway?

Broken promises, however, are not new to American politics. Nearly every president has had to alter or ignore campaign statements and promises. Perhaps this says more about our electoral process than about our elected officials. One cynical interpretation is that politicians will say anything to anyone to get elected. As a result, the electorate is so disenchanted with politicians that they have become blasé about their apparent lies and deceit. Another explanation is that we expect leaders to lead, to do what is in the best interest of the nation even if it means altering a previous stance or popular position. From this perspective, the moral character of the official is enhanced by appearing strong, righteous, and selfless.

Is ethical politics possible, or is ethical politics simply an oxymoron? Clearly, ethical conflicts, issues, and dilemmas are an essential part of *democratic* politics. A dictator has few concerns with ethics. In a democracy, however, inherent conflicts extend beyond deeds of greed, the desire for power, or blind loyalty to friends. Elected officials are expected to represent the views of their constituents as well as to act for the common good of the entire nation. Often, such judgments are at odds. At times, officials' jobs require them to lie and deny knowledge of certain classified information or actions.

Ethical considerations are also an essential element of human communication (Johannesen 1990). Human interaction gives meaning to our world and creates the reality toward which we act. Social interaction is at the core of human existence. Language usage is always selective, involving individual choice, values, and motives. Statements of policy or opinion, "conscious or not, relevant or not, provide a basis upon which an inference can be made as to the ethics and values of the individual making the choice" (Andersen 1989, 482).

Thus, the title of this book is significant. We are not providing a tome of rules describing the ethics of political communication. Rather, we are investigating *ethical dimensions* of political communication. There is an important distinction between the terms *morals* and *ethics*. Morals are the collective customs and practices of a culture. Ethics are the norms, principles, or standards upon which to evaluate morals. Our purpose, then, is to reflect upon ethical aspects of the various elements of our political culture.

In Chapter 2, Marshall Fishwick examines the ethics of popular culture. Our culture reflects, reinforces, and approves the collective values and morals of society. Beginning with Aristotle's *Ethics* and moving to to the notions of existentialism, Fishwick surveys the roots and development of standards of conduct and judgment in American culture. In response to the question "Is there any ethical consensus?" he finds the "voice of the people" uncertain and unclear about the role of ethics in public communication.

Martha Cooper's chapter investigates the potential for a postmodern ethic of political advocacy. After a review of ethical approaches to political advocacy from a postmodern perspective, she details the views of Jurgen Habermas and Michel Foucault. She argues that Habermas's discourse ethic and Foucault's ethic of resistance together provide a valuable means for reclaiming and revitalizing ethical public argument. For Cooper, without such revitalization, contemporary conditions for public advocacy threaten to restrict freedom of choice.

Bruce Gronbeck views presidential campaigns as corporate rhetorical ventures in which it becomes increasingly difficult to place ethical blame on individuals. In order to make ethical assessments, Gronbeck argues, voters reduce campaigns to comprehensible dramas where they examine the action (motives), people (characterological styles), and thought (competence as politicians) of the players. These ethical pivots can be assessed from four moral vantages: that of message maker, message consumers, messages themselves, and situational expectations. In constructing a 3 × 4 matrix, Gronbeck generates 12 questions voters may ask in assessing the ethical dimensions of presidential candidates. Interestingly, different moral questions have dominated each campaign since 1960.

Richard Johannesen reviews the major elements of character ethics in moral philosophy and argues that ethical character is a significant aspect of ethical communication. From this perspective, he explores the political communication of Presidents Johnson, Carter, and Reagan as well as the communication of Senator Joseph Biden during the 1988 presidential primary campaign. After reexamining the traditional preference for issue-oriented campaigns over image-oriented campaigns, Johannesen concludes by stressing the importance of ethical character as a legitimate dimension of political communication for citizen assessment.

My chapter investigates television as an instrument of governing and its impact upon the nature of democracy. I essentially argue that television, by its nature, is an undemocractic technology. Initially, television was destined to unite us, educate us, and, as a result, improve the actions and decisions of the polity. However, the medium counters the basic characteristics of democracy: accountability, citizen information, free marketplace of ideas, and collective deliberation. These concepts and more are illustrated by examining the primetime presidency of Ronald Reagan. The essay concludes by identifying ways to cultivate an active, democratic citizenry in light of the heavy dependence upon television.

Lois Einhorn interviewed two rhetorically trained speechwriters, Craig R. Smith and Robert Oliver. Craig Smith wrote/writes speeches for several political and business leaders, including President Ford, Lee Iacocca, and George Bush as vice president and president. Robert Oliver wrote speeches for several political leaders, including President Syngman Rhee of Korea and several Korean ambassadors. Einhorn explores the ethics of ghostwriting and concludes with a discussion of how the interviewees' remarks "fit" into the general framework of our knowledge of ghostwriting, and the similarities and differences between rhetorically trained and "accidental" ghostwriters.

Lynda Kaid's chapter on political advertising discusses the aspects that diminish democracy's goal of an informed electorate. Issues include the emotional/rational dichotomy, money and access, technological tricks, negative advertising, and oversimplification of issues. In addition to analyzing the safeguards available in the present political system, Kaid offers specific recommendations for reform.

Gary Selnow reviews the ethical problems associated with some of the latest technological advances in political communication, including the sophisticated use of polling and computers. Integrated into his discussion of the implications of such technology in campaigning and governing are the issues of responsibility, voter manipulation, the public's right to privacy, and single-issue politics. While technology has made campaigns more targeted and political communication more efficient, the same technology may be diminishing the values of democracy.

Gary Woodward, in his chapter investigating the ethics of political journalism, argues that journalists have become an essential part of the political process. Unfortunately, the inherent limitations of the journalistic enterprise fall short of journalism's noble objectives. The format and narrative presentation of events contribute to problems of objectivity, personalization of news events, and constraints of space and time. The result is the public's inability to discuss important issues.

Kenneth Andersen argues that we should return to "Aristotle's notion of the essential unity of ethics, politics, and rhetoric" (1989, 487). But such a return is not solely the responsibility of politicians and governmental officials. We often overlook the fact that democratic life carries equal responsibilities for citizens. As is true with most things in life, we get what we deserve. The polity must share the praise or blame that it heaps on its leaders. Indifferent audiences are a greater danger than uninformed ones. The greatest threat to democracy is neglect of the public forum. We need to return to a civic culture, one based on communication and persuasion, active citizen participation, and a high level of information.

Thus our efforts are aimed more at the citizens than at the politicians. By better understanding our political process and its ethical implications, we hope to empower readers with a sense of purpose and resolve to protect our civic culture. Ethical politics need not be an oxymoron but a synonym. The choice is truly ours.

NOTE

1. There are literally thousands of citations one could provide. For the best review of such works, see Richard L. Johannesen, *Ethics in Human Communication*, 3rd ed. (Prospect Heights, IL: Waveland Press, 1990).

REFERENCES

Andersen, K. E. 1989. The Politics of Ethics and the Ethics of Politics. *American Behavioral Scientist* 32:479–92.

Johannesen, Richard. 1990. *Ethics in Human Communication*, 3rd ed. Prospect Heights, IL: Waveland Press.

Taylor, Paul. 1990. *See How They Run: Electing the President in an Age of Mediaocracy*. New York: Alfred Knopf.

Chapter Two

The Ethics of Popular Culture

Marshall W. Fishwick

Who are you indeed who would talk or sing to America? Have you studied out the land, its idiom and men?"
　　　　—Walt Whitman, "By Blue Ontario's Shore"

If popular culture is people's culture—what Whitman called "the people en masse"—we do indeed have a monumental task: to "talk or sing" of those people, and relate their culture and ethics.

Let us begin by trying to define two key concepts, popular culture and ethics.

We shall use the term *popular culture* to describe events and products designed for mass consumption, to appeal to and express the tastes of the vast majority—what the Romans called *vox populi*, the voice of the people. That voice is not always easy to understand, monitor, please, or influence. No one knows just what makes a television series or play a hit, a book a best-seller, or a once-obscure individual a celebrity. Most perception comes after the fact.

Popular culture includes not only media systems and merchandising but also trends in art, architecture, advertising, and what has come to be known as "life-style."

All these things reflect and reinforce the values and patterns of thought and feeling generally dispersed through and approved by society. Under certain conditions (as in the 1960s), popular culture may serve as a vehicle for opposing prevailing conventions and tastes. It evades exact definition and is better conceived as a willingness to broaden one's range of cultural interests, to find values and meanings in the wider areas of human activity (Fishwick 1977, 12–18).

In recent years popular culture has found a place in academia, and has linked up with older, established disciplines to examine communication theory, customs, attitudes, artifacts, myths, language, fads, trends, and movements. What we do in our "time off" is crucial. Popular culture observes people watching ball games and sitcoms; selecting a soap, soap opera, or video; going to a movie, rock concert, religious revival, political rally, or theme park; playing poker, Nintendo, or "dress-up"; communicating with gestures, clichés, and applause. The patterns and rhythms of everyday life are seen not as trivial but as crucial.

The history of the study of popular culture in academia is filled with misunderstanding and opposition. From the first, proponents of the study of this major portion of life made it clear that they were interested in making popular culture a supplement to the usual courses in literature, communication, sociology, history, philosophy, and the other humanities and social sciences; nobody proposed that popular culture replace these disciplines, but many suggested that it was time to reexamine the accepted courses and see if they were still viable. Opposition to the status quo always causes anxiety and dissent, but when the issues are clarified, opposition and anxiety often melt away, as they now are doing (Browne 1990, 4).

Because it too is a new and rapidly expanding field, communication studies has proved to be a stimulating ally for popular culture. In speaking here of communication, we mean not only radio, television, print, cinema, and telecommunications (users of the electromagnetic spectrum) but also an institutionalized complex including photography, music, rhetoric, advertising, fine arts, oral interpretation, teaching machines, and information transfer—what Norbert Weiner calls "a name for the content of what is exchanged with the outer world as we adjust to it, and make our adjustments felt upon it" (Weiner 1960, 17).

Popular culture, as a discipline, has often been overused, in a flattened, one-dimensional way, to denote either commercially provided entertainment or cute-and-quaint fragments of plebeian culture. Data and documents pile up, but not theories and patterns. One is reminded of the study of folklore before a type index was devised, or of chemistry before it had a complete table of the elements (Dundes 1965, 2–9).

How, then, are we to relate popular culture to ethics, another broad and elusive word? Derived from the Greek *ethos* (character or custom), ethics is the study of standards of conduct and judgment, of moral philosophy. The interplay between ethics and popular culture is extensive—any newspaper, newscast, broadcast, or talk show demonstrates this. All sorts of laws, rules, and totems are invoked, but consensus is rare. Efforts to dictate or legislate ethics go against the grain of democracy and the much-valued Bill of Rights to the Constitution. Mark Twain said he wanted to live in a land "where everyone could go to hell in his own particular way."

Of course, we do try to set and enforce ethical standards, many of which stem from the Ten Commandments. Various groups, such as the Public Relations Society of America, adopt and revise codes of professional standards. Typical excerpts read:

"A member shall adhere to truth and accuracy and to generally accepted standards of good taste." (Who defines the truth, and just what is and isn't "good taste"?)

"A member is obligated to use care to avoid communication of false or misleading information." (What sort of "care"? And when is information "misleading"?)

Another major organization, the National Association of Broadcasters, developed a code in the 1970s that set forth this key principle: "Violence, physical or psychological, may only be projected in responsibly handled contexts, not used exploitatively. Programs involving violence should present the consequences of it to its victims and perpetrators." Members displayed the NAB Seal of Approval before broadcasts to demonstrate their compliance.

In 1976, a decision by a U.S. federal judge abolished the broadcast codes, claiming that the provisions violated the First Amendment. Today codes of ethics are voluntary, with no absolute penalties for violations. These codes are meant as guidelines. Many media organizations, such as CBS News, maintain their own detailed standards and hire people to oversee ethical conduct. Other organizations use guidelines from professional groups as a basis to develop their own philosophies.

CBS News created a national furor in 1990 when it suspended a longtime news reporter and commentator, Andy Rooney, for what was alleged to be racist and anti-gay pronouncements. So great was the outcry that Rooney was soon reinstated. Rooney's own stand on ethical reporting is worth quoting: "I will try to tell people what they ought to know and avoid telling them what they want to hear, except when the two coincide, which isn't often" (Rooney 1985, 59).

The guiding star of the networks, film studios, recording studios, and most other organs of popular culture is not ethics but profits. Not the beratings but the ratings bring about lightning change. Cloning is the name of the game. If *Rocky* works, try *Rocky II, III,* and *IV*. Do the same with *Ghostbusters, Raiders of the Lost Ark,* and *Friday the 13th.* Another tactic: try the flipside. If *The Cosby Show* goes well with an uppermiddle-class doctor and his well-groomed wife who wears designer sweaters, flip to a house full of messy clutter, overweight slobs, and baggy sweat-shirts—*Roseanne.* How can quality prevail when the bottom line is a dollar sign?

Censorship, both overt and covert, has long been part of American popular culture. Books have been banned not only in Boston (long noted for banning) but throughout the land—sometimes works by Mark Twain, J. D. Salinger, and D. H. Lawrence. In 1990 one community banned *Little Red Riding Hood*—because she was carrying a bottle of wine to her sick grandmother. For years the Hayes Office kept a close watch on Hollywood films, monitoring kissing and necking, and insisting that bedrooms have only twin beds—even if the couples involved were married. A rap group recording was banned in 1990, and Cincinnati made national news by closing its art museum's exhibit of photographs deemed by some to be obscene. That same year a group of congressmen, headed by Senator Jesse Helms, attempted to cut off funds from the National Endowment for the Arts for giving support to such exhibits. Was Big Brother alive and well long after 1984?

Had publicity and media megahype become a loose cannon on democracy's deck? Were both art and politics being manipulated by public relations? If so, what new ethical questions did this raise?

Consider the case of Saatchi and Saatchi, the London agency largely credited with Margaret Thatcher's overwhelming victories in Britain, and Paris's Jacques Seguela, whom many think did the same thing for France's François Mitterrand. Seguela's "Force tranquille" (quiet force) slogan, linked to a bucolic image of small-village France where fewer and fewer French people lived, did for French politics what Bonanzaland and the Marlboro Man did for the fast-fading American West.

As late as 1967 France had only one television channel, with no ads at all. In 1990 there are six channels, chock full of ads—some in the middle of films. America? Several dozen channels, with an unknown number of commercials, and the number ever rising.

Against this background—and these perplexing questions—we need to go back to our roots and try to find the ethical standards that have guided us for centuries.

The foundation stone of Western civilization is Aristotle's *Ethics*. After 2,500 years, it has a higher standing in our culture (elite and popular) than any other book in the field. Aristotle is realistically simple in his ethics. We can understand him. Every ideal has a natural basis, and everything natural has an ideal development.

For Aristotle the chief condition of happiness and ethical existence is the life of reason, our unique glory and power. We must strive for excellence, looking for it along the middle way, the golden mean. The qualities of character can be arranged in triads, in each of which the first and last qualities will be extremes and vices, and the middle quality a virtue or an excellence. Thus between cowardice and rashness is courage; between stinginess and extravagance is liberality; between sloth and greed is ambition; between humility and pride is modesty; between secrecy and loquacity, honesty; between moroseness and buffoonery, good humor; between quarrelsomeness and flattery, friendship; between Hamlet's indecisiveness and Quixote's impulsiveness is self-control. "Right," then, in ethics or conduct, is not different from "right" in mathematics or engineering; it means correct, fit, what works best to the best result.

This kind of thinking was still dominant in the life and work of John Stuart Mill (1806–1873), known as "the Aristotle of the Victorian Age." Mill was a liberal in politics, a modified laissez-faire thinker in economics, an empiricist in philosophy, and a secular humanist in religion. All this combined in an ethical pattern known as utilitarianism, on which much of our ethical thinking is based.

In his twenties, Mill underwent a psychological crisis brought on by his reading of Romantic poets and philosophers. Exposed to their works, he rebelled against barren, calculating rationalism and adopted a more positive and flexible point of view. While receptive to the romantic and democratic currents of midcentury European thought, Mill remained dedicated to objective, rational methods and never forsook his belief in individualism.

On Liberty (1859), Mill's greatest contribution to modern social thought, is an eloquent essay on "the nature and limits of the power which can be legitimately exercised by society over the individual," and it offers a reasoned defense of a balanced position between individual freedom and social necessity. For Mill, positive, individual liberty is essential to both the personal happiness of self-realization and the advancement of the welfare of society.

The classic statement on Mill's philosophy appeared in his book Utilitarianism (1863). In it he sought to offer to the individual, as well as to society, a more secure moral foundation than existed in his time. He believed that the moral system of past centuries, based chiefly on divine revelation, had run its course. As for the future, moral principles based on intuition ("inner conviction") might serve individuals adequately— but the personal nature of such principles could not provide a common bond for society. Utilitarianism seemed to offer what was needed: a moral system that would serve both the individual and society. Mill was certain that the wellspring of morality lay within each human being. Therefore, Mill believed that humans, when faced with two choices, will choose the alternative of higher value over that of lesser value. Consequently, the preference of the majority can normally be accepted and trusted as a sound moral choice.

This is as clear and positive a statement of the wedding of popular culture and ethics as one can find. Of course it must be amended and expanded to meet new technologies and life patterns. As inner convictions change, so must outer manifestations. Talented new writers and thinkers, espousing popular causes, insist that women and other traditionally excluded groups be brought into discussions of philosophy. How can one claim to build a "crystal palace" (as Søren Kierkegaard described G.W.F. Hegel's philosophy) if some individuals are not allowed residence inside it? One cannot write of ethics and rationality within a context where women and nonwhites have been denied access to education and then have been assumed to be inferior. Similarly, Marxist philosophy denies that "the good" or "the true" exists independently of concrete historical and material circumstances. Marxism has argued that philosophy has tended to be a reactionary tool defending bourgeois culture and values.

Pragmatism, a philosophy whose origins and roots are mainly in America, has done much to explain our culture and redefine its ethics. Derived from the Greek word *pragma* (a thing done), this school emphasizes the immediate, the actual, and the real; the validity of all concepts can be tested by the practical results. Truth, its founder Charles Sanders Peirce insisted, is a process, and the "cash-value" of an idea. It is far better to speak of how ideas work than of what truth is. Knowledge is a dynamic process rather than a static idea. The pragmatist John Dewey did much to reshape the American educational system, and his ideas turn up in many aspects of popular culture.

Since World War II, two other major nontraditional schools have entered the field: phenomenology and existentialism. Both have important messages for those concerned with ethics, actions, and the communication process. Phenomenology's slogan—"to the things themselves"—is a mandate to explore being as it reveals itself to us without bias and presuppositions about "how it ought to be."

Phenomenologists have provided rich and insightful analyses of some of the more basic, everyday aspects of human experience, including play, leisure, sexuality, and loneliness. Phenomenologists, rather than doubt the reality of the world, tend to ignore that issue and instead look at how we see or feel or taste. Analyses of popular culture can provide similar insights, allowing ethical standards to emerge from the real world of experienced desires, so prevalent in many aspects of our electronic age.

Existentialism is one of the most powerful and controversial factors in the twentieth century, and the key to relating popular culture and ethics in our time. It became Europe's popular philosophy during and after World War II. Its motto: Challenge. Scorners of abstractions, generalities, circumlocutions, and official values, its followers are blunt to the point of brutality. They refuse to have anything to do with "blah blah words." *Inauthentic existence* is another term for hell on earth. Existentialists will not stand by and see a person turned into a *thing*, a cog in the system of production and consumption. They reject the education of adjustment, which presses everyone into a pattern and condones cultural brainwashing. Blandness and complacency can destroy us. We must ask hard questions: Are we free? Have we *ever* been free? How, when, and where is creative freedom possible? Is guilt a permanent stain on the soul? Is free will a fact or an illusion? How can we choose not to choose? What does it mean to exist genuinely?

Existentialists dare to face meaninglessness as the answer to the question of meaning. They have the courage to be—or, if necessary, not to be.

Existentialism is a way of thinking about ultimate problems. This primordial concern is both its hallmark and its glory. Only when people realize their plight and have the nerve to die can they find the strength to live.

Arguments about the founders of this doctrine abound. Some argue for the fifteenth-century French poet François Villon and after him François Rabelais and Michel Montaigne. Others stress the contributions of the early Greeks; still others, nineteenth-century Germans. All those who have brought the struggle of heart versus brain into the open can be included in the line of antecedents.

Søren Kierkegaard (1813–1855) played a pivotal role. To leave this great Dane out of the story is to watch *Hamlet* minus Hamlet. Both Søren and his father dealt constantly with ethical problems—were in fact obsessed by them. The son's writings mirror the struggle of a hypersensitive soul in an unethical world.

System builders infuriated him. Kierkegaard felt that tight mental boxes confined rather than liberated the human spirit. He directed his critical attack against rationalism, which had dominated Western thought from René Descartes (1596–1650) through Hegel (1770–1831). This Danish rebel denied the possibility of public or objective solutions. We cannot deal effectively with truth, as if it is something outside us. Truth is always personal and subjective. Built on each unique individual's existence, it reveals itself through involvement.

If ordinary people do not read Kierkegaard, they see his ideas expounded (often cheapened) in popular films, television series, and best-sellers. Horror movies, chillers and thrillers, and violent bombast have found a place in the popular imagination. Recent efforts to ban records, photographs, and pictures that to some seem obscene and puerile show growing resentment of excessive permissiveness and sexploitation. But who has a right to censor and condemn?

Ethics deals with people's psychic burden, which shifts over the centuries. The ancients contended with fate, over which humans have no control. Fate culminates in death, as the Greek writers well knew. Medieval people wrestled with the problem of guilt, which culminated in condemnation. *Dies irae* was heard throughout the land; the confession was the accepted avenue to redemption. For the modern world, guilt seems less overwhelming a problem than does meaninglessness. Against this great emptiness modern people must struggle. Nothingness lies curled at the heart of being like a worm.

Modern existentialists have suggested various answers. Some favor sheer violent action. André Malraux became a soldier of fortune. Antoine de Saint Exupéry flew over the Andes in a primitive plane that could have crashed at any moment. François Mauriac and Georges Bernanos suggested that action might be moral rather than physical; the poor country priest might, in the drab routine of his work, come closest to reality.

Jean Paul Sartre insists that there are two kinds of being: *l'être en soi* (being-in-itself) and *l'être pour soi* (being-for-itself). The first is characterized by infinite density. A rock has no will, no choice, no intention. The second is characterized by mutability and desire. We have both will and intention. Project plus facility—we are haunted by the gnawing, hopeless passion to thwart meaninglessness. Existentialism's first job is to make everyone aware that the full responsibility rests with him or her. The five key propositions are the following:

1. Man exists—appears on the scene—before he can be defined.

2. Man is indefinable because (at first) he is nothing. Being negativity, he can commit *all* errors.

3. Man becomes something by making something of himself.

4. It is futile to speak of "human nature."

5. Hence man is only what he wills himself to be as he consciously moves upward toward authentic existence.

Sartre and his disciples see humans as a series of undertakings, an ensemble of relationships. Man is as he does. Action alone justifies life. Existence is action and involvement. The greatest sins are not those of commission or omission, but of *submission*. One must not allow oneself to drift into and through oblivion. Avoid inner laziness—the tendency to give up, to sell out for phony security or position. Always we gravitate toward ruts, pigeonholes, and utopias. "Stop it!" the existentialists cry. Only by struggling are you human. Social, physical, ethnic distinctions are not essential.

In *The Ethics of Ambiguity* Simone de Beauvoir gives her analysis of the types of modern men. She begins with Subman, that finite clod unmoved by a spark. He makes up the group, the herd, the "masses" (as that term was used by José Ortega y Gassett). Blind to love and desire, Subman clings to a dull, insignificant world. His spiral points downward: the less he exists, the less reason there is for him to exist.

Dangerous because he is a force for the clever to manipulate, Subman can be counted on when lynchings, pogroms, or any other dirty work arises.

Serious Man strives for permanent values by owning permanent objects. A child who never grows up, he accords ultimate meaning to the useful. Never does he ask, "*What* is this [or that] useful for?" His dishonesty comes from his obligation to renew the denial of his freedom. He abdicates his right to be truly human—in return for a bright feather to wear in his hat. The Adventurer, by contrast, doesn't try to justify himself. Interested in conquest, not consequences, he likes action for its own sake. He is a doer. Throwing himself into each new enterprise, he prefers to do or die rather than ask the reason why. Fulfilling himself by denying others' freedom, carrying within him the seed of the dictator, he is basically contemptuous of other people.

The Nihilist rejects not only his own existence but also the existences that confirm it: "If I can't be anything, I'll be nothing." He rejects existence without being able to eliminate it. Like the playwright Samuel Beckett, he comes to the zero point—and zero times anything equals zero.

Passionate Man begins as Serious Man, but allows his passions to run away with him. The object of these passions he takes as an absolute; because it proves to be ephemeral, his "absolute" fades away. Burning ambitions are never fulfilled. All that is left is angst.

Simone de Beauvoir is describing not only ambiguity but also evil. She is putting into modern parlance what mankind has discovered, with tears and anguish, time and again. The Serious Man tends to err seriously. The Adventurer sets out to save others but ends up destroying himself. The Passionate Man makes an idol of his passions and is enslaved by them. Thus the existentialists are not, as critics have claimed, antireligious or atheistic. Instead they represent an ultimate religious concern. They see the general human predicament in every particular situation. They scorn "education of adjustment," which would press everyone into a single mold, and the technological society, which turns people into things. In this, they are far more religious than many who turn out Sunday school literature or occupy pulpits on Sunday morning.

Existentialists are also attuned to the general themes of disillusionment, pessimism, unrest, the lure of destruction. They know man is a disappointing actor, full of bad faith. All too often he refuses to face up to his freedom; hides behind banalities and abstractions; worships the trivial; indulges in racial and religious prejudice; dodges responsibilities on all levels. Like the dishonest dentist, he makes his living by disguising decay. Existentialists lament the lost innocence of men who try to raise morale by turning every day into a pseudo Christmas.

German writers have been among the most successful interpreters of the existentialist position. Karl Jaspers and Martin Heidegger exerted tremendous influence on formal philosophy. Heidegger's *Sein und Zeit* (1927) draws directly from Kierkegaard in stressing the mood of dread— "what anxiety is anxious about is 'being-in-the-world' itself." Terrified by the threat of nothingness, we retreat into anonymity. Life becomes like getting a bagful of junk mail, sent to us without a name. We are lost in the lonely crowd. Somehow we must block our descent into hell, and achieve authentic existence.

Rainer Maria Rilke transmuted such thoughts into poetry. Man the sojourner can never go home. Alienation saturates Rilke's poetry. In his special world even the quick-witted animals notice that we are "none too securely at home in the world that we know." We are lost not only in the world of space but also in the world of time, which draws us into the eternal void. Nothing highlights the ethical dilemma of popular culture more than this.

Existentialism has permeated our culture as dye permeates a jar of water. Even those who have never heard the word are haunted by the questions it raises. How can I exist genuinely? Should I be content to be a couch potato—to graze among television's multiple channels, thinking I am being entertained? Overwhelmed by glitter and glitz, what can, and do, we believe? Existentialism insists that life is commitment. As we enter the final years of the twentieth century, what are we committed to?

Permeating much of Western thought, such ideas have had great impact. The school of existentialism has a strongly negative flavor. Its philosophy is one of flux and becoming. In it there is no place for the fixed or the stable. The ethical problems are often avoided. Is life livable (except on an animal level) without some structure? And does that not demand an ethic?

Existentialists are incurably individualistic. They ignore Aristotle's truism "Man is a social animal." They also ignore the Hebraic truth contained in the notion of the covenant. God made a covenant with people, rather than with a person—a consideration that has no validity in existentialism. The school is radically anthropocentric, often egocentric. Self is the alpha and omega of their concern.

Yet despite these shortcomings, existentialism is one of the most powerful weapons against explosive evil that has been devised. It isn't a theology but a way of thinking about problems. While existentialists raise critical questions, they do not purport to give final answers. Seeing a world advancing yet absurd, inescapable yet insufficient, they show us not only how to exist despite contradictions but also how to hope despite tribulations. They are tough-minded thinkers for tragic times.

Existentialists are not, of course, popular with many people who watch NFL football play-offs, scream at game shows, and cry at soap operas.

Elite writers have their effect indirectly, and in ways that many of the people affected never comprehend. Often there is a messenger who translates and popularizers such writings. A good example is Marshall McLuhan, an obscure professor of English who became the Prince of Popthink, the carrier of the Existential Word. Deejays who had never heard of Kierkegaard or Sartre were shouting, "Whatcha doin', Marshall McLuhan?" and pundits everywhere were announcing that "The medium is the message."

Other writers and intellectuals were fascinated and bemused. "Suppose McLuhan is what he sounds like," Tom Wolfe wrote in a popular magazine, "the most important thinker since Newton?" Frenchmen who had exalted existentialism began praising "le McLuhanisme." The man and his works provide a critical link between popular culture and ethics in our time.

"I am an investigator," McLuhan said time and again. "I make probes. I have no point of view. I do not stay in one position, I talk back to media and set off an adventure of exploration." He consciously assumed the role of gadfly. The deeper his bite, the more bitter the resentment. Gadflies are never easy to live with. Look what the Greeks did to Socrates.

With impressive academic credentials (graduate of Trinity College, Cambridge, positions in leading universities) he produced articles, books, disciples, and detractors in a steady stream.

For McLuhan it was Gutenberg's movable type—not Petrarch, Copernicus, or Columbus—who created the modern worldview with its special outlook. His observations had a quirk, a hook—a special angle that turned the conventional world into something startling and strange. His was a surrealism of words rather than of images. No one who has heard or read him will ever see the world in quite the same way again.

We have all come to realize that the media have been changing *what* is being communicated, not merely *how* it is communicated. The media change our perception of the outside world, but they do much more: they change how we see ourselves and what we see in ourselves.

Neither the medium nor the message determines the other, but each shapes the other. McLuhan's greatest insight is not "The medium is the message" but "Technology is an extension of man"—not just a tool (Druker 1979, 66). Technology does not master us but changes our personalities, just as much as it changes what we can do. The ethical implications are profound and far-reaching.

Like Buckminster Fuller, another popularizer of ideas, McLuhan tried to show that new approaches to our culture require that we deal with technology as "human" and "cultural," not as purely "technical." In this sense, they are two prophets for our age.

Starting in the 1960s, McLuhan began his reevaluation of mass communications and public ethics. He began to reconceive history as a pageant whose inner meaning is our metamorphosis through media. He sees an age dominated not by political or military leaders but by money ("The Poor Man's Credit Card"), photographs ("Brothels Without Walls"), and movies ("The Reel World"). Electronic media have created a global village in which all information can be shared, simultaneously, by everyone. Walls between people, nations, art, and thought come tumbling down. And McLuhan's popular culture status zoomed upward. According to a survey titled "Articles in Popular American Magazines by and about Selected Figures in 1967," he came in just behind Pope Paul VI and ahead of Martin Luther King.

Since then his pop rating has declined, but certain significant results are his legacy:

1. McLuhanism moved into the very marrow of the bones that make up mass communication theory. Even those critics who violently disagree with or berate him have to acknowledge his impact.
2. The students he so captivated are the instructors and writers from whom a new generation of students learn.
3. His strong moralistic stands (in both his personal life and his academic analyses) had an appeal in the 1980s that was ignored in the 1960s and 1970s.
4. McLuhan's linking of elite and popular culture built a bridge between the two over which many of us now cross.

Because he dreamed of a new protean mythology—and knew he must attack the old before he could reconstruct the new—McLuhan irritated many with maddening slogans, paradoxes, and puns. What he wrote and said sounded to some like utter nonsense. But, as Alfred North Whitehead pointed out, "The nonsense of today is the sense of tomorrow" (Marchand 1989, 126).

What neither McLuhan nor Whitehead could have anticipated was the rise of "non-ism" in the 1990s. We are in the Age of No. Spectacular political and economic changes have brought unexpected ethical outbursts. Bumper stickers set the tone. No Nukes. No More War. No Abortion. No More Landfills. No No No. The red circle with the diagonal line, forbidding us to enter, smoke, kiss, pollute, park, or go bump in the night is the emblem of the age.

What, then, shall we eat? Food that has no fat, no salt, no artificial chemicals, no sugar, no nitrates, no excess calories. Say NO to tuna caught in nets, coffee from El Salvador, anything from South Africa. Drink un-cola, or you'll join the un-dead.

"We don't pollute, we don't feed people unhealthy food, we don't encourage bad habits," says Rick Phipps, manager of the Noa Noa restaurant in Beverly Hills. He even equips his tables with nonpolluting

ashtrays (costing $125 each). Applauding this move away from the un-
safe, the unhealthy, and the unattractive, we still might ask, why this
dramatic change in style and substance? Why are recent symbols of
sophistication (the cigarette, the fast car, the cocktail glass, and serial
sex games) today's signs of indulgence and stupidity? Could it be that
we are seeing that we have created the Sequin Society, and are deter-
mined to get out of it?

The Greeks had their myths, the Romans had their emperors, the
early Christians had their saints. What does modern America have?
Sequins.

In a literal sense, sequins are bits of plastic or metal that add glitter
to a costume. In a figurative sense (as I want to use the word) sequins
are the bright baubles, the glitzy images, on the face of mass society.

Used in this way, sequins conjure up not only flashy objects but also
an attitude toward the world; a yuppie life-style. We use sequins
(clothes, cars, speech, crusades) to pose, posture, and primp.

Non-ism grows out of, or even coincides with, eras of easy money
and indulgence. Just say No to Reaganomics, insider trading, merger-
mania, HUD and S&L scandals, AIDS, bloated budgets, self-serving
politicians. We are ashamed of our past, fearful of our future.

We need more than a sensible budget, a credible war on drugs and
poverty, an acceptable response to *glasnost*. We must own up to a difficult
(perhaps unanswerable) question: What *do* we call a mental picture of
reality?

Sequins bedazzle us but do not sustain us. As Gilbert and Sullivan
point out in *H.M.S. Pinafore*:

> Things are seldom what they seem
> Skim milk masquerades as cream.

Nothing new here: Plato was pointing all this out 2,500 years ago. But
we have added new twists, new techniques, new illustrations. In our
time one of the first to pinpoint this was Walter Lippmann. As early as
1922, in *Public Opinion*, he identified "oversimplified patterns and al-
lures" in American life that tended "to defend our prejudices," as well
as devices that teach us "to ignore the world outside and concentrate
on the pictures in our heads." Daniel Boorstin affirmed all this, and
added new insights, in *The Image, or What Happened to the American Dream*
(1962). By now we were well into the Sequin Society. Surface overwhelmed substance. Boorstin told of the mother who, having been con-
gratulated on having such a fine baby in the carriage, replied, "Oh,
that's nothing. You should see his photographs."

Several obvious factors come to mind, especially the three "overs":
overabundance, overindulgence, and overkill. Historians prefer a single

word, which they apply whenever they see an affluent civilization coming apart at the seams: decadence.

How can we be decadent when we are the richest, proudest, most
productive nation on earth? When we have taken the hungry masses
and turned them into prosperous citizens? "Mass" is derived from the
Latin *massa*—dough used for baking bread. Thus mass, in its origins,
implies quantity of matter without definite shape. This is what Augustine had in mind when he wrote of the *massa damnata* (masses of the
damned). The term has a poignant meaning in the Age of Excess.

Mass fits nicely with *production*. All sorts of things (including sequins)
are mass-produced. I recently visited a brand-name bakery as large as
a football field. Bread, rolls, and cookies are produced for households
throughout the country by a team of machines, called a system. They
look delectable but are bland, tasteless, and unsatisfying. They belong
to our Sequin Society.

Mass eliminates the individual and intensifies the many. Hence mass
communication (whatever device is employed) works like a giant sausage
machine. Again and again it must turn out its product with the same
density, texture, and flavor. (Think of the various television genres:
news, weather, sitcom, soap opera, cop story, sports spectacle, awards
special, Miss America Pageant, etc.). Once we know the format, we
expect it—even demand it. We are caught in a McDonald's of the mind:
standardized visual hamburgers for standardized people; programs
without distinction for people without distinction. Sequins for the
masses—more glut. More overindulgence. It's time to say no.

But *will* we say no? Can popular culture adopt new ethical codes,
reconstructing the American image at home and abroad? Will we disa-
vow the "me too" philosophy that so engrossed us?

There is an inherent danger in this chapter and, I suspect, in others
in this volume. In examining a particular medium, part, or theme, we
tend to lose sight of the whole act of communication—which is the core
not only of culture but also, indeed, of life itself. "We must never forget,"
Warren Susman reminds us, "that any part, medium, or theme is per-
force related to others, sharing in some greater whole. . . . The crucial
issue of relationships is the most essential of all cultural questions" (1984,
253).

Back to basics, say many current authors and thinkers. Draw from
the great ethical truths we have inherited: Aristotle's golden mean, Mill's
utilitarianism, Kant's categorical imperative, Dewey's pragmatism. We
can solve new problems with old, time-tested remedies (Christians, Rotzoll, and Fackler 1987, 9–17).

Yet even as such books appear, so do new problems. One of the most
baffling is disinformation: a deliberate official effort to distort the truth.
For example, in October 1986, the press learned that the Reagan admin-

istration had launched a disinformation campaign to scare Libyan leader Moammar Qaddhafi. Selected U.S. government sources had planted stories that U.S. forces were preparing to strike Libya. One version appeared on August 25, 1986, in the *Wall Street Journal*.

On the basis of this story and a statement by White House spokesman Larry Speakes that the article was "authoritative," other newspapers carried the story. This brings up the ethical question of the government's responsibility not to use the press for its own ends. State Department spokesman Bernard Kalb resigned when he learned about the disinformation campaign, saying, "Faith in the word of America is the pulsebeat of our democracy." But who would, and could, take action against the U.S. government?

There are all too few Bernard Kalbs who would give up their job to support an ethical position. Most of us, in most circumstances, "go with the flow." The consequences may well be disastrous. All that is necessary for evil to triumph, Edmund Burke pointed out, is for good men and women to do nothing. The major commodity the media have to offer is information; the major one for teachers, the truth. When we succumb to untruth, bias, or "white lies," we not only violate ethical standards, we endanger the future of our nation.

We conclude our look at the the ethics of popular culture with more questions than answers. Is there any ethical consensus? Do the people who provide our public entertainment (print, radio, film, television) have the same ethical obligations as public officials, politicians, and legalists? Specifically, what about the ethics of ads and television commercials, which play such a major role in public communication? Was it right to ban television cigarette ads; and if so, should we also ban alcohol ads? And if the Marlboro Man can't ride across our television screens, should he have free access to billboards and magazines?

The voice of the people—vox populi—is heard throughout the land—indeed, around the globe; but just what that voice is saying, and how we should respond, is unclear. Popular culture seems to be a loose cannon on the deck of Planet Earth as we head into outer space. We can predict eclipses, but not uprisings and revolutions. Before dealing with cosmic questions, we have specific (sometimes local) ones to deal with right now, right here, where we live day by day.

REFERENCES

Arendt, Hannah. 1958. *The Human Condition*. Chicago: University of Chicago Press.

Biagi, Shirley. 1990. *Media/Impact*. Belmont, CA: Wadsworth.

Bigsby, C. W. E., ed. 1984. *Approaches to Popular Culture*. Bowling Green, IN: Popular Press.

Browne, Ray B. 1990. *Against Academia*. Bowling Green, IN: Popular Press.

Burke, Peter. 1978. *Popular Culture in Early Modern Europe*. New York: Harper & Row.

Christians, Clifford, Kim Rotzell, and Mark Fackler. 1987. *Media Ethics*. New York: Longman.

Denton, Robert E., Jr. 1988. *The Primetime Presidency of Ronald Reagan*. New York: Praeger.

Druker, Peter. 1979. *Adventures of a Bystander*. New York: Harper & Row.

Dundes, Alan. 1965. *The Study of Folklore*. Englewood Cliffs, NJ: Prentice-Hall.

Fishwick, Marshall W. 1977. *Parameters of Popular Culture*. Bowling Green, IN: Popular Press.

———. 1985. *Seven Pillars of Popular Culture*. Westport, CT: Greenwood Press.

Hirschfield, Charles. 1980. *The Modern World*. San Diego: Harcourt Brace Jovanovich.

Holsinger, Ralph L. 1987. *Media Law*. New York: Random House.

Hulteng, John. 1985. *The Messenger's Motives: Ethical Problems of the News Media*. Englewood Cliffs, NJ: Prentice-Hall.

Knoebel, Edgar, ed. 1988. *Classics of Western Thought—The Modern World*. San Diego: Harcourt Brace Jovanovich.

Luedtke, Luther S. 1977. *The Study of American Culture: Contemporary Conflicts*. Deland, FL: Everett Edwards.

Marchand, Philip. 1989. *Marshall McLuhan: The Medium and the Messenger*. New York: Knopf.

Rooney, Andy. 1984. "The Journalist's Code of Ethics." In *Pieces of My Mind*. New York: Atheneum.

Rotzell, Kim, James Haefner, and Charles Sandage. 1986. *Advertising in Contemporary Society*. Cincinnati: South-Western.

Schickel, Richard. 1973. "Misunderstanding McLuhan." *More* 3, no. 8 (August):21–26.

Smith, Anthony. 1980. *Goodbye Gutenberg*. New York: Oxford University Press.

Susman, Warren I. 1984. *Culture as History*. New York: Pantheon.

Weiner, Norbert. 1960. *The Human Use of Human Beings*. Garden City, NY: Doubleday.

Chapter Three

Ethical Dimensions of Political Advocacy from a Postmodern Perspective

Martha Cooper

From the time Aristotle observed that rhetoric is an offshoot of ethics and politics (1954, 1356a), rhetoricians have been concerned with ethical dimensions of public advocacy. Consequently, there exists a rich body of literature in rhetorical studies concerning the ethics of public argument (e.g., Johannesen 1990, 21–39). Ethical standards regarding strategies for public persuasion, stances for advocates, and the substance of political discourse that emerge from this body of literature are typically grounded in either a particular political ideology or a particular perspective concerning human nature. Although some of these standards remain durable, our movement into a postmodern society has called into question many of the assumptions grounding standard political and human nature perspectives for ethical judgment.

This chapter investigates the potential for a postmodern ethic regarding political advocacy. Following a review of common ethical approaches to political advocacy, the problems associated with these approaches are discussed from a postmodern perspective. Then the views of two alternative but potentially supplementary approaches to postmodernist ethics are discussed. Specifically, Habermas's discourse ethic and Foucault's ethic of resistance are investigated for their utility in opening a space for ethical considerations that take into account postmodern political communication. My argument is that Habermas's discourse ethic, which resembles traditional approaches to political communication ethics, should be supplemented by Foucault's ethics of resistance.

At the outset, several assumptions regarding the topic require careful definition. Following Chesebro, I understand that communication is political when "communication patterns" and "significant symbols" can "create, mediate, and alter dominant and subordinate relationships" (Chesebro 1976, 300). Consequently, this chapter investigates the relationship between discourse and power. Along with Foucault (1984a), I understand ethics to be concerned with what relationship we *ought* to have with ourselves and others, a position similar to that of Dance (1973), who argues that ethics is related to communication because when we communicate, we reveal ourselves and constitute ourselves in terms of others. My concern is less with ethical prescriptions concerning communication patterns and more with locating the spaces where ethical concern is pivotal, a position similar to Jensen's suggestion that "we ought to shun labeling something as 'ethical' or 'unethical,' and instead ought to think in terms of a continuum which enables us to discuss the *degree of ethical quality* in any given communicative act" (Jensen 1990, 2).

TRADITIONAL APPROACHES TO ETHICS

Traditional approaches to the ethics of political advocacy tend to rely on an instrumental view of communication derived from Classical rhetorical theory and a democratic understanding of political action derived from the Enlightenment. As Lucaites observed,

For those operating in the tradition of American rhetorical studies, with their concern for the instrumental relationship between discourse and power, the focus has been on the political as a function of the realm of "public" communication, the arena in which discourse is intentionally situated and addressed, and actively serves to empower the interests of individuals and groups in their relationship to the larger society. (1990, 51)

The instrumental approach to communication results in a focus on the means of advocacy as the area in which ethical concerns arise. Meanwhile, the Enlightenment approach to politics furnishes ethical standards such as rationality, choice, democratic procedure, and democratic values as the yardsticks by which those means of advocacy may be measured. Typical approaches to the ethics of political advocacy thus share a number of common themes.

First, the agent of ethical conduct is viewed as the citizen. All the major writers during the Classical period—Isocrates, Plato, Aristotle, Cicero, Quintilian—assumed that their guidelines for advocacy would be employed by those accorded the status of citizen (Bitzer 1981, 227). As Aristotle explained in *Politics*, a citizen is "he who has the power to take part in the deliberative or judicial administration of any state" (1943, 1275a). More contemporary treatments of the ethics of political communication make a similar assumption (e.g., Wallace 1955; Nilsen 1974; Johannesen 1990).

Second, people are invited to recognize their ethical responsibilities or obligations in terms of their unique capacities as citizens. Citizens are capable of choice (Nilsen 1974). Moreover, their choices are guided by a sense of what is reasonable or rational (Haiman 1958; Kruger 1967). Whether perceived as advocates or simply as persons exercising political choice, as elected or appointed government officials, persons labeled "citizens" are assumed capable of participating in public affairs, capable of exercising rational choice. But the rational choices of citizens are not completely unfettered; they are tempered by citizens' links to their community. Hence, a general rule of thumb for citizens is to make choices that are in the "public interest" (e.g., Wallace 1955; Thompson 1987; Nilsen 1974). *Public interest* is typically defined in terms of the shared values of a political democracy. Thus *public interest* is an ideograph for democratic values, among which the democratic process of open discussion and debate is primary (e.g., Day 1966).

Third, the means by which citizens act ethically is participation in purposeful deliberation—full and open debate. As Bitzer explains, "If we view political rhetoric as a system comprised of many competing messages, we should hold that its proper function is 'deliberation,' using the word in its general sense of inquiry on a large scale" (1981, 229). Full and open debate is assisted by a number of conditions and motives on the part of advocates. Bitzer argues:

It is obvious that we need to judge and persuade not on the basis of whimsey, falsehood, or inadequate information and methods, but rather on the basis of purposeful deliberation which employs as much truth as the subject admits and proceeds systematically through methods of investigation, evaluation, and communication suited to the subject, the audience, and the purpose. (1981, 228)

As conditions, there must exist truth, adequate information, and access to channels of communication (Johannesen 1985, 227; Johannesen 1990, 31–32).

Among the motives required of advocates are habits of search, justice, public spirit, and respect for dissent (Wallace 1955). Adherence to rules of fair play and civility are fundamental to both the conditions and the motives (Nilsen 1974). An additional practice—accountability, sometimes called publicity—supplements the primary ethical practice of full and open debate (Johannesen 1985, 227; Thompson 1987, 3). Accountability is more likely to occur when representatives or other public officials engage in retrospection on decisions made, generalization in which hypothetical situations are discussed in advance, and mediation where oversight is institutionalized (Thompson 1987, 24–39).

Finally, the telos of these practices and their attendant conditions and motives is an Enlightenment vision of the proper functioning of a democracy, defined as a political system in which citizens maintain confidence and trust in the political system and are accorded the ability to choose freely their mode of societal cooperation (Wallace 1955; Nilsen 1974; Day 1966). Ultimately, posterity will judge the speech acts that occur within such an ethical orientation as "right" or "fit," and democracy—that system of full and open debate as a means for resolving disputes, inducing cooperation, and allocating power—will persist (Bitzer 1981; Thompson 1987).

Thus, traditional approaches to the ethics of public advocacy advise advocates on the disposition appropriate to their role as citizens and on the means of advocacy appropriate to the continuation of a democratic system of free and open discussion. The model of political advocacy assumed by those theories rooted in the Classical and Enlightenment tradition is based on a vision of face-to-face communication in which advocates have the possibility of obtaining accurate information and choosing among policy alternatives. An image of autonomous individuals who possess the participatory rights of citizenship and are motivated by a sense of public interest completes this vision.

POSTMODERN CONDITIONS OF POLITICAL ADVOCACY

Contemporary social theorists have called into question many of the assumptions regarding discourse, knowledge, and power common to philosophy from the Classical age to the Enlightenment (e.g., Lyotard 1984; Kellner 1988; Aronowitz 1987). Within this context it is appropriate to question that vision so fundamental to the liberal democratic understanding of civic politics, for in postindustrial Western democracies, political advocacy and decision making appear to occur in a situation somewhat different from that assumed by Classical and Enlightenment theorists. And, as Charland observed: "Rhetorical theory usually does not render problematic the categories of the rhetorical situation. It tells us neither why certain occasions, speakers, and topics are privileged, nor what unspoken interests are served, nor what audiences [are] excluded" (1990, 262). Several unique features of contemporary political discourse are worthy of note for their implications regarding the conditions and motives necessary for full and open discussion.

First, much political advocacy is mediated rather than occurring in face-to-face forums specifically designed to ensure full and open discussion. The influence of the media is usually characterized in terms of their agenda-setting function. Cobb and Elder point out "the role of the media in defining both the systemic agenda of community concerns and the formal agenda of government," in providing "important channels for communication among policymakers," in "acting as sources of readily usable policy-relevant information," and in presenting and interpreting the public record (1981, 392). Regarding this last function, they note that

actors within the political system have come to rely more on the mass media, mass mailings, selective targeting and mobilization techniques, direct individual contacting and professional or issue-based channels as the principal means for policy-relevant communication. (Cobb and Elder 1981, 398)

Not only do the media provide a channel for exchange of political information, but their use by political advocates often has the effect of moving discussion and debate from formal forums for advocacy to a realm in which the rules for fair and open discussion are much less codified. Cobb and Elder note the "continuing 'individualization' of American politics manifested by declining reliance on traditional intermediate institutions such as groups and parties to structure the relationships between policy makers and the public" (1981, 398). And McGee reminds us:

The effect of an "imperial presidency" is a general political consciousness that permits and tolerates short-circuiting of the rhetorical process at will by the president—whenever "leadership" is required, a president may appeal *ad populum* from the responsibility to convince another branch of government, in reasonable argumentation, of the soundness of a policy. Indeed, thanks to the amplification of mass communication technology, a president can be assured of a national audience for a speech, press conference, or news coverage of any event at any time on any issue. (1985, 163)

The less formal court of public opinion provided by media is sought by interested but unelected political advocates as well. Thus, any interest group or social movement tends to spend considerable resources in order to obtain media coverage of its point of view. In addition, the commercial nature of American media often encourages such advocates to package their positions as a form of entertainment. One result of this commercial influence is that what used to be considered merely popular culture, extraneous to "real" political discourse, often manifests a strong political component. As Wander (1981) argues, the content of popular culture, as displayed through the media, is pregnant with political implications. But the discourse of popular culture occurs in a context where aesthetic standards concerning our tastes prevail rather than in a context where democratic standards of fair play and public interest prevail. As Aronowitz has observed, "Mass politics signifies the end of public discourse, where there is face to face communication and decisions are arrived at through consciously applying the rules of evidence and argument" (1987, 107).

Second, much of the substance of political advocacy, policy making and decisions about implementation, occurs in professional and bureaucratic settings rather than in forums designed for full and open debate. Cobb and Elder note "the growing complexity of policy and policy making resulting in, and stimulated by, increasing professionalization and bureaucratization of policy making and implementation" (1981, 397). The administrative agencies and bureaus empowered to carry out policies foster a process for decision making that relies on "insiders" who provide technical expertise and act as social planners on behalf of the rest of the citizenry. Cobb and Elder describe the new policy innovator and power broker in political circles as a "policy entrepreneur" (1981, 410–11). Hedrick Smith's analysis of decision making in the Pentagon and his reports concerning the growth in importance of professional experts in Washington are illustrative of this trend. Similarly, Nancy Fraser's characterization of the social welfare system as a "juridical-administrative-therapeutic state apparatus (JAT)" that translates "political issues concerning the interpretation of people's needs into legal, administrative, and/or therapeutic matters," and thus "executes political policy in a way that appears nonpolitical and tends to be depoliticizing," points to another example of this trend (1989, 154).

The danger of such professionalization and bureaucratization of political advocacy was recognized by John Dewey:

No government by experts in which the masses do not have the chance to inform the experts as to their needs can be anything but an oligarchy managed in the interests of the few. And the enlightenment must proceed in ways which force the administrative specialists to take account of their needs. (1954, 208–9)

McGee explains that the reliance on technical expertise and professionalized policy making results in the use of "technical reasoning," a "culture of critical discourse," to which ordinary citizens have little access (1985, 172–73).

Academics lend their ethos and "knowledge" to government at the price of scholarly objectivity and a position as social critic. Governments lend their power and money to academics at the price of settling on policies that academics approve as "reasonable" according to prevailing conceptions of what counts as "reasonable" in the academy. (McGee 1985, 169–70)

Reid and Yanarella make a similar point, arguing that the "objective processes" and "technical rationality" which dominate contemporary political communication and action provide a poor breeding ground for consciousness and intentionality (1974, 95, 128–29). Moreover, as elite experts construct the public vocabulary and enjoy special access to the means of communication, their actions alter the meaning of an "open society" and "full and open discussion" (Lucaites 1990, 59; Condit 1987, 83). Cobb and Elder summarize the situation accordingly:

Changes in communication capabilities have contributed to the continuing fragmentation of the policy process, making it more difficult to fathom by citizen and analyst alike. They have undermined intermediate structures that have traditionally served to make the process comprehensible and meaningful to the average citizen. These changes have also contributed to the growing "knowledge gap" that is likely to put the disadvantaged at greater disadvantage and frustrate the many for whom participation is a civic duty but not a full-time commitment. (1981, 413–14)

Confronted as it is with a forum for public advocacy that reduces, if not totally inhibits, face-to-face communication and requires considerable resources to gain media access, and faced with a sprawling bureaucracy in which experts make many political decisions, a third feature of contemporary political communication is less surprising. Characteristic of contemporary public life is a growing public antipathy toward government. Cobb and Elder point out that there is "growing concern about the appropriateness, intrusiveness, costs, and effectiveness of public policy and governmental action generally" (1981, 398). Such antipathy is demonstrated by low voter turnouts, public opinion polls that show a lack of confidence in government officials, taxpayer revolts, and the general retreat of many from involvement in the public sphere that has been documented by critics such as Sennett (1977) and Lasch (1979).

Some scholars have suggested that such alienation on the part of citizens has led to a generalized pessimism regarding political life. Aronowitz, for example, claims that as "more people [have] chosen to withhold their ballot, public life withers in all late-capitalist and state socialist societies" (1987, 102). In place of public life, people have transferred their sense of community to the workplace and the market, and have transformed themselves from citizens to consumers (Aronowitz 1987, 100–101; Lanigan and Strobl 1981, 153). In more extreme cases, people may substitute violent reaction to the public sphere for mere withdrawal from it. Defining terrorism as "acts of violence against those who 'represent' legitimate power" and explaining that "contemporary terrorism of this type results from the disillusionment of the generation of the 60s with conventional radical politics," Aronowitz suggests that the rise of terrorism "is a major kind of postmodern politics" (1987, 102).

As many have withdrawn from public affairs and civic responsibility, those citizens remaining active have tended to collect themselves into single-issue interest groups that find their guidance more from limited ideologies than from a generalized public interest. "The emergence of

prominent new actors in the form of single-issue and ideologically oriented groups that seemingly defy the accepted logic of group politics and
fail to abide by the norms of that politics" is recognized by numerous
scholars (Cobb and Elder 1981, 398). According to McGee, "the result can
be the creation of such mutually inconsistent views of the world that ordinary argumentation is impossible" (1985, 161). And, McGee notes,
"the rhetorical separation of factions within the community is so common
and so successful that one major theorist sees warlike 'confrontation' as a
defining characteristic of political movements" (1985, 161; Cathcart 1978,
1980). McGee explains that the warlike rhetoric common to American political discourse, as practiced by interest groups, calls into question the possibility of full and open discussion by dehumanizing those who oppose the
ideological tenets of a particular advocacy group:

In theory, there is a contradiction between commitment to rationality in government and participation in a rhetorical vision of fervent, passionate response
to any problem that seems to subvert our faith. In practice, there is a contradiction
between our insistence that we are rational, tolerant of diversity, and peace-
loving; and our habitual use of a rhetoric of war that pits the forces of civilization
against dehumanized humans who are alleged to be bestial, irrational, intolerant,
and violent. (1985, 165–66)

Confronted with a society in which many of the features common to
liberal democracy have seemingly disappeared, many interested in the
connection between rhetoric and social theory have lamented the state
of public moral argument (e.g., Fisher 1984; Frentz 1985; Farrell 1986;
McGee 1985; Wander 1984). They seem to recognize that if our political
advocacy is now conducted through a medium to which not all are given
equal access and in which those formal rules of advocacy which encourage open discussion are missing; if decisions are made in bureaucratic forums where technical reasoning predominates; and if the most
viable "public" participation is expressed in warlike rhetoric, then citizen
withdrawal from the public sphere seems likely. In such a context, traditional guidelines for ethical communication are at least problematic,
if not impossible to carry out.

Amid such despair, Condit (1987) sounds a more optimistic note concerning political advocacy. She argues that the public realm still exists
as a viable place in which to resolve disputes and construct public morality. The polemic and warlike tendencies of special-interest groups are
not so threatening, she explains, because "competing rhetors persuade
third parties—audiences—and create a 'public consensus' that does not
require the approval of every individual on every point" (1987, 81).
Furthermore, because a "public rationale for an action must always be
expressible in the form of general goods," it matters less that decisions

may actually be based on technical reason or partisan ideologies (Condit 1987, 82). In other words, advocates must ultimately repair to the "public interest," if only for the pragmatic reason that they must publicly justify their actions. Finally, Condit states that "sociopolitical philosophy advocating equality in communication as a base for morality," like that advocated by Habermas, points the way toward continued expansion of the availability of the means for public participation in civic communication (1987, 84). If Condit is correct, then there appears to remain a viable space for ethical considerations in public advocacy, but that space is configured quite differently from the liberal democratic vision on which traditional approaches to ethics are based.

POSTMODERN APPROACHES TO ETHICS

Just what that space for ethical considerations looks like can be informed by turning to the works of the postmodern social theorists who offer a variety of alternative explanations of the workings of discourse, power, and knowledge. Consonant with other commentaries about postmodern social theories, "it should be pointed out in advance that there is nothing like a unified 'postmodern social theory' " (Kellner 1988, 241). Instead, theories ranging from Jurgen Habermas's brand of critical theory, Jacques Derrida's deconstruction, Michel Foucault's new historicism, and Jean Baudrillard's avant-garde aestheticism, to Nancy Fraser's democratic-socialist-feminism are often treated as postmodern because, despite their obvious conceptual differences, they question many of the same assumptions common to traditional social theory.

The assumptions they question provide a convenient reminder of the features of contemporary political communication just reviewed and focus attention on the problems attendant to ethics in contemporary political communication. Baudrillard, for example, questions whether there even exists a realm that we could call "public" or "social," arguing that "the main force in rendering the masses an apathetic silent majority seems to be the proliferation of information and media" (1983, 25–26; cf. Kellner 1988, 246). Foucault, meanwhile, questions the very existence of autonomous citizens who may engage in rational discourse, suggesting that the role of the individual knower is heavily constrained by the regime of established discourse (1980a, 131; cf. Code 1987, 237).

Among the postmodern social theorists, two—Habermas and Foucault—seem to address the question of ethics most directly. Habermas's project of constructing a "discourse ethic" testifies to the centrality of ethics in his work. And Foucault, when asked to describe his interests in one of the last interviews before his death, responded: "What interests me is much more morals than politics or, in any case, politics as an ethics" (1984c, 375). As a consequence, several commentators have attempted to explore the ethical implications of their work (e.g., Richters 1988; Boyne and Lash 1984; Van Hooft 1976; Rajchman 1986).

Although Habermas and Foucault seem to offer radically different positions in contemporary debates regarding postmodernism (Richters 1988, 613–14; Fraser 1989, 35–53) and Habermas (1985) himself has launched attacks on the work of Foucault as incommensurate with his own, those commentators who have explored their viewpoints concerning ethics suggest several ways in which their work may be complementary (Richters 1988, 640; Fraser 1989, 182; Boyne and Lasch 1984). Both Habermas and Foucault appear to have retained some link to the philosophical assumptions grounding traditional approaches to ethics in political communication. Habermas seems to hold to the Enlightenment objective of using intellect (communicative rationality) to improve everyday life, while Foucault retains an affinity for the Enlightenment idea of individual autonomy when he advises adoption of a thoughtful, self-reflexive attitude (Richters 1988, 617). By reviewing the ethical stance of Habermas and Foucault, both their differences and their points of commonality come to light.

Since Condit (1987) builds her optimistic vision of public moral argument partially on the work of Habermas, it is appropriate that we begin with his position. Habermas (1976) sees ethics as a branch of sociology, arguing that ethical norms arise from the nature of society (Van Hooft 1976, 150–51). Since society is the product of a social construction of reality that occurs through the process of communication, according to Habermas's view, the bases for communication are also the bases for society. Habermas's argument is not unlike John Dewey's explanation that "men live in a community in virtue of the things which they have in common; and communication is the way in which they come to possess things in common" (1916, 4). The requirements for genuine communication, therefore, become the requirements for a moral society, according to Habermas.

In *Legitimation Crisis* (Habermas 1975, esp. 107–8), as well as in numerous essays and interviews (e.g., Habermas 1979, 1970), Habermas outlines the requirements for genuine communication and refers to this outline as the "ideal speech situation." In an ideal speech situation, participants are able and willing to suspend the pragmatic, or strategic, dimension of speech in order to question the background consensus that is necessary for speech to occur. Four questions are common to the engagement in "discourse" that Habermas recommends. First, is the speech comprehensible, free from confusion or obfuscation? Second, is the speech true, congruent with reality as the participants understand reality? Third, is the speech truthful, reflecting the genuine or sincere intentions of the participants. And fourth, is the speech appropriate, suitable to and reflective of the generalizable interests of the participants?

It is the ability and willingness to engage in these four questions that Habermas identifies as the "moral principle for discourse" (Van Hooft 1976, 162; Lanigan and Strobl 1981, 148–52; see also Ingram 1982; Beiner 1983, 25–30; Johannesen 1990, 50). By encouraging advocates to suspend strategic considerations, Habermas's moral principle emancipates by allowing participants to construct their own roles in communicative situations (Lanigan and Stroble 1981, 153–54).

This moral principle has been elaborated both as a set of prescriptions for bringing into existence a vibrant public sphere and as a set of cautions for avoiding the systematically distorted communication that occurs when the requirements of the ideal speech situation are not met. Hauser identifies four "conditions that are essential to the smooth functioning of the public sphere" that are based on Habermas's model:

First, it must be accessible to all citizens. . . . Second, there must be access to information. . . . Third, specific means for transmitting information must be accessible to those who can be influenced by it. . . . A fourth feature of the public sphere: there must be institutional guarantees for the public sphere to exist. (1989, 324–26)

These features can be read as ethical requirements for the process of public advocacy, as ethical imperatives for organizations or systems, as well as for individuals. The notion suggested is that there may be systemic dimensions of ethics as well as ethics that apply to individual responsibility.

On the other hand, Habermas's discourse ethic also implies cautions for how to avoid illegitimate public discussion. Van Hooft summarizes the point well:

The political challenge that Habermas' arguments issue is to create discourse wherever and whenever possible. We may not rest on a realized ideal. Rather we should oppose all those decision-making processes which are not rational and not discursive but which rely in some way or another on power or privilege or on the suppression of discourse. Any decision making that does not permit the discursive involvement of those affected or which is based on faulty or partially withheld relevant information must be opposed. Concerted political action must be taken to ensure access to unbiased media and to relevant information; to ensure sound and proper debate, and so forth. Furthermore, any political campaign must itself instantiate the ideal speech situation and not proceed in a manner which cannot be rationally justified. (1976, 174–75)

In other words, Van Hooft suggests that "Habermas has given us a map for political activism," an outline of what to oppose in order to behave ethically in political communication (1976, 175). Again, the emphasis is on processes and systems, the means by which decisions are made and campaigns are ordered. We are invited to engage in ethical behavior by performing a sort of watchdog function that takes advocates and their mediators to task when the requirements for the ideal speech situation do not seem to be met and to attend to the operation of sprawling bureaucracies and other institutions—from government agencies to private media conglomerates—in order to ensure the realization of a discourse ethic.

Many commentators suggest that Habermas's ideal speech situation is counterfactual and does not actually exist (e.g., Cushman and Dietrich 1979). Consequently, Habermas has been accused of offering simply another variant of a universal ideal, a grand metanarrative that is common to modernist thinking but unproductive for a postmodern world (Lyotard 1984, 65–66). But Van Hooft points out that it is the assumption by participants in discussion that such questions may be asked which allows conversation to occur (1976, 171). Without assuming that what takes place is understandable, true, truthful, and appropriate, the motive to engage in public discussion would wither. This is not to suggest that all persons who communicate in the public forum do adhere to Habermas's four requirements. But as Hauser has noted, "without this condition propaganda prevails and public opinion becomes managed in ways that deny its significance in shaping institutional policies" (1989, 324). Habermas explains that when these questions are not part of accepted communicative practice, then strategic considerations predominate and systematically distorted communication occurs that can result in a crisis of legitimacy and a threat to individual freedom. Thus, whenever people gather to resolve public issues through communication and are convinced that what they are saying and hearing is genuine, the ideal speech situation is in fact real, not just a hypothetical construct (Habermas 1985, 196).

The potential reality of the ideal speech situation has prompted others to accuse Habermas of offering an ideal that is potentially partial and biased (e.g., Fraser 1989, 113–43). If, as Richters explains, the ideal speech situation is not a universal ideal but, rather, a historically situated reality, then "the most difficult aspect of his ethics is the avoidance of ethnocentrism" (1988, 633; see also 628–29). This problem arises primarily because of Habermas's insistence that discourse be appropriate, that it conform to generalizable interests. Frequently, "public" interests exclude the interests of marginalized groups. If some are not defined as interested parties within a prevalent worldview, then how can Habermas's discourse ethic ensure that they will be accorded equal access to the public sphere and that their interests will become a part of generalizable interests? This concern is particularly important, given reviews that observe the conservative, legitimizing, and potentially elitist character of much contemporary political communication (e.g., Rogin 1967;

Joslyn 1986; Wander 1990). Recalling the cool rationality of the architects of the Nazi holocaust and the frame of reference common to the Nazi party, Habermas's requirements could have been met in the disastrous political propaganda initiated by Joseph Goebbels.

Even when the consensus regarding what is in the public interest appears to take marginalized groups into account, problems may still arise. Foucault put the problem succinctly when asked to comment on Habermas's position: "The 'best' theories do not constitute a very effective protection against disastrous political choices; certain great themes such as 'humanism' can be used to any end whatever—for example, to show with what gratitude Pohlenz would have greeted Hitler" (1984c, 374). Foucault's observation suggests that a prevailing political rationality, worldview, or ideology may appear to represent generalizable interests while in actuality serving oppressive ends.

It is precisely at this juncture, in consideration of this problem of potential ethnocentrism, that some commentators have suggested a wedding of Habermas and Foucault, finding in Foucault a possible corrective for Habermas and in Habermas a useful complement for Foucault (e.g., Richters 1988, 637; Fraser 1989, 182; Boyne and Lash 1984). Therefore, a brief summary of Foucault's ethical position is in order before proceeding to an exploration of how the ideas of both Habermas and Foucault may point to areas for ethical consideration in postmodern political communication.

In contrast with Habermas's discourse ethic, Foucault's work suggests what has been termed an ethics of "resistance" or "transgression" (Richters 1988, 627). The central feature of Foucault's position is his belief that by analyzing whom we have been constituted to be, we can ask whom we might become. This principle arose from his studies of the constitution of the moral subject, principally from his three-volume *History of Sexuality* (Foucault 1980a, 1985, 1986). Defining ethics as the relationship you ought to have with yourself and others, Foucault investigated discursive practices from the Classical to the Modern periods to expose "a historical ontology in relation to ethics through which we constitute ourselves as moral agents" (Foucault 1984a, 352). His concern for whom we might become emphasizes the value of autonomous choice, while his suggestion that we may better consider whom we might become by examining whom we have been constituted to be fosters a self-reflexive attitude common to Enlightenment thinking.

Foucault's discussion of ethics was grounded in his observation that any discursive practice entails three dimensions: knowledge, power, and ethics. Because the production of discourse inherently posits meaning that may constitute knowledge, and because whenever knowledge is at stake, relations among those who know and those who do not know are constructed, discursive action always entails dimensions of power and ethics. In other words, any discursive event contains the potential for both political and ethical implications because of the epistemic nature of discourse. As Foucault put it, "The relationship between rationalization and excesses of political power is evident. And we should not need to wait for bureaucracy or concentration camps to recognize the existence of such relations" (1982, 210). Code borrows from Foucault to make a similar point in her discussion of epistemic responsibility:

The crucial point is that there is, indeed, power inherent in knowledge, a power that can be exercised over those who do not know. This power, misused and abused, is manifest in totalitarian societies whose modus operandi is controlled ignorance. It is manifest, too, in situations where, for reasons of vested interest, findings about harmful effects of certain drugs—for instance, cortisone or estrogen—are suppressed to prevent financial loss in business enterprises. Here we find an intersection between epistemic and moral considerations where, in the worst rather than the best sense, the former are used to control the latter. (1987, 238–39)

The implication of Foucault's explanation of the epistemic dimension of discourse is a call for resistance through skepticism (Rajchman 1986, 168; Richters 1988, 619–20). Rather than receiving information as sensible and accurate, participants in political discussion should exercise reasoned skepticism. In regard to politics, Foucault argued that "what we need is a new economy of power relations. . . . The role of philosophy is to keep watch over the excessive powers of political rationality" (1982, 210).

In addition, Foucault argued that discursive action entails an ethical dimension because participants in conversation, whether that conversation is blatantly political or not, inevitably position one another as subjects. In particular, Foucault noted that political institutions frequently position their citizens as individuals rather than as members of groups, and as producers and consumers rather than as citizens (1982, 208–9). Fraser provides an illustration of Foucault's idea in her analysis of the social welfare system. She explains that the unemployment compensation and Social Security systems position individuals as purchasing consumers who receive monies that are rightfully theirs, while other welfare programs, such as AFDC, Medicaid, and the food stamp program position their recipients as dependent clients who are the beneficiaries of public charity (1989, 149–53). Such positioning is, of course, the result of a variety of discursive practices that are common to the communication of administrative agencies.

The social relationships created during and as a result of political discourse invite questions about the relationships that one should have with self and others. By liberating ourselves from the state, from the sense of ourselves that the state has created, we may create a new type of subjectivity, a new position for ourselves, a new relationship between ourselves and others (Richters 1988, 631–32). Rather than relying on moral codes that arise from various institutions as a means for understanding and locating ourselves as moral subjects, Foucault recommended "an ethic of 'choosing' the forms of experience through which we constitute ourselves" (Rajchman 1986, 167). In other words, his ethic of resistance advises that individuals resist the positions offered to them by others in favor of choosing their mode of experience. His discussion of the women's movement in various of his writings offers a case in point. As Rajchman observes:

For Foucault, "the real strength of the women's liberation movement is not that of having laid claim to the specificity of their sexuality and the rights pertaining to it, but that they have actually departed from the discourse conducted under the apparatuses of 'sexuality'." Thus one might say that the kind of "femininity" invented by feminine writing was one which departed from the "hysterization" of the female body, and invented another image than that of "the Mother with the negative image of 'nervous woman'." As such, "femininity" would become an ethical issue of the choice of a beautiful existence not a moral issue of universal obligation or duty. (1986, 180)

Foucault's ethics of resistance, understood as resistance to political rationality and political positioning, is not dissimilar to Habermas's call for a willingness and ability to engage in discourse, an arena of communicative action in which the background assumptions of political discourse can be questioned. The similarity is particularly striking given Foucault's discussion of two alternative orientations toward discussion. Asked to explain why he didn't engage in polemics, Foucault responded:

A whole morality is at stake, the morality that concerns the search for the truth and the relation to the other.

In the serious play of questions and answers, in the work of reciprocal elucidation, the rights of each person are in some sense immanent in the discussion. They depend only on the dialogue situation. The person asking the questions is merely exercising the right that has been given to him: to remain unconvinced, to perceive a contradiction, to require more information, to emphasize different postulates, to point out faulty reasoning, etc. As for the person answering the questions, he too exercises a right that does not go beyond the discussion itself; by the logic of his own discourse he is tied to what he has said earlier, and by the acceptance of dialogue he is tied to the questioning of the other. (1984b, 381–82).

This dialogue is both pleasant and difficult. Each participant exercises only the rights given by the partner and dictated by the dialogue's form. Foucault described the polemicist as the opposite of the participant in dialogue, explaining that for the polemicist, the game consists in abolishing the partner rather than in recognizing him as a subject with a right to speak (Foucault 1984b, 382). Describing it as "a parasitic figure on discussion and an obstacle to the search for truth," Foucault observed that political polemics "defines alliances, recruits partisans, unites interests and opinions, represents a party," and establishes the other as an enemy that must be defeated (1984b, 382–83). By engaging in polemics, he continued, "one gesticulates: anathemas, excommunications, condemnations, battles, victories, and defeats are no more than ways of speaking, after all. And yet, in the order of discourse, they are also ways of acting which are not without consequence. There are the sterilizing effects: Has anyone ever seen a new idea come out of a polemic?" (1984b, 383).

The dialogue that Foucault favored over polemics bears close resemblance to Habermas's discourse ethic. But, unlike Habermas, who values the rationality that emerges from a willingness and ability to question the assumptions grounding discussion, Foucault valued the integrity given to individuals that emerges from participation in dialogue. Thus, Foucault's concern was for the individual's position within a system of advocacy, for the implications of a system of advocacy for individual subjects.

Foucault's concern for how individuals relate to a system of political communication led him to provide some rather specific advice on how people may engage in the ethics of transgression that is less similar to, but possibly corrective for, Habermas's position. Following a discussion of antiauthority struggles generally, he observed:

These struggles are not exactly for or against the "individual," but rather they are struggles against the "government of individualization." They are an opposition to the effects of power which are linked with knowledge, competence, and qualification: struggles against the privileges of knowledge. But they are also an opposition against secrecy, deformation, and mystifying representations imposed on people. . . . all these present struggles revolve around the question: Who are we? They are a refusal of these abstractions, of economic and ideological state violence which ignore who we are individually, and also a refusal of a scientific or administrative inquisition which determines who one is. (Foucault 1982, 212)

In other words, Foucault saw struggles against categorization as fundamental to resisting administrative political power. Those categories which position people might well arise from arenas, such as the academy, that are not explicitly political but could be put into service for the administration of various government agencies.

It is precisely the sort of struggles that Foucault outlined to which Fraser refers when she suggests that Habermas's discourse ethic be modified to correct for potential ethnocentrism that could vitiate the effectiveness of social movements. She argues:

A discourse ethic could take into account that dominant and subordinated groups stand in different and unequal relations to the means of interpretation and communication. It could do this by maintaining a kind of suspicion or distance from any given vocabulary for interpreting needs, defining situations and pressing claims. It could keep open the possibility that it could come to pass that biases might become apparent in even what have been thought to be relatively neutral forms of discourse; that such forms could themselves become stakes in political deliberation; that subordinated groups could contest such forms and propose alternatives, and thereby gain a greater measure of collective control over the means of interpretation and communication. (Fraser 1986, 426)

Fraser goes on to build a new discourse ethic informed by Foucault's notion of transgression. She explains that in late capitalist political culture, "talk about people's needs is an important species of political discourse" and "has been institutionalized as a major vocabulary of political discourse" (1989, 161–62). Following Foucault, Fraser argues that needs talk arises in the context of three struggles: the struggle to establish or deny the political status of a given need; the struggle over how to define, interpret, and therefore determine how to satisfy that need; and the struggle to secure or withhold provision of that need (1989, 164). Because contemporary political advocacy is dominated by experts engaging in technical reason, "the people whose needs are in question are repositioned. They become individual 'cases' rather than members of social groups or participants in political movements," and as a consequence "are rendered passive, positioned as potential recipients of predefined services rather than as agents involved in interpreting their needs and shaping their life conditions" (Fraser 1989, 174).

A way of reclaiming the participatory role of citizenship for these cases is resistance, according to Fraser. That resistance works according to four steps:

First, individuals may locate some space for maneuver within the administrative framework of a government agency. . . . Second, informally organized groups may develop practices and affiliations that are at odds with the social state's way of positioning them as clients. . . . Third, individuals and/or groups may resist therapeutic initiatives of the social state while accepting material aid. . . . Fourth, in addition to informal, ad hoc, strategic and/or cultural forms of resistance, there are also more formally organized, explicitly political organized kinds. (Fraser 1989, 177–80)

Fraser illustrates these steps by referring to various ways in which recipients of public aid have attempted to reposition themselves (1989,

177). She notes, for example, that by involving caseworkers in the operation of the family—within the framework of administrative agencies—needs concerning child and wife abuse were brought to light. Similarly, she reviews examples of "domestic kin networks" that distribute food and AFDC allowances among groups larger than the household as illustrative of practices that create affiliations at odds with the social state's way of positioning clients.

Through such means of resistance, then, people may challenge the potential ethnocentrism of an otherwise apparently ethical system of political advocacy by asserting their own interpretations of needs and claiming their own status as interested citizens rather than accepting the noncitizen positions assigned to them by those with administrative power. Thus, Foucault's ethic of resistance can operate as a useful supplement to Habermas's discourse ethic.

CONCLUSION

The merger of Habermas's discourse ethic and Foucault's ethic of resistance points to a postmodern ethic for political advocacy that takes into account the unique features of contemporary political advocacy while remaining sensitive to traditional approaches that grow out of an image of liberal democratic politics. In doing so, such a merger both reinforces and extends Condit's claim that public moral argument is still possible in liberal Western democracies.

A discourse ethic that includes resistance maintains the traditional interest in democratic procedure but elevates the importance of preserving the possibility of citizens, freely choosing their mode of societal cooperation. For Habermas (1971), the objective of his moral principle is the assurance of freedom, a concept he equates with a sense of identity that allows autonomous action (Van Hooft 1976, 153–54). For Foucault, his definition of ethics itself is predicated on the notion that by struggling with limits imposed on the self, people can better exercise autonomous choice (1984d, 42; Richters 1988, 617).

From the perspective I have called traditional, citizens are invited to exercise ethical behavior by participating in full and open discussion. Habermas's ideal speech situation seems to be a quintessential description of such full and open discussion. And Foucault's preference for dialogue over polemics makes his position appear consistent with full and open discussion. But the way in which a discourse ethic that includes resistance invites ethical action extends the conditions and motives common to traditional views that speak of sound evidence and rational arguments. It is in that extension that postmodern theorists such as Habermas and Foucault contribute ethical dimensions which take into account unique features of contemporary political communication.

The importance of the mass media as a forum for public discussion and the growth of administrative agencies as forums for decision making make participation in full and open discussion problematic for many citizens. In response to this problem, Habermas advises a concern for the systems of advocacy and the institutions of decision making that focuses our attention on whether people have access to these forums. Foucault extends our concern to other arenas where the nature of the human being is defined because he recognizes that the notion of who a human being is may radically alter whether that person is granted access to the means of communication so vital to participation in political action.

The centering of decision making in forums where technical reasoning predominates and the growing importance of special interest groups call into question the possibility of discussion that promotes the "public interest." Professional administrators and special interest groups run the risk of basing their arguments on partial ideologies or elitist conceptions of problems that neglect the interests of all members of the public. Condit, returning to familiar notions like accountability and publicity, argues that this is not really a problem, since ultimately public decisions must be justified in public, where a vocabulary of "public interest" must be used. Habermas's discourse ethic supports Condit's idea by explaining that the ability and willingness to engage in discourse, to examine the notions that background particular decisions, is a historical reality when the public accepts political decisions. Foucault's work, on the other hand, offers an alternative by suggesting that through antiauthority struggles, citizens can resist biased, partial ideologies used to guide political affairs. Such resistance may provide a way of coping with the systematically distorted communication that worries Habermas and his critics alike.

Antipathy toward government, withdrawal from public participation, and the general tone of warlike rhetoric that predominates in what political advocacy remains, call into question whether there still exist citizens—agents capable of ethical advocacy. Condit's suggestion that Habermas's moral principle can expand public participation provides a partial answer to this question. But her observation that advocates need not convince each other, but must convince only audiences, is problematic. If access is broadened and pluralistic perspectives are included in public discourse—if the public sphere is broadened as she and Habermas recommend—then the division between advocate and audience blurs. Moreover, condoning warlike rhetoric as a modus operandi for political advocacy sidesteps the ethical question of what the relationship between advocates and their audiences *should* be. Habermas's discourse and Foucault's dialogue seem to offer a better alternative. At least for Foucault, the fundamental issue is one of how an advocate positions his or her adversary and audience. The way a subject is constructed is a matter of ethical concern insofar as people may be positioned as citizens or consumers or clients, as people with equality or people to be excommunicated and symbolically killed. The telos of free choice and democratic procedure common to traditional approaches and the work of Habermas and Foucault alike seem to demand an ethical consideration for the subject of the type Foucault recommends.

A postmodern ethic for political advocacy, then, centers on the need to re-create the citizen. As with traditional approaches, postmodern theory connects ethics with a concern for individual freedom and choice (see Boyne and Lash 1984, 154). But unlike traditional approaches that take individual freedom and choice as the ground for what constitutes ethical behavior, postmodern approaches take such individual freedom and choice to be the end that ethical behavior seeks. Consequently, political advocacy can be examined for its impact on individual freedom and choice. That examination should incorporate two dimensions.

First, like traditional approaches, postmodern theory suggests that ethics is concerned with procedures for discussion. But unlike traditional perspectives that value truth and adequate information, postmodern perspectives recognize that truth may be elusive and information partial, and therefore place more value on access to the means of communication. Consequently, political advocacy can be examined for its procedural adherence to an open system in which people are allowed to participate in decision making and are given access to the media and other information networks through which advocacy occurs.

Second, postmodern theory suggests that ethics is concerned with the outcomes for participants in discussion. A willingness and ability to suspend strategic considerations like that proposed by Habermas and Foucault is similar to the respect for dissent and public-spiritedness proposed in traditional perspectives toward ethics. However, postmodern thinking recognizes that the "public interest" can be the product of partial interests and that when it is taken to extremes, "dissent" can position opposing advocates or potential audiences out of existence. Therefore, from a postmodern perspective, the guiding principle for motives of political advocates is the preservation of others as autonomous subjects. Consequently, political advocacy can be examined for its inclusiveness in substance as well as in procedure.

In practical terms a postmodern ethic creates new demands for individuals engaged in political advocacy. For example, Murphy and Callaghan (1988) advise administrators in community agencies of the need for citizen participation in the planning and delivery of social services as a way of enacting the call for greater inclusiveness. From a more macroscopic perspective, Gregg (1989) applauds the work of those who provide alternative interpretations of social problems on the grounds that such alternity can change prevailing political ideologies and enhance individual and collective freedom.

Nancy Fraser provides a fitting illustration of the ethical considerations that emerge from a consideration of postmodern thought in her description of a democratic-socialist-feminist ethic for the interpretation of needs in contemporary society. She writes:

First, there are procedural considerations concerning the social processes by which various competing need interpretations are generated. For example, how exclusive or inclusive are various rival needs discourses? How hierarchical or egalitarian are the relations among the interlocutors? In general, procedural considerations dictate that, all other things being equal, the best need interpretations are those reached by means of communicative processes that most closely approximate ideals of democracy, equality, and fairness. In addition, considerations of consequences are relevant in justifying need interpretations. This means comparing alternative distributive outcomes of rival interpretations. For example, would widespread acceptance of some given interpretation of a social need disadvantage some groups of people vis-a-vis others? Does interpretation conform to, rather than challenge, societal patterns of dominance and subordination? (1989, 182)

As Fraser's outline of questions suggests, a postmodern ethic for political communication tries to balance democracy and equality, procedure and consequences. While traditional approaches to the ethics of political advocacy remain durable in their contribution to a concern for procedures and means of advocacy, postmodern perspectives add a concern for the substantive consequences of political advocacy, allowing us to explore the ethics of political communication in terms of its outcomes as well as of its means. Concern for outcomes that enhance individual choice encourages a search for procedures that are more inclusive. More inclusive procedures, in turn, increase the likelihood of substantive results that enhance individual freedom. The ethical quality of political advocacy can thus be evaluated according to its contribution to the construction of citizens—agents who can participate in government. In short, procedures for advocacy and the social relationships that result from advocacy may be judged to be of greater ethical quality when people are invited to act as citizens than when they are invited to withdraw from the public sphere. Instead of assuming the existence of ethical subjects in the form of citizens, as is the case in traditional approaches, a postmodern ethic problematizes the agent of ethical action and suggests that ethical considerations focus on reestablishing the possibility of citizenship.

REFERENCES

Aristotle. 1943. *Politics*. Trans. Benjamin Jowett. New York: Modern Library.
———. 1954. *Rhetoric*. Trans. W. Rhys Roberts. New York: Modern Library.
Aronowitz, Stanley. 1987. Postmodernism and politics. *Social Text* 18:99–115.
Baudrillard, Jean. 1983. *In the shadow of the silent majorities*. New York: Semiotext.
Beiner, Ronald. 1983. *Political judgment*. Chicago: University of Chicago Press.
Bitzer, Lloyd F. 1981. Political rhetoric. In *Handbook of political communication*, ed.
    Dan D. Nimmo and Keith R. Sanders, 225–48. Beverly Hills, CA: Sage.
Boyne, Roy, and Scott Lash. 1984. Communicative rationality and desire. *Telos*
    61:152–58.
Cathcart, Robert S. 1978. Confrontation as a rhetorical form. *Southern Speech
    Communication Journal* 43:233–47.
———. 1980. Defining social movements by their rhetorical form. *Central States
    Speech Journal* 31:267–73.
Charland, Maurice. 1990. Rehabilitating rhetoric: Confronting blindspots in dis-
    course and social theory. *Communication* 11:253–64.
Chesebro, James W. 1976. Political communication. *Quarterly Journal of Speech*.
    62:289–300.
Cobb, Roger W., and Charles D. Elder. 1981. Communication and public policy.
    In *Handbook of political communication*, ed. Dan D. Nimmo and Keith R.
    Sanders, 391–416. Beverly Hills, CA: Sage.
Code, Lorraine. 1987. *Epistemic responsibility*. Hanover, NH: University Press of
    New England.
Condit, Celeste Michelle. 1987. Crafting virtue: The rhetorical construction of
    public morality. *Quarterly Journal of Speech* 73:79–97.
Cushman, Donald C., and David Dietrich. 1979. A critical reconstruction of
    Jurgen Habermas' holistic approach to rhetoric as social philosophy. *Jour-
    nal of the American Forensic Association* 16:128–37.
Dance, Frank E. X. 1973. Speech communication: The revealing echo. In *Com-
    munication: Ethical and moral issues*, ed. Lee Thayer, 277–86. New York:
    Gordon and Breach.
Day, Dennis G. 1966. The ethics of democratic debate. *Central States Speech Journal*
    17:5–14.
Dewey, John. 1916. *Democracy and education*. New York: Free Press.
———. 1954. *The public and its problems*. Reprint of 1927 ed. Chicago: Swallow
    Press.
Farrell, Thomas B. 1986. Rhetorical resemblance: Paradoxes of a practical art.
    Quarterly Journal of Speech 72:1–19.
Ferrara, Alessandro. 1990. A critique of Habermas' *Discursethik*. In *The interpre-
    tation of dialogue*, ed. Tuillo Maranhao, 303–37. Chicago: University of
    Chicago Press.
Fisher, Walter R. 1984. Narration as a human communication paradigm: The
    case of public moral argument. *Communication Monographs* 51:1–22.
Foucault, Michel. 1980a. *The history of sexuality*, Vol. 1, *An introduction*. Trans.
    Robert Hurley. New York: Vintage Books.
———. 1980b. Truth and power. In *Power/knowledge*. Trans. Colin Gordon, Leo

Marshall, John Mephar, and Kate Soper. Ed. Colin Gordon, 208–16. New York: Pantheon.

———. 1982. The subject and power. Trans. Leslie Sawyer. Afterword to Hubert L. Dreyfus and Paul Rabinow, *Michel Foucault: Beyond structuralism and hermeneutics*, 208–26. Chicago: University of Chicago Press.

———. 1984a. On the genealogy of ethics: An overview of work in progress. In *The Foucault reader*, ed. Paul Rabinow, 340–72. New York: Pantheon.

———. 1984b. Polemics, politics, and problemizations. Trans. Lydia Davis. In *The Foucault reader*, ed. Paul Rabinow, 381–90. New York: Pantheon.

———. 1984c. Politics and ethics: An interview. Trans. Catherine Porter. In *The Foucault reader*, ed. Paul Rabinow, 373–80. New York: Pantheon.

———. 1984d. What is enlightenment? Trans. Catherine Porter. In *The Foucault reader*, ed. Paul Rabinow, 32–50. New York: Pantheon.

———. 1985. *The use of pleasure*. Vol. 2 of *The history of sexuality*. Trans. Robert Hurley. New York: Pantheon.

———. 1986. *The care of the self*. Vol. 3 of *The history of sexuality*. Trans. Robert Hurley. New York: Pantheon.

Fraser, Nancy. 1986. Toward a discourse ethic of solidarity. *Praxis International* 5:425–29.

———. 1989. *Unruly practices: Power, discourse and gender in contemporary social theory*. Minneapolis: University of Minnesota Press.

Frentz, Thomas S. 1985. Rhetorical conversation, time, and moral action. *Quarterly Journal of Speech* 71:1–18.

Gregg, Richard B. 1989. The rhetoric of denial and alternity. In *American rhetoric: Context and criticism*, ed. Thomas W. Benson, 385–417. Carbondale: Southern Illinois University Press.

Habermas, Jurgen. 1970. Towards a theory of communicative competence. In *Recent sociology #2*, ed. Hans Peter Dreitzel, 114–48. London: Collier Macmillan.

———. 1971. *Knowledge and human interest*. Trans. Jeremy Shapiro. Boston: Beacon Press.

———. 1975. *Legitimation crisis*. Trans. Thomas McCarthy. Boston: Beacon Press.

———. 1976. Some distinctions in universal pragmatics. *Theory and Society* 3:155–67.

———. 1979. *Communication and the evolution of society*. Trans. Thomas McCarthy. Boston: Beacon Press.

———. 1981. Modernity versus postmodernity. *New German Critique* 22:3–14.

———. 1985. Questions and counterquestions. In *Habermas and Modernity*, ed. R. J. Bernstein. Cambridge, MA: MIT Press.

Haiman, Franklyn S. 1958. Democratic ethics and the hidden persuaders. *Quarterly Journal of Speech* 44:385–92.

Hauser, Gerard A. 1989. Administrative rhetoric and public opinion: Discussing the Iranian hostages in the public sphere. In *American rhetoric: Context and Criticism*, ed. Thomas W. Benson, 323–84. Carbondale: Southern Illinois University Press.

Ingram, David. 1982. The possibility of a communication ethic reconsidered. *Man and the World* 15:149–61.

Jensen, J. Vernon. 1990. Directions to consider in communication ethics. In

Proceedings of the first national communication ethics conference, 1–16. Hickory Corners, MI: Kellogg Biological Station Educational Center on Gull Lake.

Johannesen, Richard L. 1985. An ethical assessment of Reagan rhetoric: 1981–1982. In *Political communication yearbook, 1984*, ed. Keith R. Sanders, Lynda Lee Kaid, and Dan Nimmo, 226–41. Carbondale: Southern Illinois University Press.

———. 1990. *Ethics in human communication*, 3rd ed. Prospect Heights, IL: Waveland Press.

Joslyn, Richard A. 1986. Keeping politics in the study of political discourse. In *Form, genre, and the study of political discourse*, ed. Herbert W. Simons and Aram A. Aghazarian, 301–38. Columbia: University of South Carolina Press.

Kellner, Douglas. 1988. Postmodernism as social theory: Some challenges and problems. *Theory, Culture, and Society* 5:239–69.

Kruger, Arthur N. 1967. The ethics of persuasion: A re-examination. *The Speech Teacher* 16:295–305.

Lanigan, Richard L., and Rudolf L. Strobl. 1981. A critical theory approach. In *Handbook of political communication*, ed. Dan D. Nimmo and Keith R. Sanders, 141–68. Beverly Hills, CA: Sage.

Lasch, Christopher. 1979. *The cult of narcissism: American life in an age of diminishing expectations*. New York: W. W. Norton.

Lucaites, John Louis. 1990. A rhetorical response: Or towards a rhetorical consciousness of 'politics' in the realms of culture and the public. *Communication* 12:49–64.

Lyotard, Jean-François. 1984. *The postmodern condition: A report on knowledge*. Trans. Geoff Bennington and Brian Massami. Minneapolis: University of Minnesota Press.

McGee, Michael Calvin. 1985. 1984: Some issues in the rhetorical study of political communication. In *Political communication yearbook, 1984*, ed. Keith R. Sanders, Lynda Lee Kaid, and Dan Nimmo, 155–82. Carbondale: Southern Illinois University Press.

Murphy, John, and Karen Callaghan. 1988. Postmodernism and social research: An application. *Social Epistemology* 2:83:91.

Nilsen, Thomas R. 1974. *Ethics of speech communication*, 2nd ed. Indianapolis: Bobbs-Merrill.

Rajchman, John. 1986. Ethics after Foucault. *Social Text* 13/14:165–83.

Reid, Herbert G., and Ernest J. Yanarella. 1974. Toward a postmodern theory of American political science and culture: Perspectives from critical Marxism and phenomenology. *Cultural Hermeneutics* 2:91–166.

Richters, Annemeik. 1988. Modernity-postmodernity controversies: Habermas and Foucault. *Theory, Culture, and Society* 5:611–43.

Rogin, Michael Paul. 1967. *The intellectuals and McCarthy: The radical spectre*. Cambridge, MA: MIT Press.

Sennett, Richard. 1977. *The fall of public man*. New York: Knopf.

Shusterman, Richard. 1988. Postmodernist aestheticism: A new moral philosophy? *Theory, Culture, and Society* 5:337–55.

Smith, Hedrick. 1988. *The power game*. New York: Ballantine Books.

Thompson, Dennis F. 1987. *Political ethics and public office*. Cambridge, MA: Harvard University Press.

Van Hooft, Stan. 1976. Habermas' communicative ethics. *Social Praxis* 4:147–75.

Wallace, Karl R. 1955. An ethical basis of communication. *The Speech Teacher* 4:1–9.

Wander, Philip. 1981. Cultural criticism. In *Handbook of political communication*, ed. Dan D. Nimmo and Keith R. Sanders, 497–528. Beverly Hills, CA: Sage.

———. 1984. The ideological turn in modern criticism. *Central States Speech Journal* 34:1–18.

———. 1990. The politics of despair. *Communication* 11:277–90.

Chapter Four

Ethical Pivots and Moral Vantages in American Presidential Campaign Dramas

Bruce E. Gronbeck

To assemble and contemplate the series of ethical decision points that Americans use in calling moral fouls during presidential campaigns is a daunting task. For one thing, a presidential campaign is no longer, if it ever was, merely an extension of the characters or *ethoi* of the competing candidates. Stirred into any campaign effort are the so-called kingmakers (Chagall 1981), that is, the handlers and advisers known to us by name and by reputation (thanks to journalistic probing), and the press itself, which filters the words and events reaching the voter and which puts "spin" on those words and events in its daily exhibition of interpretive expertise. If presidential campaigns are corporate or institutionalized rhetorical acts available to voters only as mass-mediated events, then traditional rhetorical standards for assessing an individual's ethical culpability may need to be rethought.

In the second place, finding the ethical issues upon which voters make their decisions is complicated by the duration of the American electoral process. We now live in what Sidney Blumenthal (1980) called the permanent campaign; his reference was to the attached advisory, polling, and communication industries that need year-round campaign activity to make money, though in our time the reference can also comprehend the candidate conglomerates: given the complexities of the American electorate and the cost of doing electoral business, presidential candidates simply cannot stop seeking the Oval Office. Federal matching funds demand small contributions ($250) from numerous citizens in at least 20 states, and it takes time to raise that money. And the search for votes is a continual process in a time of 50 primaries and caucuses; facing Democratic candidates are 19 caucuses, and the GOP aspirants, 14, with the rest of the 50 states holding primaries between February 8 and June 7 (in 1988). The early caucus states, especially, demand considerable personal attention from candidates well before primary season because of press concern for initial voter interest (Lichter, Amundson, and Noyes 1988). Overall, campaigns in all 50 states are time-consuming and expensive.

Third, given the length of a presidential campaign, the occasions for ethical assessment are highly variable. The perpetual quality of the campaign season gives us not only more political discourse but also more different kinds of messages. When searching out "political speeches," for example, we are faced with state-of-the-nation talks at Jefferson-Jackson Day banquets by Democratic politicians hoping someone will think of them as presidential timber, speeches in support of local candidates (to justify the "unannounced" candidate's presence in your home town), pre-announcement speeches, announcement speeches, acceptance speeches, news conferences, debates and other joint appearances, apologies in response to gaffes or presumed gaffes, victory speeches or explanations justifying a second- or third-place finish in a primary, and good ol' state fair encomiums for the citizens down home. On television, in addition to video clips from those speeches there are biographical ads, issue ads, comparative ads, attack ads, God-mother-hood-and-country tableaux of candidates and their families, five-minute discussions of the "big" issues during the last two weeks of the campaign, half-hour biographies and campaign summaries by the political parties, panel and talk-show appearances, and any number of other "press opportunities" prepared by the candidate's publicists.

Nor can you escape politics by turning off your electronic boxes. In your mailbox will be letters from the candidates, broadsides, pamphlets, questionnaires, position papers aimed purposively at someone like you living in your nine-digit ZIP code, sample ballots, appeals from county organizations, congressional newsletters, and celebrity-signed requests for contributions. On the street will be billboards, car-top posters, bumper stickers, headquarters window displays, parades, calls to city park corn roasts, street-corner rallies, factory-gate handshakes, malt-shop and church basement meet-the-candidate gatherings, and walks through ghettos. You can easily pick up a League of Women Voters' guide to issues, a campaign biography at a bookstore, and multiple magazines' and newspapers' reports on and evaluations of the candidates. The American voter is awash in political messages of such varied types that simple ethical calls are impossible to make.

What I am suggesting is that the nature of the rhetorical acts we call "campaigning for president" and the range of ethical judgments voters are asked to make have changed markedly in the twentieth century. No longer does the presidency call someone to it; Richard Gephardt (D-

Missouri) started his 1988 campaign in neighboring Iowa during 1985. In an important sense, Ronald Reagan started running for the presidency in the mid–1960s, when he toured the country giving "The Speech" (Ritter 1968). No longer are dense speeches the essence of political rhetoric; electric rhetoric—from computerized letters to video clips and sound bits—is the discourse with which most of us are presented in the name of campaigning. No longer do we have the luxury of judging candidates' performances in offices as separate from campaigning, for campaigning is there perpetually. While the Federal Election Commission controls some of the fund raising and money management (*Compliance* 1983), nonfederal sources—and individuals—do most of the ethical assessment. How are voters to make ethical judgments in a political system where campaigning is forever and where political personas are presented to us like terribly expensive video games?

THE ETHICAL PIVOTS IN PRESIDENTIAL CAMPAIGNS

While we must recognize that presidential campaigns are permanent, complex, and composed of far more messages than any single human being (including the candidate) can grasp, they are not formless. We can comprehend, understand, and evaluate them. To do so thoroughly means that we must live the life of syndicated columnist David Broder, eating and breathing politics every day of the week. The rest of us take shortcuts; we search out social-psychological structures that capture and freeze the campaigning process in simple forms. Those structures, I would submit, are usually sociodramatic.

Many have written about campaigns, especially presidential campaigns, as dramas (e.g., Bennett 1977; Stillman 1977; Nimmo and Combs 1980, 231–39; Combs 1980, ch. 6; Trent and Friedenberg 1983; Gronbeck 1985, 1987). Understanding campaigns as sociodramas helps us comprehend the variety of messages needed in different phases or acts. It also suggests that the power of campaign communication lies less in facts and figures, causes and effects, and statistical trends than in the stories campaigners tell and the rites they act out in order to materialize their qualifications, their hopes, and their values. Third, dramatic frames help us—as scholars and as voters—to essentialize campaigns; the dramas of "Bring Us Together" (Nixon's slogan of 1968) and "Re-elect the President" (his slogan in 1972) were very different, the first symbolizing a campaign taking aim at the Democratic Party's discord of 1968 (Hubert Humphrey vs. the peaceniks) and the second affirming Richard Nixon's leadership abilities. In 1968 and 1972 we witnessed campaign dramas with most of the same players yet quite different plots.

Thinking of campaigns as sociodramas, in the fourth place, gives us another way into the analysis of campaign ethics. As we learned from

Aristotle's *Poetics* long ago, the three primary dimensions or features of drama are action or plot (*mythos*), character (*ethos*), and thought (*dianoia*). It is possible to use these three dimensions of all drama to frame an analysis of the *ethical pivots* around which assessments of campaign morality are made. Ethical pivots are like the support bars for teeter-totters; they are the central social-psychological structures around which more specific political issues of morality are organized.In 1988, if voters believed Michael Dukakis was a dangerous liberal who overtaxed the state of Massachusetts and took rights to decide away from individuals, they would likely use that ethical pivot to negatively evaluate his welfare proposals, tax schemes, and urban reform plans. If voters believed George Bush was a politically expedient person who always pointed in the direction the voters wind was blowing, they likely used that ethical pivot to explain away his assertions about federal support of education, environmentalism, and what was called the Pledge of Allegiance issue in 1988.

Voters and public commentators thus seem to find a series of dramatic structures—plots, characters, and topics—around which to build the "story" of any given presidential campaign. Those structures determine the kind of morality play or mythic fable we construct quadrennially to help us assess the competing claims and, ultimately, to direct and rationalize our votes. As complex as campaigns really are, ethical judgments come down to the following:

1. Candidates' actions and the *motives* they offer in justification of those actions
2. Candidates' *character* (to Aristotle, the degree to which they exhibit good sense, goodwill, and acceptable morals in their talk)
3. Candidates' discussions of issues and the extent to which they illustrate their *competence* as governors.

Let me explain more fully what I mean.

Campaigning for the presidency is a billion-dollar game of "what if": What if this person were president of the United States? That is a most difficult question to answer, of course, because America's president plays so many different roles: chief of state, chief executive, commander in chief of the armed forces, chief diplomat, chief legislator, chief of party, voice of "the people," protector of the peace, manager of prosperity, and world leader (Rossiter 1960). Not only are the roles varied, but voters are forced to make complex judgments between and among them: Will a person exercise his or her world leadership via skillful diplomacy or militaristic saber rattling? When a person faces a choice between party and the people, whose interests will he or she serve? Will the person be able to negotiate successfully between his or her executive and legislative roles?

Our principal clues in seeking answers to such questions are to be found in actions and their underlying motives, outlines of character as seen in word and deed, and the competence with which candidates handle complex issues. Motive, character, and competence are the three primary ethical pivots of a presidential campaign.

The Assessment of Motive

Any good leader is expected to reflect the basic mores and political values of his or her society. In a complex world where right and wrong are not easily distinguished, where defense budgets seem obscene yet necessary, and where everyone believes in helping the poor but no wants to foot the bill, a political actor's motives must be assessed. As used here, "motive" should not be confused with "motivation" (deep-set psychological springs to action) or "cause" (physical or physiological forces that produce predictable consequences).

"Motives" are public rationalizations of justifications of human action. The war hero who says he fell on a grenade "so that my buddies wouldn't get hurt" has said nothing, really, about motivation (how did he develop such an extreme sense of self-sacrifice?) or cause (the operation of his autonomic nervous system that allowed him to move before he thought about it). "So that my buddies wouldn't get hurt" is a socially acceptable justification for human action, one that recognizes the claim of the collectivity and its protection by the individual. Or, as Ted Kennedy in 1969 discussed the poor lighting, twisting road, rickety bridge, and cold water when explaining why he had an accident on Chappaquiddick Bridge and why he acted as he did afterward, he offered rationalizations most could understand; and when, at the end of the speech, he surrendered the authority to judge his actions to the people of Massachusetts, whom he represented as senator, he left the impression he had nothing to hide—pure, publicly acceptable motives (Ling 1970).

We want to know the general motives from which our presidential candidates operate. An attack upon an opponent must not be "merely political," that is, offered only for personal gain, but somehow must be made publicly acceptable by being tied to "the public's right to know" or to previous assertions made by the opponent. Or, when candidates push to increase defense spending, it must be related to "peace through strength," the cliché that expresses general beliefs about "proper" reasons for arming a democracy in the late twentieth century. Candidates are judged on the motives they assert to rationalize or justify their positions.

The Assessment of Character

If motives are socially acceptable reasons to act that we assess in order to check out a candidate's grounding in his or her culture, character is a matter of less specific judgments. Motives are assessed situation by situation, while character—what the Greeks called *ethos*—is a more transcendent aspect of candidates' persons.

James David Barber (1972, 8) defines presidential character generally as "the way the president orients himself toward life." That orientation, however, is understood by voters not simply as a personal orientation, something idiosyncratic, but as a *type* of orientation—a social type of orientation. "Character" must be, as James Combs notes, "presented, staged, and performed" (1980, 82). When critics discuss Jimmy Carter's "populist style," the "Camelot" style of John F. Kennedy, or the "coolness" of Michael Dukakis in 1988, they are probing not simply an individual ethos but also social vocabularies for talking about individuals in collective ways. Populism is, roughly, a kind of bottom-up, citizen-based orientation to politics that we contrast with "aristocratic," "elite," and "oligarachic" orientations; references to Camelot associate the largeness of Kennedy's vision with the Arthurian myth of strength in democracy, where individuals are both strong and moral. Michael Dukakis is charged with being a cool "technocrat" because of his refusal to be angered by personal attacks and his emphasis on organizational solutions even to individual problems; his orientation is seen as uninvolved, merely efficient, in an election where his opponent worked hard alternately at being angry and at calling for "a kinder, gentler nation."

Richard Nixon's ruthlessness (1960, 1968, 1972), Barry Goldwater's overzealousness (1964), George McGovern's blinded commitment to surrender (1972), Gerald Ford's physical and verbal clumsiness (1976), Walter Mondale's blandness (1984), and Joseph Biden's exaggerations of his own record (1988) caused each of these candidates to be accused of having important flaws of character, of orientation. More positively, of course, Ronald Reagan was depicted as a humble, warmhearted, homey sort whose character mimicked that of the "everyday" people he praised in his 1989 inaugural address, and Jesse Jackson was adjudged the most moral man in the 1988 candidate by the Iowa voters (Gronbeck 1989a).

As noted earlier, such judgments of character seldom are tied to specific events or actions. They are ethical assessments we make transcendentally—by a kind of abstracting process difficult to specify. Thus, it becomes difficult to argue someone into or out of a characterological judgment. Such judgments tend to change slowly, over long sweeps of time. Nixon worked hard to rid himself of the ruthless label, and probably never did get rid of the characterization "tricky Dick" even before the Watergate debacle, despite two victories as presidential aspirant. It takes many words and multiple image constructions to make or remake voters' assessments of character. That large number of verbal and visual constructions comes to us primarily in the bombardment of political advertisements that seek us out in every election. Over the duration of a presidential campaign, bits and pieces of verbal and visual rhetorical tiles are assembled in our minds to construct a mosaic of political character (Becker 1971).

The Assessment of Competence

Campaigns, of course, are full of promises; we do not really see what candidates *will* or *can* do as president but only what they *think* or *project* they will accomplish. The assessment of someone's competence as a leader, in an important sense, therefore is based on our assessments of that person's thoughts and projections. To be sure, we can base part of our judgment of competence on previous records: Jimmy Carter (1976), Ronald Reagan (1980), and Michael Dukakis (1988) told the electorate to examine their records as governors to see how competent they were as executives; John Anderson (1980), John Glenn (1984), and Robert Dole (1988) produced ads discussing their managerial skills as legislators. But the office of president is different, in kind and in magnitude, from any other political office, and hence we must make our assessments of competence on more than personal history. Candidates' thoughts and projections are crucial.

How do we assess competence? That is a difficult question. One answer that is useful for analysts of presidential aspirants is to say that, as is the case with all judgments being discussed in this chapter, we assay competence from our own sense of what is useful yet prudent, effective yet moral. We attempt to assess the degree to which common sense is exhibited by a candidate. In the history of rhetorical thought, common sense, *sensus communis*, has meant many different things (Schaeffer 1990). Always present in its rhetorical meaning, though, is the idea that a people share understandings—usually, at least since Descartes (Schaeffer 1990, 2), a kind of practical sense of how one should act in a specific situation.

Take the example of Gary Hart's actions in the spring of 1987. Thanks to a tip, reporters discovered he was being accompanied on sea and on land by model Donna Rice. His motive, a weekend-long dalliance by a married man with a sexually attractive woman, was clear enough. For that, women found him "unacceptable, intolerable and unforgivable"; men, interestingly, found him "stupid"—that is, "incompetent" (*Newsweek* 1988, 47). In not immediately responding to the negative ads focused on the Massachusetts criminal furlough program (the so-called Willie Horton ads), on Boston harbor, and on his lack of knowledge of foreign and military affairs (the so-called tank ads), Dukakis was deemed incompetent (Editors of *Time* 1988, 213–43).

Sensus communis, acting practically, as can be seen in relationships between women's and men's reactions to Hart, is closely associated with assessments of motive. Both stem from voters' attempts to understand and appreciate (or not) candidates' actions; both also assume that individual behavior is somehow grounded in the *doxa*, the generally received opinions, of a society. Yet they are distinct judgments; there is a difference between saying someone acted out of illiberal motive and saying that person did something impractical—something dumb. Thus, each is a ground for positive or negative assessment of political candidates.

Some may find it odd to consider "competence" an ethical matter. In a sense, assessments of competence are amoral, matters of getting from A to B with a minimum of hassle. But, as ought to be clear from this discussion, being a person of prudent action and acting within a culture's or subculture's *sensus communis* are matters with ethical features; participating within the ethic, the ethos, of a society is at root an ethical matter, for a "like us" assessment is being made. The ancient Greek ideal of *phronesis*, of demonstrating practical wisdom in one's concrete actions, is still with us; controlling one's self and the environments within which the self operates is as much a moral as an efficient good in all societies. The competent presidential candidate must offer us thoughts and projections that we see as demonstrating practical wisdom.

ETHICAL PERSPECTIVES ON PRESIDENTIAL CAMPAIGNS

Identifying ethical pivots is only half the problem we face in discussing campaign morality. The other knotty question is *From what vantages can we assess motive, character, and competence? In traditional rhetorical studies, four ethical perspectives have been discussed.*

The Ethics of Political Message Makers

As noted earlier, a traditional rhetorical perspective on ethics has worked from the vantage of the rhetor, the message maker. When Quintilian wrote in the first century about *vir bonus peritus dicendi*, the goodman speaking well, he urged his readers to assess the morality of a discourse by the morality of its maker. The judgment was a dual one: (1) To what extent do we see virtue in the speaker (*vir bonus*)? (2) To what extent is the message well made (*peritus dicendi*)? The good man, to Quintilian, was the product of a careful upbringing and education, a person steeped in the social wisdom of the culture and tutored for public life. Such people, of course, tended to be aristocratic—products of the gentry class because only there were time and money available for such socialization. The person had to be "good" ethically and civically, and the message had to be the product of systematic preparation and doxatic thought, that is, well considered and sensitive to the beliefs, attitudes, and values of the population to which it would be delivered.

In spite of the impossible complexities of contemporary campaigning, which in reality make the moral assessments of message makers inadequate, there persists among many voters a desire to hold *somebody* responsible for campaign messages. After viewing a particularly obnoxious ad or reading a fear-mongering solicitation letter, we all sooner or later are ready to scream, "I want to know who's responsible for this!" Some of our judgments in campaigns about motive, character, and competence are centered on the rhetor or messenger. Judgments of candidates' motives are comparatively absolutist; that is, voters who assess message makers tend to use hardened moral measuring sticks. To those who focus on communicators, people have acceptable or unacceptable motives, characterological styles, and levels of competence; they tend to be deeply committed to one candidate and deeply antagonistic toward opponents.

The Ethics of Political Message Consumers

An equally viable rhetorical tradition is the ethics of caveat emptor, buyer beware. From the beginning of his *Rhetoric*, Aristotle justified his work in that field in part by arguing it would make us more discerning consumers of persuasive talk. Consumerism as we know it in this century has been the outcome of both the industrial revolution, which mechanized (depersonalized) production while creating inexpensive mass-manufactured items, and the communications revolution, which not only accelerated the spread of the consumption culture but also framed the means of resisting it. The communications revolution was enslaving in its creation of an ersatz cultural environment, a product not of life but of fictions about life. It also, however, was liberating in that the telephone, telegraph, and computer-generated letter could link geographically distant individuals; as well, the very formulization of radio and television fare contained within itself the grounds for critique.

In terms of presidential campaign politics, consumerist thinking has three consequences. First, we campaign not only via mass media but also via mini media. The communications revolution has surrounded us with point-to-point technologies such as phones, fax machines, satellite hookups, modems, and coaxial cable (Armstrong 1988). These media tend to reduce the dominance of such mass media as radio, television, and film. Second, because of repetition and the formulary nature of mass-mediated messages, they inevitably spawn their own dissent. As a formula (e.g., a standard political biographical ad or an attack-on-voting-record ad) is employed again and again in a limited number of ads, it becomes commonplace and recedes into perpetual background. Overuse dissipates the force of appeals and, in psychologically disposing of clichés, consumers take command.

Third, modern electronic media, together with rigorous pursuit of the democratic ideal, have produced a fragmented or splintered society; "consumers" do not comprise a monolithic bloc of product users but, rather, various sets of audiences. We are separated from each other by many demographic characteristics: two genders, multiple ethnic backgrounds, varied religious practices, socioeconomic strata, educational levels, and age groups that allow advertisers to appeal to us as teens, young adults, baby boomers, and the elderly. We also can be aligned for and against each other around specific clusters of beliefs, attitudes, and values; these alignments are especially visible politically in the "single-issue" groups or lobbies—groups pro and contra the legalization of abortion, the National Rifle Association and its detractors, nuclear freeze and disarmament coalitions, K–12 and higher education lobbies, and the like. Thus, there are "women's issues" that function as litmus tests of presidential candidates for members of the National Organization for Women, stands on abortion for certain religious groups and social organizations, questions about citizens' rights to own "Saturday night specials" and AK–47 machine guns that strongly interest NRA members. Litmus tests thus are questions that arise from particular sets of voters (political consumers); in some elections, at least, they seemingly have guided significant numbers of votes.

We do not, however, always rely solely on ourselves as experienced consumers or even on our reference groups when making ethical judgments in campaigns. The issues are too difficult, too complex, too specialized for most of us to call (Fisher 1987). As suggested earlier, campaigns become dramas for most of us because that is the only way we can cope with them—as narrative stories about quests, about life in the past, present, and future. We look for important narrators—the candidates themselves, their "spin doctors," journalists, organizational spokespersons, party leaders—to suggest useful ways of looking at what candidates do and say. As well, since 1952 (Mickelson 1989), we have looked at electronically analyzed images of our own beliefs and attitudes, at poll results, to compare our personal reactions with those of a hard-wired "public"; "public opinion" today, with its scientific aura, becomes an odd but influential kind of "expert" on domestic and foreign affairs. As buyers, we face a world too formidable to be able to determine for ourselves of what we must be wary.

And yet the consumerism movement supplies us with useful ethical vantages, as we see in the rise of Common Cause and other "public" lobbies in the 1960s and 1970s and in the vigorous entry of so-called single-issue organizations with money into the campaign finance business. Most of us want to think that we are the lifeblood of democratic society and that we occasionally can assert our own consumer rights; most of us hope that Buyer Beware! occasionally can be turned around to Seller Beware! Occasionally it is.

The Ethics of Political Messages

In the Platonic dialogues on rhetoric (especially the *Gorgias* and the *Phraedrus*) there are suggestions that the good rhetor can know and articulate the Truth. Many of us hold a deep item of faith—one for which we seldom have direct evidence, unfortunately—that yearns to search for Truth. Truth becomes important to us, one must assume, in part because certitude is comforting in a world of flux, in part because truths are measuring rods against which we can assess the motives, character, and competence of others. Truth thus is important for our own sense of well-being and for our relationships with others. And hence we use a truth criterion in assessing rhetorical messages, including political messages.

Truth telling is related to the first ethic discussed here, that of the message maker; that is, "telling the truth" is an important means by which we assess the good sense, good will, and morals of rhetors. It also is, more strictly speaking, a way of assaying messages. We test the truth of speeches by examining their claims or propositions, checking out the supporting materials, comparing the reasons given to support some cause with the reasons most people fall back on in such situations, and the like. When Karl Wallace articulated "An Ethical Basis of Communication," the first two of his bases were related specifically to message characteristics: a speaker's commitment to search for information and inquire after ideas with an open mind, and unswerving "allegiance to accuracy, fairness, and justice in the selection and treatment of ideas and arguments" (1955, 9). Further, Haiman (1958) worried about messages that short-circuited reasoning by the way they were constructed. Here, too, is a message- or text-based judgment, for the "reasoning" of concern here is visible in linguistic constructions. Truth, we think, ought to be visible in the words we use to describe and characterize the world.

This, of course, is an impossibility. None of us can know if Columbus *really* sailed for the New World in 1492, because the past is inaccessible to us; we rely upon the testimony of others—others writing before the calendar was adjusted in the eighteenth century. Is the phrase "All men are created equal" *true* or not? That depends, of course, upon whether "men" is taken to be a generic noun and whether "are created equal" is seen as a factual assertion or a valuation assumption about life; both language usage and the force of statements can change over time, making truth linguistically and temporally relative.

Yet again, when push comes to shove in presidential campaigns, truth tests abound. Like assessments made of candidates themselves (as message makers), moral judgments here tend to be absolutist and determinative of one's vote. During Campaign '88, we worried a good deal about the truth about Dukakis's furlough program, whether Gary Hart could rhetorically justify his liaison with model Donna Rice, and if Joseph Biden knowingly plagiarized part of his Iowa State Fair speech in 1987. These candidates rose or fell on the messages they offered in self-defense and response to attacks.

The Ethics of the Situation

Probably the most controversial ethical system of our time is situational ethics, the idea that ethical principles in society vary from context to context. This position was articulated generally by Edward Rogge:

The extension of the democratic principle suggests that speech critics must evaluate the ethics of a speech by the standards developed by the society. The critic must recognize that the standards vary as factors in the speech situation vary, that they vary as the necessity for the implementation of the persuader's proposal varies, that they vary as his degree of leadership varies.(1959, 425)

This position is often condemned because it can degenerate into relativism, one of the philosophical swear words of our age. Yet, of course, it need not collapse into an "anything goes" attitude. We may apply one set of standards or expectations to preaching from a pulpit, and another set to beseeching on the used-car lot, yet both can be rule-governed communication situations. We have come to expect exaggeration in political campaigning but more straightforward analyses of domestic and foreign problems in state-of-the-union addresses, yet both can be assessed by situation-specific ethical rules.

The foundations of this ethical perspective are the ideas of *rules* and *roles*. Acculturation is a matter of learning rules—positive and negative guides to behavior and sanctions you face for not following them. You learn rules for eating in the presence of others, for what you may and may not touch, for how to address everyone from a sibling to a grand-dame aunt—and how to campaign for public office. *How* you talk is a matter of *where* you are and *what* role you are playing. You talk one way as a son or a daughter, another as a nephew or a niece, another as a student or a teacher, another as a Presbyterian or a Muslim, another as a Norwegian or an African-American; your speech varies with those aspects of your roles which are relevant to particular situations.

And, it can be argued, the same is true of campaign communication. The ethical rules we use to assess acceptance speeches are quite different from those which apply to commercials. We come to expect different kinds of talk in joint appearances (debates) than in half-hour televised campaign biographies. Judging the ethical posture of candidates situation by situation, thus, is terribly complicated; situational ethics by its very nature is comparative rather than absolutist, and demands of its adherents a willingness to make multiple readings over time and a power to factor in many candidate performances before drawing moral conclusions about the person.

Complicated or not, however, we see signs that situational ethics are employed by a significant number of voters. If we can assume that an "undecided" response to a public opinion poll is in part, at least, the result of a delayed, reasoned moral judgment of the candidates, then the fluctuation of the undecided vote throughout a campaign and the size of that vote even in the last two weeks of a campaign are signs that some voters take multiple moral readings of candidates across numerous campaign settings. Situational judgments affect electoral outcomes.

All in all, therefore, as we consider the ethics of presidential campaigning, we are left with three ethical pivots (motives, character, and competence) that can be assessed from four moral vantages (message maker, message consumer, message, and situation). These are arrayed in Table 1. Considering the social-psychological interaction of the ethical pivots and moral vantages, we arrive at twelve questions that can guide voters' moral assessments of presidential candidates.

MORAL QUESTIONS TO WHICH WE SEEK ANSWERS IN CAMPAIGNS

Not all moral inquiries are featured in every presidential campaign (though presumably somebody is asking each of the 12 questions every four years). The critic interested in exploring voters' ethical judgments, however, can use those 12 questions as assessment tools; that is, critics can attempt to see which questions became matters of public concern in particular elections, and then use the results of their researches to generally characterize the moral tone and ethical dynamics of those campaigns.

We certainly do not have room in a short chapter to do a complete study of even a single election, let alone enough to fully illustrate all 12 questions. We can, however, at least offer examples of each moral inquiry and briefly contrast campaigns with different ethical vortices; in

Table 1
Questions That Can Guide Voters' Ethical Judgments in Presidential Campaigns

	ETHICAL PIVOTS		
MORAL VANTAGES	Motives	Character	Competence
Message Makers	Are candidates' motives acceptable?	Are candidates' characterological styles acceptable?	Have candidates demonstrated political competence?
Message Consumers	What political motives do sets of voters find acceptable?	What characterological styles do sets of voters find acceptable?	What measures of political competence are used by particular sets of voters?
Messages	Are candidates' motives expressed in acceptable ways?	Are candidates' characterological styles depicted in acceptable ways?	Are candidates illustrating their political competence in messages and responses to opponents' messages?
Situations	What movitves are acceptable in various situations	What characterological styles are expected in various situations?	Are candidates handling various political situations competently?

that way, the potential utility of the 3 × 4 matrix offered in Table 1 will be presented.

The 12 Questions

First, let us examine the 12 cells of the matrix, identifying each by the interaction between ethical pivot and moral vantage:

Motives of Message Makers. When former Alabama governor George Wallace ran for president in 1964 and 1968, first as a Democrat and then as a third-party candidate, his motives were regularly questioned: Was he running seriously as a well-rounded candidate or simply as a racist seeking to intensify an already bad situation in race relations?

Character of Message Makers. When Joseph Biden plagiarized a speech by British Labour Party leader Neil Kinnock and exaggerated his law school record, character traits unacceptable in a presidential aspirant were attributed to him.

Competence of Message Makers. When Michael Dukakis refused to deal with the charge that he was a "liberal," made by George Bush at the GOP convention and regularly thereafter, he demonstrated a dual incompetence: an incompetence to deal directly with attack (absolute assessment of competence) and an unwillingness to defend an important constituency within the Democratic party (assessment by liberal voters, that is, consumers, as discussed below).

Motives Viewed by Message Consumers. Women's groups in 1984 questioned Ronald Reagan's articulated motives for not supporting the Equal Rights Amendment, and positively assessed Walter Mondale's when he not only strongly endorsed the ERA but also selected a female running mate, Geraldine Ferraro.

Character Viewed by Message Consumers. Hubert Humphrey's support as vice president of President Lyndon Johnson up to the general election of 1968 was seen as unacceptable by the Union of Concerned Democrats and other antiwar groups. Then, when Humphrey seemingly turned on Johnson during the fall campaign, centrist Democrats found his disloyalty reprehensible. Various sets of voters thus found his ethos irreparably flawed.

Competence Viewed by Message Consumers. President Jimmy Carter in 1980 began campaigning with the "Rose Garden strategy." He stayed in the White House, he said, in order to run the country and focus his attention on the Iranian hostage situation, talking only briefly to reporters in the Rose Garden. This made him appear to many voters as a candidate avoiding the communication of his thoughts and projects for the next four years. It was deemed an incompetent political strategy. (Carter's leadership abilities also were found wanting in public discussion of his job performance—his handling of both inflation and the Iranian hostage crisis.)

Motives Written into Messages. Many found George Bush's promise in 1988 to not raise taxes in spite of a mounting national debt and a deficit budget to be a "merely political" stand—one he could not possibly maintain as president. His "no new taxes" statement was questioned regularly by the press and featured in the presidential debates.

Character Written into Messages. Ronald Reagan's most powerful ads in 1984 were built around an "It's morning in America" theme; they depicted a prosperous, happy, patriotic citizenry whose *ethoi* were presumably reflected in Reagan's own values—concerns for positive achievement, self-satisfaction, commitments to America and Americans' dreams. The ads thus attempted to isolate and to make isomorphic moral characteristics of Ronald Reagan and the people whose votes he pursued.

Competence Written into Messages. "Slips of the tongue" or "lapses of judgment" often become grounds for assessing a candidate's competence. George Wallace's racist jokes in 1964, Jimmy Carter's 1976 disclosure in a *Playboy* interview that he had "committed adultery in his heart," Gerald Ford's assertion during his debate with Carter that Poland was a free country, and Reagan's stumbling for words in his first debate with Mondale in 1984 (seen by the press as a sign of old age) were examples where the press, and presumably some voters, made assessments of competence by examining specific aspects of political messages.

Candidates' Motives in Specific Situations. Various candidates' refusal to debate their opponents in 1964, 1968, and 1972 were taken to be signs of political insecurity and weakness. George Bush's choice of Dan Quayle was questioned throughout the 1988 campaign, as was his use of a fear appeal in airing the Willie Horton ads (an African-American prisoner convicted of raping and murdering a white woman while participating in a prison furlough program).

Candidates' Character in Specific Situations. Voters saw Barry Goldwater's assertion that "Extremism in the pursuit of liberty is not vice" during the 1964 Republican national convention as a moral shortcoming, and his acknowledgment that he would not categorically rule out tactical nuclear weapons in the Vietnam war, as a deviation from the *sensus communis* of the citizenry.

Candidates' Competence in Specific Situations. Senator John Glenn (D-Ohio) blew his chances to be Jimmy Carter's vice presidential candidate when he gave a flat speech at the 1976 Democratic convention. Carter, in turn, was blamed for the incompetence of the American rescue attempt in Iran in the 1980 campaign. Reagan's team of advisers got many competence points for the production of his ads but lost them for the way his handlers prepared him for the first 1984 presidential debate.

These are some examples of ways that moral vantages interact with ethical pivots to raise specific questions about particular candidates, their words, and their actions. Let us now turn to a more abstract matter, the general moral tone of particular campaigns.

The Moral Centers of Presidential Campaigns

It is possible, at least in principle, to identify and comment on the moral vortex for a particular campaign. While many ethical issues are raised by multiple candidates and their myriad campaign messages, the press and the voters often boil down a campaign to central moral issues. Reductionist strategies are important as we attempt to find the plots in the sociodramas that comprise our presidential campaigns.

Thus, the press pitted John Kennedy's competence as a young, untried national leader against Richard Nixon's fundamental character—the "tricky Dick" heritage he carried from the early 1950s—in the general election of 1960. Concern for Lyndon Johnson's character as a backroom manipulator was put into ethical dialogue with Barry Goldwater's conservative motives and general competence in 1964. Nixon's speeches carefully construed his experience as the basis of his leadership and general political character in 1968, which commentators contrasted with Humphrey's incompetence and suspected motives (the vindication of

Johnson's domestic and foreign policies). The GOP-Democratic contrast was turned into a matter of who better affirmed the basic vision of American citizens and who could be charged with subverting that dream in the Nixon-McGovern contest of 1972 (Fisher 1973).

In 1976 Ford's competence as a leader was tested by the construction of Jimmy Carter's "outsider" character; Ford's generally prosaic vision and his pardon of Richard Nixon were contrasted with Carter's lack of true national experience (but also his lack of pollution by the crimes of Watergate), with Carter getting the moral nod. By 1980, it was Carter's competence under attack by Ronald Reagan, whose motives were depicted as perfectly in tune with those of the everyday American heroes he praised in his first inaugural address. And in 1984, motives again were the center of controversy, as Mondale's "liberalness" was everywhere maligned by the GOP and as Reagan's heartlessness, his insensitivity to women, minorities, and the average laborer, was attacked in multiple Democratic speeches and ads. Campaign '88 ultimately hinged on three moral fulcrums: the motives behind Bush's and Dukakis's negative ads, the relationships between their basic characters and those of the American electorate, and their respective abilities to govern competently. Bush was overwhelmingly adjudged to be the man with the purer motives, the more acceptable characterological style, and the talents to govern more competently.

This brief tour of the presidential elections since 1960, it must be emphasized, is dangerously abstract and glib. Each of the critical propositions offered for the various years needs defense by careful, systematic analysis of multiple speeches, position papers, responses to questions asked in presidential debates, and ads from various stages of the campaigns. (For an excellent study of the ads, see Jamieson 1984.) I mean the list only to be suggestive—suggestive of abstract themes that seem to guide the campaign dramas acted in various years, and suggestive of the ways in which specific issues vary even within particular categories of voters' ethical judgments.

CONCLUSION

As we conclude this chapter on the ethics of presidential campaigning, it is well to return to our starting point. Technological innovations, changes in the length of campaigns, party reforms that have put a premium on individual voters, and shifting demographics in America have combined to radically alter presidential campaigning since 1960 (Gronbeck 1989b). The permanent campaign we now face has wiped out the last vestiges of the founding fathers' idyllic world wherein important offices called great men to public service, and wherein campaigns were waged by surrogate warlords as the candidates themselves sat at home, awaiting the outcome. That world has been replaced by a postmodern one in which electric bursts of hot-pink political rhetoric pulsate through audiences traced on computer printouts.

In our brave new world, ethical judgments are not made of politicians we know personally and of messages we receive in the whole. Rather, we are fed bits and pieces of political talk and action in video clips and sound bites. Out of those rhetorical scraps we stitch together comprehensible stories about political actors who seemingly believe in this-or-that vision, who apparently hold these-or-those social-political values. The sources for our stories about any given politician are legion—some from the politician and his or her staff, some from the opponent's campaign committee, some from news media or public lobbies, some from reminiscences we call up from our own memories of campaigns past. Out of the bits and pieces we build plots (*mythoi*), characters (*ethoi*), and thoughts about issues (*dianoia*). And then, on the basis of these plots, characters, and thoughts, we make our social-political judgments and cast our votes.

In large-scale, public political campaigns, we never have direct, absolute knowledge of people and events, for our knowledge is always selected by someone else and presented to us in symbolic, usually mass-mediated, ways. Nor are our judgments merely moral—ethical knee-jerk reactions to the raw world around us. Rather, ethical assessment is a complex negotiatory process, whereby the causes and effects, rights and wrongs, that politicians, the press, and other public commentators isolate and assess are framed in sociodramas that each of us views and judges in terms of our individual experiences. Meaning making and moral assessment are social-psychological processes of negotiation between those who would have us believe and accept one thing and those who interpret what has been communicated.

In a world where meanings are negotiated, a series of ethical pivots and moral vantages are employed by voters to make the ethical judgments upon which ballots are cast. Those of us who are critics of politics must search out the pivots and vantages that seem to occupy the public mind each time we elect a president of the United States. If we can find and comprehend them, we will be able to understand much about what Americans value both in their leaders and in themselves.

REFERENCES

Armstrong, Richard. 1988. *The Next Hurrah: The Communications Revolution in American Politics*. New York: Beech Tree Books.

Barber, James David. 1972. *The Presidential Character*. Englewood Cliffs, NJ: Prentice-Hall.

Becker, Samuel L. 1971. Rhetorical Studies for the Contemporary World. In *The*

Prospect of Rhetoric, edited by Lloyd F. Bitzer and Edwin Black, 21–43. Englewood Cliffs, NJ: Prentice-Hall.

Bennett, W. Lance. 1977. The Ritualistic and Pragmatic Bases of Political Campaign Discourse. *Quarterly Journal of Speech* 63:219–38.

Blumenthal, Sidney. 1980. *The Permanent Campaign: Inside the World of Elite Political Operatives*. Boston: Beacon Press.

Chagall, David. 1981. *The New Kingmakers*. San Francisco: Harcourt Brace Jovanovich.

Combs, James E. 1980. *Dimensions of Political Drama*. Santa Monica, CA: Goodyear.

Compliance with Federal Election Campaign Requirements: A Guide to Candidates. 1983. 4th ed. New York: American Institute of CPAs.

Editors of *Time*. 1988. *The Winning of the White House 1988*. New York: Time, Inc.

Fisher, Walter R. 1973. Reaffirmation and Subversion of the American Dream. *Western Journal of Speech Communication* 59:160–67.

———. 1987. *Human Communication as Narration: Toward a Philosophy of Reason, Value, and Action*. Columbia: University of South Carolina Press.

Gronbeck, Bruce E. 1985. The Presidential Campaign Dramas of 1984. *Presidential Studies Quarterly* 15:386–93.

———. 1987. Functions of Campaigns. In *Political Persuasion in Presidential Campaigns*, edited by L. Patrick Devlin, 137–58. New Brunswick, NJ: Transaction Books.

———. 1989a. Mythic Portraiture in the 1988 Iowa Presidential Caucus Bio-Ads. *American Behavioral Scientist* 32:351–64.

———. 1989b. Electric Rhetoric: The Remaking of American Presidential Campaigns. In *Conference in Rhetorical Criticism 1989*, edited by John Hammerback and Karen L. Fritts. Hayward, CA: Department of Speech Communication, California State University, Hayward.

Haiman, Franklyn S. 1958. Democratic Ethics and the Hidden Persuaders. *Quarterly Journal of Speech* 44:385–92.

Jamieson, Kathleen H. 1984. *Packaging the Presidency: A History and Criticism of Presidential Campaign Advertising*. New York: Oxford University Press.

Lichter, S. Robert, Daniel Amundson, and Richard Noyes. 1988. *The Video Campaign: Network Coverage of the 1988 Primaries*. Washington, DC: American Enterprise Institute.

Ling, David A. 1970. A Pentadic Analysis of Senator Edward Kennedy's Address to the People of Massachusetts, July 25, 1969. *Central States Communication Journal* 21:81–86.

Mickelson, Sig. 1989. *From Whistle Stop to Sound Bite: Four Decades of Politics and Television*. New York: Praeger.

Nimmo, Dan, and James E. Combs. 1980. *Subliminal Politics: Myths & Mythmakers in America*. Englewood Cliffs, NJ: Prentice-Hall.

Ritter, Kurt W. 1968. Ronald Reagan and "The Speech": The Rhetoric of Public Relations Politics. *Western Journal of Speech Communication* 32:50–58.

Rogge, Edward. 1959. Evaluating the Ethics of a Speaker in a Democracy. *Quarterly Journal of Speech*. 45:419–25.

Rossiter, Clinton, 1960. *The American Presidency*, rev. ed. New York: New American Library.

Schaeffer, John D. 1990. *Sensus Communis: Vico, Rhetoric, and the Limits of Relativism*. Durham, NC: Duke University Press.

Stillman, Peter R. 1977. *Introduction to Myth*. Rochelle Park, NJ: Hayden.

Trent, Judith S., and Robert V. Friedenberg. 1983. *Political Campaign Communication: Principles and Practices*. New York: Praeger.

Wallace, Karl R. 1955. An Ethical Basis of Communication. *The Speech Teacher* 6:1–9.

Chapter Five

Virtue Ethics, Character, and Political Communication

Richard L. Johannesen

The contemporary philosophy of ethics has been dominated by an emphasis on duties, obligations, rules, rights, principles, and the resolution of complex ethical dilemmas, quandaries, or borderline cases (Jonsen and Toulmin 1988; Kupperman 1988; Pincoffs 1986). This dominant emphasis has been true whether as variations on Immanuel Kant's categorical imperative, on John Rawls's depersonalized veil of ignorance to determine justice, on statements of intrinsic ultimate goods, or on Jeremey Bentham's or John Stuart Mill's utilitarian/consequentialist views. The past several decades, however, have seen a growing interest among ethicists in a largely ignored tradition that goes back at least as far as Plato's and Aristotle's philosophies of ethics (Adler 1970, 235–65; Geatch 1977; MacIntyre 1984, 146–64; Mayo 1958, 200, 209–12; Palmour 1987; Rorty 1980, 106). This largely bypassed tradition typically is called virtue ethics or character ethics. Indeed, Alderman argues that "Aristotle's moral philosophy is *properly* to be construed as the first important virtue theory" (1982, 128).

Most ethicists of virtue or character see that stance as a crucial complement to the current dominant ethical theories (Becker 1975, 1986; Brandt 1981; Frankena 1970; Kupperman 1988, 123; Meilaender 1984, 4–5; Pincoffs 1986, 5, 35; Sichel 1988, 82; Wallace 1978; Walton 1988, 7). A few elevate character ethics to the position of "primary moral category" and argue that "character is a more adequate final court of appeal in moral philosophy than either rights, goods, or rules" (Alderman 1982). But Hudson (1981) contends that a complete moral theory should encompass *both* rules and principles "which specify a person's moral obligations and duties" *and* the significant role of the virtues of character in guiding moral action. The strengths and weaknesses of a character or virtue ethics approach are explored in an anthology edited by French, Uehling, and Wettstein (1988).

Some philosophers draw distinctions between ethics and morals as concepts. *Ethics* denotes the general and systematic study of what ought to be the grounds and principles for right and wrong human behavior. *Morals* (or morality) denotes the practical, specific, generally agreed-upon, culturally transmitted standards of right and wrong. Other philosophers, however, use the terms *ethics* and *morals* more or less interchangeably—as will be the case here.

THE NATURE OF ETHICAL CHARACTER

In *After Virtue*, MacIntyre views moral character as "the arena of the virtues and vices" (1984, 168). Ethicists describe virtues variously as deep-rooted dispositions, habits, skills, or traits of character that incline us to see, feel, and act in ethically right and sensitive ways. Virtues also are described variously as learned, acquired, cultivated, reinforced, capable of modification, capable of conflicting, and ideally coalesced into a harmonious cluster (see Hauerwas 1981a, 115; Hauerwas 1981b, 49; MacIntyre 1984, 149, 154, 205, 219; Mayo 1958, 101–2, 214; Meilaender 1984, 6–11; Pinckaers 1962; Pincoffs 1986, 73–100; Sichel 1988, 75, 83; Slote 1983).

Consider the nature of moral character as described at some length by three ethicists and a theorist of rhetoric. According to Richard DeGeorge,

As human beings develop, they tend to adopt patterns of actions, and dispositions to act in certain ways. These dispositions, when viewed collectively, are sometimes called character. A person who habitually tends to act as he morally should has a good character. If he resists strong temptation, he has a strong character. If he habitually acts immorally, he has a morally bad character. If despite good intentions he frequently succumbs to temptation, he has a weak character. Because character is formed by conscious actions, in general people are morally responsible for their characters as well as for their individual actions. (1986, 89)

Karen Lebacqz believes that

Indeed, when we act, we not only *do* something, we also shape our own character. Our choices about what to do are also choices about whom to be. A single lie does not necessarily make us a liar; but a series of lies may. And so each choice about what to *do* is also a choice about whom to *be*—or, more accurately, whom to become. (1985, 83)

In line with this view, Joseph Kupfer (1982; also see Michell 1984; Minnick 1985) contends that the "moral presumption against lying" rests on two lines of argument that demonstrate ultimate negative effects on the "character" *of the liar*. First, lying causes immediate restriction of the freedom of the deceived. Lying inclines the liar toward a general disrespect for persons—toward abuse of the uniquely human capacity for language as necessary for understanding and reflective choice. Second, lying involves the self-contradiction of "repudiating in speech what we believe." Liars disguise their "real self" from others by contradicting their real beliefs and, thus, who they really are. This self-opposition threatens the integration or coherence of the liar's personality. By disguising the self, the liar rejects the opportunity for self-knowledge; reactions of others useful for self-definition are possible only in response to truthful self-disclosure of beliefs.

Both of the negative effects on the liar—an attitude of disrespect for persons and threat to coherence of personality—weaken his or her moral character. Walter Fisher considers character to be an "organized set of actional tendencies" (1987, 47) and observes: "If these tendencies contradict one another, change significantly, or alter in 'strange' ways, the result is a questioning of character. . . . Without this kind of predictability, there is no trust, no community, no rational human order (1987, 147–48).

Significant in many discussions of character ethics is the concept of "vision" (Birkhead 1989; Palmour 1987, 20–22). Moral character involves a spectrum of moral excellences or a range of reasons for our actions that provide moral vision (Hauerwas 1981b, 59; Sichel 1988, 256–258). To live morally, believes Hauerwas, "we must not only adhere to public and generalizable rules but also see and interpret the nature of the world in a moral way. The moral life is as much a matter of vision as it is a matter of doing" (1981b, 66). Meilaender describes *"vision* as a central theme of any ethic of virtue" (1984, ix). "Our virtues do not simply fit us for life; they help shape life. They shape not only our character but the world we see and inhabit" (1984, 5). He concludes: *"Being* not *doing* takes center stage; for what we ought to do may depend on the sort of person we are. What duties we perceive may depend upon what virtues shape our vision of the world" (1984, 10).

SOME FUNCTIONS OF ETHICAL CHARACTER

In living the ethical life, what functions may be served by the virtues of character? Our formed ethical character does influence our choices and actions (Adler, 1970, 162, 253; Adler 1988, 247, 253–55, 266; Cunningham 1970; Hauerwas 1981b, 62). "Character surrounds action" and often is "a set of limitations restraining or shaping actions in certain ways. . . . Action occurs within the context of character" (Wilbur 1984, 176). In urging us to take virtues seriously, Hudson maintains that "an ethic of virtues can require both that we be of a certain character and that we perform certain kinds of acts. Human good *consists* (in part) both in virtuous action and in being a person of a certain character" (1981, 198–99). He explains that while a coward occasionally may do a courageous thing, this "does not make him a courageous" person, for the courageous person acts courageously as a matter of course or "second nature." Mayo says that according to character ethics, "there is another way of answering the fundamental question 'What ought I to do?' Instead of quoting a rule, we quote a quality of character, a virtue: we say 'Be brave', or 'Be patient' or 'Be lenient'" (1958, 213). Sommers explains that the virtue-based theorist, by "concentrating attention on character rather than action, tacitly assumes that a virtuous person's actions generally fall within the range of what is right and fair" (1985, xii–xiii).

Our ethical character sensitizes us to ethically difficult or problematic situations, motivates our concern so that the situation matters to us, and undergirds our commitment—our long-term loyalty—to necessary values and actions (Kupperman 1988, 115–21). Hauerwas believes that only "if we have a morally significant character can we be relied upon to face morally serious questions rather than simply trying to avoid them" (1981b, 64). Also, however, as Meilaender argues, in redressing the overemphasis in current ethical theory on "troubling moral dilemmas" and on "borderline cases":

An ethic of virtue seeks to focus not only on such moments of great anxiety and uncertainty in life but also on the continuities, the habits of behavior which make us the persons we are. Not whether we should frame one innocent man to save five—but on the virtue of justice, with its steady, habitual determination to make space in life for the needs and claims of others. Not whether to lie to the secret police—but on that steady regard for others which uses language truthfully and thereby makes a common life possible. (1984, 4–5)

Ethical character influences what *roles* we play in life and how we play them. The roles that we choose should be appropriate to and reflective of our character, not supplant that character (Cochran 1982, 17–21). The ethical virtues and commitments that comprise our moral character "control which roles can be accepted" and "influence how any role is actually lived" (Sichel 1988, 229–30; also see MacIntyre, 1984, 204–8). Ethical character also is related to the *rules* and abstract principles specified by various ethical theories. MacIntyre (1984, 150, 232–35, 257, 268) traces some of these relationships throughout the history of ethical theory. But particularly important is the way in which ethical character can humanize the application of abstract rules and principles. According to Sichel, the virtues of character "interject concern for concrete persons and foster more humane and sensitive feelings, compassion and sympathy, concern for moral ideals and qualities that abstract principles often seem to ignore" (1988, 266; see also Williams 1981, 1–19).

ETHICAL CHARACTER AND COMMUNICATION

A virtue is not a "habit" in the sense of dictating a "weary repetition of identical acts" (Cunningham 1970, 98) or in the sense of automatic, mechanistic repetition (Simon 1986). Rather, Pinckaers (1962) argues at length that moral virtues are formed by the repeated exercise of "interior acts" of practical reason and will that "insure their mastery" over exterior actions. Varied exterior acts in various circumstances may reflect the same internal disposition of virtue. Moral virtues reflect creativity and inventiveness in both their formation and their application, and they dispose a person to produce the maximum of what he or she "is able to do on a moral plane." Although a virtue does not involve "a series of identical material acts tirelessly reproduced," it is characteristic of a moral virtue "to permit an action to be performed without further need for lengthy reflection, without hesitation, and without interior conflict" (Pinckaers 1962, 65, 81).

Ethical communication is not simply a series of careful and reflective decisions, instance by instance, to communicate in ethically responsible ways (Cochran 1982, 32–33; Hauerwas 1977, 20, 29; Klaidman and Beauchamp 1987, 17–20; Lebacqz 1985, 77–91; Sichel 1988, 26, 33–37). Deliberate application of ethical rules sometimes is not possible. Pressure may be so great or a deadline so near for a decision that there is not adequate time for careful deliberation. We may be unsure what ethical criteria are relevant or how they apply. The situation may seem unique and thus applicable criteria do not readily come to mind. In such times of crisis or uncertainty, our decision concerning ethical communication stems less from deliberation than from our "character." Furthermore, our ethical character influences the terms with which we describe a situation and whether we believe the situation contains ethical implications.

In Judeo-Christian or Western cultures, good moral character usually is associated with the habitual embodiment of such virtues as courage, temperance, prudence (or practical wisdom), justice, fairness, generosity, patience, truthfulness, and trustworthiness. Contemporary feminist scholars would interject additional vital virtues: caring for self and others, compassion, nurturance of relationships, responsiveness to growth and appreciation for change, resilient good humor and clear-sighted cheerfulness, attentive and realistic love, and a humble "sense of the limits of one's actions and of the unpredictability of the consequences of one's work" (Ruddick 1980; Gilligan 1982; Gilligan et al. 1988;

Noddings 1984). Martin Buber's dimensions of true dialogue could be viewed as virtues of ethical character: authenticity, inclusion, confirmation, and presentness (Johannesen 1990, 57–77). Other cultures may praise additional or different virtues that they believe constitute good ethical character. Instilled in us as habitual dispositions to feel, see, and act, such virtues guide the ethics of our communication when careful or clear deliberation is not possible.

CODES OF ETHICS AND THE CHARACTER-DEPICTION FUNCTION

We turn to the possible connection between formal codes of ethics and the concept of character ethics. Formal codes of ethics have been proposed by various communication-oriented professional associations, corporations, and citizen-action groups in such fields as commercial advertising, public relations, technical writing, organizational consulting, print and broadcast journalism, and political communication. While varied objections have been raised concerning the usefulness of formal codes, and while a number of significant functions for formal codes of ethics have been identified (Johannesen 1990, 169–91), I will concentrate on one important and largely ignored function of such codes.

In her book *Professional Ethics* (1985, 63–91), Karen Lebacqz suggests that formal ethical codes, especially in the professions, should be seen as having a function quite different from the typical one, namely, as rules for specific behavior or as admonitions concerning specific instances. In her view, we must look beyond the action-oriented language of most codes ("do this," "avoid that") to the "overall picture of the type of person who is to *embody* those actions." As reconceptualized by Lebacqz, a code embodies a picture of the moral "character" to be expected of a professional in a given field; it would depict, for example, an ethical communicator's "being" collectively and over time. She contends that "codes do not give specific guidance for action as much as they say something about the character traits necessary for someone to be a professional." "In short," she says, "codes are geared primarily toward establishing expectations for character." On this view, codes are "guideposts to understand where stresses and tensions have been felt within a profession and what image of the good professional is held up to assist professionals through those stresses and tensions."

According to Lebacqz, a wide range of professional codes reflect a core of central character traits, ethical principles, or obvious duties: "justice, beneficence, non-maleficence, honesty, and fidelity." She believes that a "professional is called not simply to *do* something but to *be* something." At a fundamental level codes depict a professional as "bound by certain ethical principles *and* as incorporating those principles *into his or her very character."* Ideally a code depicts the professional as "a person of integrity who not only does the 'right' thing, but is an *honorable person."* As illustration Lebacqz says that a trustworthy person not only keeps a confidence but is "thoughtful about the impact" of decisions on others and is "sensitive to their needs and claims." An honest person "tries to avoid any kind of deception, not just explicit lies." As noted earlier, Lebacqz contends that "when we act, we not only *do* something, we also shape our own character. . . . And so each choice about what to *do* is also a choice about whom to *be*—or, more accurately, whom to become."

This function of ethical codes as depicting desirable virtues of character more than (or at least as much as) specific rules for specific actions is exemplified by a code urged by the Josephson Institute for the Advancement of Ethics. The institute is a nonprofit organization established to "advance ethical awareness, commitment and behavior in both the public and private sectors of society." In its journal, *Ethics: Easier Said Than Done*, the Josephson Institute published a code of "Ethical Values and Principles in Public Service" (Spring/Summer 1988, 153). The institute believes that these are the "characteristics and values that most people associate with ethical behavior." Although the code does not specifically focus on communication ethics, many of its elements appropriately could be adapted for communication.

Each of the eleven values presented in the Josephson code might be viewed as a character virtue for persons in public service—whether elected public official, political campaigner, or appointed bureaucrat: honesty; integrity; promise keeping; fidelity; fairness; caring; respect; good citizenship; excellence; accountability; and public trust (Johannesen 1990, 182–84). Each of the values or virtues is briefly explained in the code by describing obligations stemming from it. For example, promise keeping: "Persons worthy of trust keep promises, fulfill commitments, abide by the spirit as well as the letter of an agreement; they do not interpret agreements in an unreasonably technical or legalistic manner in order to rationalize noncompliance or create justifications for escaping commitments." Or consider caring: "Concern for the well-being of others manifests itself in compassion, giving, kindness and serving; it requires one to attempt to help those in need and to avoid harming others." The Josephson code does, I believe, serve a character-depiction function.

ETHICAL CHARACTER AND POLITICAL COMMUNICATION

A social/institutional ethic for assessing political communication can be rooted in the values and procedures central to the health and growth of our system of governing, representative democracy. Among them are the intrinsic dignity and worth of all persons; equal opportunity for fulfillment of individual potential; enhancement of citizen capacity to reach rational decisions; access to channels of public communication; access to relevant and accurate information on public issues; maximization of freedom of choice; toleration of dissent; honesty and clarity in presenting values relevant to problems and policies; honesty in presenting motivations and consequences; thoroughness, accuracy, and fairness in presenting evidence and alternatives; and recognition that the societal worth of an end seldom should be the sole justification of the ethics of the means to achieve that end (Johannesen 1990, 21–37, 236–37, 255). Often informal standards and formal codes of ethics for various types of political communication are founded implicitly or explicitly on such fundamental values (Johannesen 1990, 31–34, 184–91).

In contrast, a number of scholars are suggesting that virtue ethics or character must have a significant place in political ethics. Such books as *Character, Community, and Politics* (Cochran 1982) and *Character: An Individualistic Theory of Politics* (Homer 1983) represent attempts to situate character ethics at the center of the philosophy of political ethics. In ancient Greece, according to MacIntyre (1984, 135, 138, 219), whether the ethical views of the older sophists, Plato, or Aristotle are considered, all took "it for granted that the milieu in which the virtues are to be exercised and in terms of which they are to be defined is the *polis*." Today ethical character is no less important for politics and public service.

Today's leaders have neglected the whole issue of moral character in both theory and practice and no longer encourage informed public reflection on the kind of people we are becoming and on our responsibilities to one another now and in the future. . . . The reality of moral character is unavoidable . . . in the so-called 'character' issue of the public's trust in politicians. (Palmour 1987, 14–15)

If the concept of ethical character were given a preeminent place in political philosophy, contends Homer, the result would be "a profound change in the way we think about politics. . . . Character would force us to re-examine the way we bring up our children to think about politics, the way we should know political institutions, and the way we should act in the world." Emphasis on character would "refocus the debate in political theory on the enduring question of how to live well in the proximity of others" (1986, 166–67). Lilla laments the overemphasis in the education of students preparing for public service on ethical rules for application and on the study of ethical dilemmas and catastrophic cases. The moral life of the public official primarily consists, Lilla believes, of "a set of virtues which the official has acquired through his education and it reveals itself in the attitudes and habits he displays to the political process and the public in his day-to-day work" (1981, 5). And what Gilligan (1982; et al. 1988) describes as the male moral voice of rights, rules, justice, and fairness and the female moral voice of care, compassion, relationships, and responsiveness *both* must be legitimized as encompassing virtues necessary for the moral conduct of politics broadly defined (Ruddick 1980, 345, 361; Sichel 1988, 218–24).

CYNICAL VIEWS

Humbuggery and Manipulation is F. G. Bailey's analysis of the art of leadership—primarily political leadership. One of his main arguments is that "no leader can survive as a leader without deceiving others (followers no less than opponents) and without deliberately doing to others what he would prefer not having done to himself" (1988, ix). Bailey summarizes his view:

Leaders are not the virtuous people they claim to be: they put politics before statesmanship; they distort facts and oversimplify issues; they promise what no one can deliver; and they are liars. But I have also insisted that leaders, if they are to be effective, have no choice in the matter. They could not be virtuous (in the sense of morally excellent) and be leaders at the same time. I do not mean that a leader should necessarily behave immorally. . . . I mean only that he must have the imagination (and—a paradox—the moral courage) to set himself above and beyond established values and beliefs if it is necessary to do so to attain his ends. (1988, 174–75)

To what degree should we accept Bailey's viewpoint? Does he believe that leaders must lie and deceive routinely or only occasionally? Do political leaders really have no "choice," as he argues? From his perspective, Bailey seems to describe not only what *is* the case but also what *ought to be* the case. I would contend that while we might agree with the former, we should reject the latter view.

Although scholars continue to debate the meaning of Niccolo Machiavelli's conception of *virtù* (Garver 1987; Hannaford 1972; Plamenatz 1972; Wood 1967), arguably Machiavelli saw prudence and practical wisdom as intellectual virtues more than as moral virtues; described other traditional moral virtues, such as honesty and courage, simply as means to be used strategically (even violated) to preserve the state; and urged that a leader must exercise the practical virtue of self-control. Machiavelli also believed that private moral virtues were inappropriate and ineffective for public political life and that at best a leader need only pretend to possess these moralities (Hariman 1989; O'Leary 1989).

During his presidential campaign and his administration, Jimmy Carter "offered a vision of authority based entirely on character" and "argued that virtue was the sole criterion for leadership" (O'Leary 1989,

123). Carter explicitly offered the virtues of honesty, efficiency, competence, compassion, and love. He assumed that essentially private virtues also appropriately operate in the conduct of public duties. In the long run, however, Carter was unable to translate these virtues into effective public policies and into sufficient public support. Indeed, contends O'Leary, Carter's reliance on a classical conception of virtue was "ultimately bound to fail in a world that has accepted the assumptions of the Machiavellian ethic" (1989, 123). Furthermore, he argues, "To a public that has accepted the assumption that it is not only permissible, but necessary, for a politician to lie in the performance of his duties, Carter's promise of honesty (to the extent that it was believed) could only serve as direct evidence of his incompetence" (1989, 126).

PRESIDENTS JOHNSON AND REAGAN

In her book *Character*, Gail Sheehy describes the "habit of deceit" that had developed throughout Lyndon Johnson's lifetime; it was the "aspect of his character most deeply engraved and evident as a pattern throughout his youth and adulthood" (1988, 16). His public duplicity on the Vietnam war as candidate and as president "played a crucial role in the disillusionment of a political generation." The legacy of the "credibility gap" and a "long-term mistrust of the president . . . can be laid directly at the door of one man's character" (1988, 17).

Throughout his two terms as president, Ronald Reagan continued a long-standing habit of playing fast and loose with the facts (Barber 1985, 491–96; Green and MacColl 1987; Johannesen 1990, 235–52; Sheehy 1988, 257–303). In his news conferences, informal comments, and speeches, Reagan routinely misstated facts, statistics, and situations. Another aspect of playing fast and loose with the facts was Reagan's misuse of factual illustrations and stories for proof, characterized satirically by the press as his "anecdotage" problem. Reagan frequently used vivid and dramatic real-life stories to prove this point or that. Unfortunately, these anecdotes, even when not misstated, often were found to be misleading or unrepresentative. Reagan's misstatements of facts and misuse of anecdotes were not rare, occasional, or on minor matters. Rather, they were routine, sometimes repeated even after exposure, and often on matters of important public policy. The standard is not perfect accuracy. Occasional slips on minor details may be expected. The obligation is not to ultimate truth in some absolute and invariable sense. But given the major resources at his or her command for verifying information, a president does have an obligation regularly to present highly probable conclusions and data that are as accurate and fair as possible.

Is what James David Barber terms Reagan's attitude of "contempt for the facts" an ethical character flaw, a vice? Reagan was "literally shameless when it came to the question of factuality" (Barber 1985, 493; Green and MacColl 1987, 11). His unconcern for accuracy was, in view of Green and MacColl, "a habit he apparently cannot unlearn." Indeed, they characterize Reagan as "incorrigible" on this matter. "He is simply incapable of entertaining information that conflicts with his ideology. When facts differ from his beliefs, he changes the facts, not his beliefs. He has sunk to a point where he can't make a major statement without making a major misstatement" (Green and MacColl 1987, 18).

THE 1988 PRESIDENTIAL CANDIDATES

During 1987 and 1988 intense news media scrutiny of presidential primary candidates focused on the "character issue" and the search for significant "character flaws." Democratic candidate Gary Hart temporarily withdrew from the race after allegations of a pattern of sexual indiscretion in his private life. If nothing else, the virtues of temperance, fidelity, and prudence were at issue. Republican television evangelist Marion "Pat" Robertson denied any pattern of deception in the numerous exaggerated, misleading, or erroneous statements about himself in his résumé, speeches, and books (see Alter 1987b; Reid 1987; Wills 1987).

The withdrawal of Senator Joseph Biden from the Democratic presidential primary race clearly illustrates the relation of moral character and communication ethics. A pattern of plagiarism was a major issue of communication ethics in Biden's case. *Plagiarism* stems from the Latin word for kidnapper. It involves a communicator who steals another person's words and ideas without properly acknowledging their source and who presents those words or ideas as his or her own. Plagiarism may take such varied forms as repeating almost word for word another's sentences, "repeating someone else's particularly apt phrase without appropriate acknowledgment, paraphrasing another person's argument as your own, and presenting another's line of thinking in the development of an idea as though it were your own" (Gibaldi and Achtert 1988, 21).

Previously the press had characterized Biden positively as the most eloquent of the Democratic contenders or negatively as glib and shallowminded. Now the press revealed that in campaign speeches Biden often presented as his own, without acknowledgment, various phrases, sentences, and long passages from speeches by John F. Kennedy, Robert Kennedy, and Hubert Humphrey. On two occasions Biden plagiarized a lengthy segment from a speech by British Labour Party leader Neil Kinnock. In this case, however, Biden also inaccurately presented parts of Kinnock's life history as his own. Biden falsely claimed that his ancestors were coal miners and that he was the first in his family to attend college. In addition, evidence surfaced that while a first-year law student, Biden had plagiarized, word for word, five pages from a law journal article. Although not a matter of plagiarism, a final element in Biden's flawed character emphasized by the news media involved his false claims in an informal interview with a small group of New Hampshire voters. Biden claimed that he graduated with three degrees and was given an award as the outstanding political science student. Further, he claimed that he attended law school on a full academic scholarship and won an international moot court competition. In fact none of these claims were true ("Biden's Borrowings" 1987; "Biden Was Eloquent" 1987; Kaus 1987; Margolis 1987a, 1987c).

What defenses and excuses were offered by Biden and his staff? Staff members pointed out that on some occasions Biden had credited Kinnock and Robert Kennedy as sources. Biden contended that the episodes of plagiarism stemmed from ignorance, stupidity, or inattention to detail rather than from intentional deceptiveness. Concerning the plagiarism from Kinnock's speech by Biden at the Iowa State Fair, an aide explained: "He's under a huge amount of pressure. He didn't even know what he said. He was just on automatic pilot" (Coffey 1987; Margolis 1987b).

To what degree, if at all, should any of these defenses justify Biden's communication or soften our ethical judgment? In what ways should inattention to detail or lack of conscious intent to deceive influence our ethical assessment (Johannesen 1990, 10–11)? Biden's case illustrates patterns or habits of communication that the news media interpreted as serious character flaws. Lack of judgment to restrain impulses, falsification of facts, and inflation of his intellectual and communication abilities became the elements of Biden's doubtful character. At issue were such ethical virtues as humility, prudence, temperance, fairness, truthfulness, and trustworthiness (Broder 1987; Kaus 1987).

CHARACTER, IMAGE, AND ISSUES IN CAMPAIGNS

Praise of an issue-oriented campaign as responsible and condemnation of an image-oriented campaign as superficial, even as unethical, has become a conventional judgment in political commentary (Bennett 1989). However, some political and rhetorical scholars do not share this automatic preference for issues over image in political campaigns. These scholars argue that issues and stands on issues are too transitory and too complex for voters to make dependable judgments. For example, an issue vital today often soon fades, to be replaced by one unforeseen during the campaign. Or issues may have to be created if none loom large in the public mind at the inflexible time when the campaign must occur. Instead, suggest some scholars, the basic dimensions of a candidate's image, largely defined as character, are as important as, if not more important than, particular stands on particular issues for citizen evaluation of political candidates during campaigns (Sheehy 1988, 21). One view describes images and issues as inextricably intertwined through the values espoused and contested by a candidate (Fish 1989; Weiss 1981; Werling et al. 1987).

Granted, image stereotypically is viewed as intentionally deceptive and misleading—as largely unrelated to the candidate's actual nature. But image also may be conceived of as a composite audience perception of the candidate's actual personal qualities and abilities as reflected in her or his record of choices. With image defined in this manner, the key questions in the long run become the following: Does the candidate's past record demonstrate strength of moral character, decisiveness of action, openness to relevant information and alternative viewpoints, thoroughness in studying a problem, respect for the intelligence of other persons, and ability to lead through public and private communication (Barber 1985, 1–11; Hahn and Gonchar 1972; Gonchar and Hahn 1973)?

Rhetorician Lloyd Bitzer contends that "the stuff of ordinary campaigns consists of arguments, position statements, testimonials, commercials, and other materials relating to the prudence, good character, and right intentions of the candidate—to the image" (1981, 242–43). He argues

The public forms fairly reliable judgments about the candidates by observing their mistakes—especially their flaws in reasoning, character, and prudence. Most voters are not well educated about details of issues and legislation, although they should be; consequently, most are not good judges of a candidate's pronouncements on complicated issues. But most voters do have sound views on the constituents of logical reasoning, good character, and prudence. Thus when a candidate makes a mistake of reasoning, or of practical wisdom, or a mistake resulting from a flaw in character, the public is quick to recognize and, by and large, competent to judge it. (1981, 242)

Michael McGee, from the viewpoint of a rhetorician, argues that the conventional wisdom of preferring "issues" over "images" actually may be "ultimately unjustifiable and dangerous." Citizens generally

do not have the necessary information to judge measures; such information could not be communicated to them in the context of an election campaign because the decisions to be made are too complicated for the limited time available; and, finally, the information needed for decision seems so technical and esoteric that most of "the people" could not judge it properly if it were available. (1978, 53)

Indeed, contends McGee, the only "issue" that the citizen is competent to judge is "the general character and trustworthiness displayed by candidates for office." Even when we believe that our choice stems from our evaluation of "the issues, we are in fact judging the character and the general trustworthiness of those who tell us what 'the issues' are" (1978, 154).

In her book *Eloquence in an Electronic Age*, Kathleen Jamieson describes the current era as one in which

voters are searching behind the promises for clues about whether a candidate is honest, knowledgeable, high principled, and temperamentally suited to lead the nation. In voter decisions, the candidate's character is now more central than his or her stands on issues and party identification. (1988, vii–viii)

However, in contrast with eras with fewer filters of communication mediation interposed between candidate and citizen, Jamieson views the present era as a time in which assessment of ethos—of practical wisdom, goodwill, and worthy moral character—is increasingly difficult. She concludes:

With the advent of an electorate of millions and a country spanning oceans, direct experience of the character of a speaker is unattainable for most called on to judge public discourse. When we see a potential leader through the filter provided by pseudo-events, news bites, or nuggetized ads and then can know for certain only that most politicians do not speak their own words, *ethos* is a less reliable anchor for belief. (1988, 240)

In a synthesis of political theory and empirical survey research, Miller, Wattenberg, and Malanchuk argue that

Evaluating candidates on the basis of personal qualities has for years been regarded as emotional, irrational, and lacking in political relevance. . . . The evidence now suggests that a reinterpretation is clearly needed. Rather than representing a concern with appearance, previously labeled "personality," the candidate assessments actually concentrate on the manner in which a candidate would conduct the affairs of office. (1985, 210)

Such assessments indeed may be "reasonable and intelligible performance evaluations." Miller et al. (1985) believe that voters primarily assess candidates along four dimensions of personal qualities: (1) competence—political experience and statesmanship, comprehension of political issues, realism, and intelligence; (2) integrity—trustworthiness, honesty, and sincerity; (3) reliability—dependable, strong, hardworking, decisive, and aggressive; and (4) charisma—leadership, dignity, humbleness, patriotism, and ability to communicate with people and inspire them.

"Of course issues are important. . . . But can any issue be more im-

portant in a presidential election than character?" Marshall Manley, chief
executive officer of an insurance company, elaborates this position in a
"My Turn" citizen editorial in *Newsweek*. He contends that

No matter how much we know about a candidate's views on specific issues, we
can't really predict how he, or she, will react to the shifting demands and crises
of an actual term in office. . . . Most voters wisely look beyond a candidate's
stand on the issues to something more important: qualities of mind and character
(1988, 8).

Manley suggests five qualities of character essential for a president:
(1) trustworthiness and integrity; (2) toughness in the sense of courage,
stamina, and determination; (3) gregariousness, including ability to build
coalitions, shape consensus, and work with peers; (4) a grasp of the
lessons of history, both problems and solutions; and (5) a capacity for
"love of country, love of family, and love of the rough and tumble of
politics" (1988, 8).

As guidelines for assessing the character of a political candidate, we
can reflect on the adequacy of the four dimensions described by Miller
et al. and the five qualities suggested by Manley. Are there additional
dimensions or qualities that should be significant for evaluating a candidate's character? Which of the dimensions or qualities seem to focus
primarily on *ethical* characteristics? For example, to what degree should
competence, determination, a grasp of the lessons of history, or love of
the rough and tumble of politics be viewed as matters of ethics generally
or more specifically as ethical virtues?

CONCLUSIONS

Political columnist Stephen Chapman (1987) offers three reasons why
media scrutiny of character was so intense on the 1988 presidential
candidates. First, voters are imposing increasingly higher ethical standards. Second,

Personal integrity is one of the few matters that lend themselves to firsthand
judgments by the voters. Most voters may feel unable to judge whether a politician is right about the defense appropriations bill. But they are able to consider
evidence about a politician's ethics and reach a verdict, since they make similar
evaluations about people every day. (1987, 3)

Third, voters "tend to vote for general themes, trusting candidates to
apply them in specific cases. A politician who creates doubt about his
personal honesty . . . creates doubt that his concrete policies will match
his applause lines" (1987, 3).

In greater depth, Gail Sheehy probes three reasons why it is essential that "we examine the character of those who ask us to put our country in their hands" (1988, 20). Primarily, "it is to protect ourselves from electing a person whose character flaws, once subjected to the pressures of leading a superpower through the nuclear age, can weaken or endanger the course of our future" (1988, 21). With issues a less sure guide than we once thought, we "are left to search out those we can believe in as strong and sincere, fair and compassionate: real leaders to whom we can leave the responsibility to use good judgment when crises catch us unaware" (1988, 29).

Second, "We need the cold slap of insight to wake us up from the smoothly contrived images projected by highly paid professional media experts who market the candidates like perfumed soap" (1988, 29). Of course, candidates and their managers can exploit the "character issue" to their own advantage. But reporters, editorialists, commentators, and investigative journalists could assist citizens in major ways by providing information about a candidate's character development—about past and present relevant virtues and vices—about significant contexts and influences through which the moral character was formed, so that the manufactured pseudo character can be penetrated to judge character more realistically. "In judging character," Sheehy reminds us, "one can never be sure the judgment is 100 percent accurate." But to that reminder I would add that it is crucial that we continue to make the most informed judgment that we can.

A final reason that we should examine the moral character of our leaders and potential leaders is to learn about ourselves. In Sheehy's view, the case histories of the characters of political leaders

instruct us in how, and how not, to conduct ourselves to win at life. We can use these characters as mirrors of our own character—reflecting both our flaws and strengths. Seeing how their various attempts to change and adapt have played out from earliest childhood through public life can be a catalyst for taking steps to change ourselves. (1988, 29)

In *The Virtuous Journalist*, Klaidman and Beauchamp argue that citizens "should expect good character in our national leaders, and the same expectations are justified for anyone in whom we regularly place trust" (1987, 17). The *Wall Street Journal* ("Oliver North" 1987) surveyed dozens of top executives of American companies to see if they would hire Lt. Col. Oliver North (of the Iran-Contra scandal) if he applied for a job. Many executives enthusiastically said they would hire him, but some would restrict his responsibilities. Among those who would refuse to hire him, one especially pinpointed the matter of character, saying, "It is a real character flaw when someone is willing to lie, cheat, and steal to accomplish the end of his superiors. That flaw will ultimately hurt the company. It's a character flaw that I would find unacceptable despite the strengths of his loyalty. The integrity flaw outweighs any other" ("Oliver North" 1987, 35). Here we see the virtue of fidelity in conflict with the virtues of truthfulness and trustworthiness. An emphasis on virtue ethics or character ethics as a viable approach to ethics in organizations, both business and governmental, is reflected in such essays and books as Des Jardins's "Virtues and Corporate Responsibility" (1984); Kolenda's *Organizations and Ethical Individualism* (1988); Scott and Mitchell's "The Problem or Mystery of Evil and Virtue in Organizations (1988); Walton's *The Moral Manager* (1988); and Wilbur's "Corporate Character" (1984).

Admittedly, the news media (or anyone) may at times be overzealous and focus on trivial or irrelevant character traits. But in general the emphasis on moral character in evaluating presidential candidates is central "to what the electorate seems to value most in its presidents—authenticity and honesty" (Taylor 1987, 23; Broder 1987, 7). To aid in assessing the ethical character of any person who is in a position of responsibility or who seeks a position of trust, we can modify guidelines suggested by journalists (Alter 1987a). Will the recent or current ethically suspect communication probably continue? Does it seem habitual? Even if a particular incident seems minor in itself, does it "fit into a familiar pattern that illuminates more serious shortcomings?" If the person does something inconsistent with his or her public image, "is it a small miscue or a sign of hypocrisy?"

"At this point in our political history," Sheehy emphasizes, "the concentration on character issues is unparalleled in its intensity" (1988, 11). The reason, she says, "is simple and stark." "By the time they become national leaders, the candidates' characters are sown. And if the character is destiny, the destiny they reap will be our own. . . . We must therefore know our would-be leaders in a deeper way than ever before" (1988, 21).

Communication ethics should encompass both individual ethics and social ethics. What are the ethical virtues of character and the central ethical standards that should guide individual choices? What are the ethical standards and responsibilities that should guide the communication practices of organizations and institutions—public and private, corporate, governmental, or professional? For an ethically suspect communication practice, where should individual and collective responsibility be placed? The study of communication ethics should suggest standards both for individual daily and context-bound communication choices and also for institutional/systemic policies and practices.

In her provocative essay "Ethics Without Virtue," Christina Hoff Sommers (1984) warns that the present "system of moral education is silent about virtue." She condemns moral education as presented in most

American universities today for addressing itself "not to the vices and virtues of individuals, but to the moral character of our nation's institutions." She argues:

> Inevitably the student forms the idea that applying ethics to modern life is mainly a question of learning how to be for or against social and institutional policies. . . . In that sort of ethical climate, a student soon loses sight of himself as a moral agent and begins to see himself as a moral spectator or protojurist. . . . The result of identifying normative ethics with public policy is justification for and reinforcement of moral passivity in the student. (1984, 388)

A curriculum of ethics without virtue, Sommers concludes, "is a cause for concern."

REFERENCES

Adler, Mortimer J. 1970. *The time of our lives: The ethics of common sense.* New York: Holt, Rinehart and Winston.

──────. 1988. *Reforming education: The opening of the American mind.* New York: Macmillan.

Alderman, Harold. 1982. By virtue of a virtue. *Review of Metaphysics* 36 (September):127–53.

Alter, Jonathan. 1987a. The search for personal flaws. *Newsweek* 19 October, 79.

──────. 1987b. A change of Hart. *Newsweek* 28 December, 12–16.

Bailey, F. G. 1988. *Humbuggery and manipulation: The art of leadership.* Ithaca, NY: Cornell University Press.

Barber, James David. 1985. *The presidential character: Predicting performance in the White House.* 3rd ed. Englewood Cliffs, NJ: Prentice-Hall.

Becker, Lawrence C. 1975. The neglect of virtue. *Ethics* 85 (January):110–22.

──────. 1986. *Reciprocity.* London: Routledge and Kegan Paul.

Bennett, W. Lance. 1989. Where have all the issues gone? Explaining the rhetorical limits in American elections. In *Spheres of argument,* ed. Bruce E. Gronbeck, 128–35. Annandale, VA: Speech Communication Association.

Biden was eloquent—if not original. 1987. *Chicago Tribune* 12 September, sec. 1, 1–2.

Biden's borrowings become an issue. 1987. *Chicago Tribune* 16 September, sec. 1, 4.

Birkhead, Douglas. 1989. An ethics of vision for journalism. *Critical Studies in Mass Communication* 6 (September):283–94.

Bitzer, Lloyd F. 1981. Political rhetoric. In *Handbook of political communication,* ed. Dan D. Nimmo and Keith R. Sanders, 225–48. Beverly Hills, CA: Sage.

Booth, Wayne C. 1988. *The company we keep: An ethics of fiction.* Berkeley: University of California Press.

Brandt, R. B. 1981. W. K. Frankena and the ethics of virtue. *Monist* 64 (July):271–92.

Broder, David S. 1987. The latest departed candidate. *Indianapolis News* 25 September, A–7.

Chapman, Stephen. 1987. How seriously has Joe Biden hurt his presidential effort? *Chicago Tribune* 20 September, sec. 4, 3.

Cochran, Clarke E. 1982. *Character, community, and politics.* University, AL: University of Alabama Press.

Coffey, Raymond. 1987. Biden's borrowed eloquence beats the real thing. *Chicago Tribune* 18 September, sec. 1, 23.

Cunningham, Stanley B. 1970. Does "does moral philosophy rest upon a mistake?" make an even greater mistake? *The Monist* 54 (January):86–99.

DeGeorge, Richard T. 1986. *Business ethics.* 2nd ed. New York: Macmillan.

Des Jardins, Joseph. 1984. Virtues and corporate responsibility. In *Corporate governance and institutionalizing ethics,* ed. W. Michael Hoffman, Jennifer Mills Moore, and David A. Fedo, 135–42. Lexington, MA: D. C. Heath.

Fish, Duane R. 1989. Image and issue in the second Bush-Dukakis debate: The mediating role of values. In *Spheres of argument,* ed. Bruce E. Gronbeck, 151–57. Annandale, VA: Speech Communication Association.

Fisher, Walter R. 1987. *Human communication as narration: Toward a philosophy of reason, value, and action.* Columbia: University of South Carolina Press.

Foot, Phillipa. 1978. *Virtues and vices and other essays in moral philosophy.* Oxford: Basil Blackwell.

Frankena, William K. 1970. Pritchard and the ethics of virtue. *Monist* 54 (January):1–17.

French, Peter A., Theodore Uehling, Jr., and Howard K. Wettstein, eds. 1988. *Midwest studies in philosophy.* Vol. XIII, *Ethical theory—character and virtue.* Notre Dame, IN: University of Notre Dame Press.

Garver, Eugene. 1987. *Machiavelli and the history of prudence.* Madison: University of Wisconsin Press.

Geatch, Peter. 1977. *The virtues.* Cambridge: Cambridge University Press.

Gibaldi, Joseph, and Walter S. Achtert. 1988. *MLA handbook for writers of research papers.* 3rd ed. New York: Modern Language Association.

Gilligan, Carol. 1982. *In a different voice: Psychological theory and women's development.* Cambridge, MA: Harvard University Press.

Gilligan, Carol, et al. 1988. *Mapping the moral domain: A contribution of women's thinking to psychological theory and education.* Cambridge, MA: Harvard University Graduate School of Education.

Gonchar, Ruth, and Dan Hahn. 1973. Rhetorical biography: A methodology for the citizen-critic. *Speech Teacher* 22 (January):48–53.

Green, Mark, and Gail MacColl. 1987. *Reagan's reign of error.* Rev. and enl. ed. New York: Pantheon Books.

Hahn, Dan, and Ruth Gonchar. 1972. Political myth: The image and the issue. *Today's Speech* 20 (Summer):57–65.

Hannaford, I. 1972. Machiavelli's concept of virtù in *The Prince* and *The Discourses* reconsidered. *Political Studies* 20 (June):185–89.

Hariman, Robert. 1989. Before prudence: Strategy and the rhetorical tradition. In *Spheres of argument,* ed. Bruce E. Gronbeck, 108–16. Annandale, VA: Speech Communication Association.

Hauerwas, Stanley. 1977. *Truthfulness and tragedy.* Notre Dame, IN: University of Notre Dame Press.

————. 1981a. *A community of character: Toward a constructive Christian social ethic*. Notre Dame, IN: University of Notre Dame Press.

————. 1981b. *Vision and virtue*. Notre Dame, IN: University of Notre Dame Press.

Homer, Frederic D. 1983. *Character: An individualistic theory of politics*. Lanham, MD: University Press of America.

Hudson, Stephen. 1981. Taking virtues seriously. *Australasian Journal of Philosophy* 59 (June):189–202.

Jamieson, Kathleen Hall. 1988. *Eloquence in an electronic age: The transformation of political speechmaking*. New York: Oxford University Press.

Johannesen, Richard L. 1990. *Ethics in human communication*. 3rd ed. Prospect Heights, IL: Waveland Press.

Jonsen, Albert R., and Stephen Toulmin. 1988. *The abuse of casuistry: A history of moral reasoning*. Berkeley: University of California Press.

Josephson Institute. 1988. Ethical values and principles in public service. *Ethics: Easier said than done* 1 (Spring/Summer):153.

Kaus, Mickey. 1987. Biden's belly flop. *Newsweek* 28 September, 23–24.

Klaidman, Stephen, and Tom L. Beauchamp. 1987. *The virtuous journalist*. New York: Oxford University Press.

Kolenda, Konstantin, ed. 1988. *Organizations and ethical individualism*. New York: Praeger.

Kupfer, Joseph. 1982. The moral presumption against lying. *Review of Metaphysics* 36 (September):103–26.

Kupperman, Joel. 1988. Character and ethical theory. *Midwest studies in philosophy*, Vol. XIII, *Ethical theory: Character and virtue*, ed. Peter A. French, Theodore E. Uehling, Jr., and Howard K. Wettstein, 115–25. Notre Dame, IN: University of Notre Dame Press.

Lebacqz, Karen. 1985. *Professional ethics*. Nashville, TN: Abingdon Press.

Lilla, Mark T. 1981. Ethos, "ethics," and public service. *The Public Interest* 63 (Spring):3–17.

MacIntyre, Alasdair. 1984. *After virtue*. 2nd ed. Notre Dame, IN: University of Notre Dame Press.

Manley, Marshall. 1988. Going beyond "the issues." *Newsweek* 18 January, 8.

Margolis, Jon. 1987a. Biden threatened by accusations of plagiarism in his speeches. *Chicago Tribune* 17 September, sec. 1, 3.

————. 1987b. Biden on quote furor: I've done some dumb things. *Chicago Tribune* 18 September, sec. 1, 3.

————. 1987c. For Biden, as for Hart, it's the stupidity that hurts. *Chicago Tribune* 22 September, sec. 1, 15.

Mayo, Bernard. 1958. *Ethics and the moral life*. London: Macmillan.

McGee, Michael. 1978. "Not men, but measures": The origins and import of an ideological principle. *Quarterly Journal of Speech* 64 (April):141–54.

Meilaender, Gilbert C. 1984. *The theory and practice of virtue*. Notre Dame, IN: University of Notre Dame Press.

Michell, Gillian. 1984. Women and lying: A pragmatic and semantic analysis of "telling it slant." *Women's Studies International Forum* 7:375–83.

Miller, Arthur H., Martin P. Wattenberg, and Oksana Malanchuk. 1985. Cognitive representations of candidate assessments. *Political communication yearbook 1984*, ed. Keith R. Sanders, Lynda Lee Kaid, and Dan Nimmo, 183–210. Carbondale: Southern Illinois University Press.

Minnick, Elizabeth. 1985. Why not lie? *Soundings* 68 (Winter):493–509.

Noddings, Nel. 1984. *Caring: A feminine approach to ethics and moral education.* Berkeley: University of California Press.

O'Leary, Stephen D. 1989. Machiavelli and the paradox of political hypocrisy: The fragmentation of virtue in the public and private spheres. In *Spheres of argument*, ed. Bruce E. Gronbeck, 117–27. Annandale, VA: Speech Communication Association.

Oliver North, businessman? Many bosses say that he's their kind of employee. 1987. *Wall Street Journal* eastern ed. 14 July, sec. 2, 35.

Palmour, Jody. 1987. *On moral character: A practical guide to Aristotle's virtues and vices.* Washington, D.C.: Archon Institute for Leadership Development.

Pinckaers, Servais. 1962. Virtue is not a habit. *Cross Currents* 12 (Winter):65–81.

Pincoffs, Edmund L. 1986. *Quandaries and virtues: Against reductivism in ethics.* Lawrence: University of Kansas Press.

Plamenatz, John. 1972. In search of Machiavellian "virtù." In *The political calculus: Essays on Machiavelli's philosophy*, ed. Anthony Parel, 157–78. Toronto: University of Toronto Press.

Reid, T. R. 1987. Rewriting the book on Pat Robertson. *Washington Post National Weekly Edition* 15 October, 15.

Rorty, Amelie Oksenberg, ed. 1980. *Essays on Aristotle's* Ethics. Berkeley: University of California Press.

Ruddick, Sara. 1980. Maternal thinking. *Feminist Studies* 6 (Summer):342–67.

Scott, William G., and Terence R. Mitchell. 1988. The problem or mystery of evil and virtue in organizations. In *Organizations and ethical individualism*, ed. Konstantin Kolenda, 47–72. New York: Praeger.

Sheehy, Gail. 1988. *Character: America's search for leadership.* New York: William Morrow.

Sichel, Betty A. 1988. *Moral education: Character, community, and ideals.* Philadelphia: Temple University Press.

Simon, Yves R. 1986. *The definition of moral virtue.* New York: Fordham University Press.

Slote, Michael. 1983. *Goods and virtues.* New York: Oxford University Press.

Sommers, Christina Hoff. 1984. Ethics without virtue. *The American Scholar* 53 (Summer):381–89.

———, ed. 1985. *Vice and virtue in everyday life.* New York: Harcourt Brace Jovanovich.

Taylor, Paul. 1987. Our people-magazined race for the presidency. *Washington Post National Weekly Edition* 2 November, 23.

Wallace, James D. 1978. *Virtues and vices.* Ithaca, NY: Cornell University Press.

Walton, Clarence C. 1988. *The moral manager.* Cambridge, MA: Ballinger.

Weiss, Robert. 1981. The presidential campaign debates in their political context: The image-issue interface in the 1980 campaign. *Speaker and Gavel* 18:22–27.

Werling, David S. 1987. Presidential debates: Epideictic merger of images and issues in values. In *Argument and critical practices*, ed. Joseph W. Wenzel, 229–38. Annandale, VA: Speech Communication Association.

Wilbur, James B., III. 1984. Corporate character. In *Corporate governance and institutionalizing ethics*, ed. W. Michael Hoffman, Jennifer Mills Moore, and David A. Fedo, 173–84. Lexington, MA: D. C. Heath.

Williams, Bernard. 1981. *Moral luck*. Cambridge: Cambridge University Press.

Wills, Gary. 1987. Hart's guilt trick. *Newsweek* 28 December, 17–18.

Wood, Neal. 1967. Machiavelli's concept of virtù reconsidered. *Political Studies* 15 (June):159–72.

Chapter Six

Primetime Politics: The Ethics of Teledemocracy

Robert E. Denton, Jr.

The only cure for the evils of democracy is more democracy.
—Al Smith

Historically, television was heralded as the ultimate instrument of democracy. It was, as no other medium, destined to unite us, educate us, and, as a result, improve the actions and decisions of the polity.

Television requires no special literacy. As a source of timely public information, it provides the greatest potential for understanding ourselves, our society, and even the world. Marshall McLuhan (1964) predicted that television would break down national barriers and transform the world into a "global village." In the 1950s, television showed us what life "could be." In the 1960s, it showed us what life "should be." In the 1970s, it showed us what life "was." And in the 1980s, it portrayed life "as it was" in an idealized past. For the 1990s, some claim television will become the vehicle of direct democracy (Naisbitt 1982, 159–61; Toffler 1980, 416–32). As notions of freedom and liberty spread throughout eastern Europe and the Pacific Rim, television is the instrument of unification and definition.

But we tend to forget that television also serves as an instrument of power and control (Innis 1964, 1972). To control content is to control public perceptions and attitudes. In America, television has become the primary medium and tool of both political campaigning and governing, culminating in the presidency of Ronald Reagan (Denton 1988). The central question before us, then, is whether television can make us more informed in our electoral choices or more democratic in terms of electoral participation. Is "teledemocracy" the twenty-first-century equivalent of fifth-century-B.C. Athenian democracy? Is the risk really "telefascism"?

Traditional textbooks in mass media (Bittner 1986; Hiebert et al. 1988; Jeffres 1986) argue that technology itself has no inherent values. The ethical dimensions or decisions lie not in the machinery but in the people who use the machinery. From my perspective, however, this rationale is too simplistic. Of course, intentionality is a variable of ethics, but so is capability. Television, by its nature, is an undemocratic technology. At best our attempts to make it an instrument of direct democracy have been less than successful, not because of users of the medium but because of the inherent constraints of the medium.

This chapter investigates television as an instrument of governing and its impact upon the nature of democracy. My concerns are qualitative and conceptual. I offer no empirical evidence. Such a normative exploration may be less satisfying to some of my political science colleagues, but the influence of the media is so subtle and complex that mere quantitative data alone cannot reveal all aspects of their nature and function in society. I also am not prepared to argue for the superiority of direct democracy over other forms, such as representational democracy. In fact, direct democracy is not very appealing. The question is simply whether television can aid democracy. The assumption is equally simple. Informed citizens can best protect self and public interests.

DEMOCRATIC CONCERNS

Without undertaking a philosophical discussion of democracy, one can identify several critical characteristics of a democratic form of government that are relevant to this discussion. The notion of accountability is essential to the notion of democracy. Because citizens delegate authority to those who hold office, politicians are answerable to the public for all actions and deeds. Elections are just one method of accountability. In America, news journalism serves as another check on political power and authority. The "watchdog" function is a long-standing tradition of the American press.

Information is critical for citizens to make informed judgments and evaluations of elected officials. Television news is the prime source of information for the public. The electorate receives 65 percent of its political information through television programming (Kaid and Davidson 1986, 185). Incomplete or inaccurate information can lead to bad public decisions.

A free marketplace of ideas is vital to a thriving democracy. Diversity of thought and respect for dissent are hallmarks of the values of freedom and justice. When multiple viewpoints are heard and expressed, the "common good" prevails over "private interest."

Finally, democracy is a process of what Dennis Thompson (1987, 3) calls "collective deliberation" on disputes of issues and fundamental values. It is the national and public debate that determines the collective wisdom and will of the people.

Television, as a medium, limits and in some cases inhibits the characteristics of democracy. However, I am not prepared to label the users or handlers of the medium as unethical, because officials do not have greater responsibilities than citizens in maintaining the quality of our democracy. As a nation, we often get what we deserve. It is too simplistic to blame politicians or journalists for media abuse or manipulation.

TELEVISION AND DEMOCRACY

With the development of national cable systems, satellite delivery systems, videotex, and other television technologies, futurists in the 1980s predicted a major transformation of American politics (Toffler 1980; Naisbitt 1982; Barber 1984). Teledemocracy promised electronic voting, more civic programming, and greater citizen participation. What we witnessed, however, was declining rates of voting, increasing levels of cynicism, and lower levels of political knowledge. By considering the impact of television upon the characteristics of democracy, we gain some insight into the unfulfilled promise of teledemocracy.

Accountability

Television increases the accountability of politicians when it provides sufficient information to enhance public awareness and decision making. But the medium has been co-opted by politicians as an instrument of advocacy. Politicians surround themselves with media professionals who advise on ways of nurturing the proper image, persona, or personality. It is very easy for politicians to manipulate media access and control. Thus, television is more beneficial for politicians as a medium of self-promotion than as one of information for the public.

According to Tony Schwartz (1973), constant exposure to television results in the sharing of common "TV stimuli" by everyone in society. This creates a reservoir of common media experiences. The way politicians can "connect" with citizens is to present stimuli that "resonate" with information already stored within individuals. Schwartz even argues that "experiences with tv and radio stimuli are often more real than first-hand, face-to-face experiences" (1973, 44). In fact, he asserts that the "captured reality" of media is preferred to personal experience. We make inferences about politicians based not on objective experience but on previous stored knowledge, likes, dislikes, and so on. Television especially encourages focus on personalities rather than upon abstract issues. Personalities are more salient and easier to understand than issues.

Most research shows that there is a great deal of stability in citizen criteria for presidential and candidate personalities (Miller et al. 1985). This symbiotic relationship is demonstrated in a study by Rodger Streitmatter (1985) on the impact of presidential personality on news coverage. He found that a president receives 50 percent more coverage if his personality is robust and outgoing, appealing to both the public and journalists.

For candidates, the process of image projection and media manipulation is rather easy. Pollsters identify the desired qualities, and candidates act accordingly. Candidates, of course, need the help of media and polling professionals to project the desired image to the public. Once elected, officials utilize the medium for image maintenance and control.

One result is that television has created a short-term political environment. The reactive nature of the medium makes it too costly to endorse long-term, controversial policies. One problem of democracy, according to our founders, is the potential impact of the momentary passions of the people upon policy. The short-term focus of television further distorts the information necessary for political judgment and exacerbates one of democracy's most dangerous characteristics.

The politics of popularity results in plebiscitary leadership. Samuel Kernell makes the argument that presidents "going public" is a strategic adaptation to the information age. "Going public," according to Kernell, is "a leadership style consistent with the requirements of a political community that is increasingly susceptible to the centrifugal forces of public opinion" (1986, 212). Thus, he predicts that "going public" will occupy a prominent place in the strategic repertoire of future presidents. The proliferation of "unmediated news" allows politicians to control media outlets, bypassing news reporters and journalists (Abramson et al. 1988).

Roderick Hart's (1984, 1987) studies reveal that presidents are talking to us more than ever before, primarily because of the mass media. He concludes that "presidential speechmaking—perhaps presidential communication in general—has now become a tool of barter rather than a means of informing and challenging the citizenry" (1987, 212). Thus, as Iyengar and Kinder recognize, "To the extent that the president succeeds in focusing public attention on his accomplishments while distracting the public from his mistakes, he contributes to his popularity, and eventually, to the influence he can exercise over national policy" (1987, 122). The public is not only left out of the decision-making process of national policy but is also unaware of the manipulation. Authoritarian politics, according to Jean Elstain, can be carried out "under the guise of, or with the convenience of, majority opinion. That opinion can be registered by easily manipulated, ritualistic plebiscites" (1982, 108).

The greatest danger in the politics of popularity is the encouragement of demagoguery. Demagogues play up false issues to divert public attention from true issues, relying heavily on propaganda, capitalizing on a contemporary social issue or problem, with the primary motive being self-interest and promotion (Johannesen 1990, 125–26). Robert Entman argues that "the media now provide an overwhelming temptation for politicians and other political figures to engage in demagoguery" (1989, 126). He claims that "the media feed a spiral of demogoguery, diminished rationality in policymaking, heightened tendency toward symbolic reassurance and nostalgic evasion of concrete choices, and ultimately misrepresentation of the public" (1989, 128).

Traditionally the public has empowered the press to serve as the collective watchdog over elected officials. If the public is unable or unwilling to hold officials accountable for their actions, the press is there, on a daily basis, to ensure fair representation. Despite the perception of an adversarial relationship with government officials, those officials still benefit more from mass media presentations than do outsiders or critics of elected officials. In a study by Leon Sigal (Bennett 1983, 53–54), government officials provided 75 percent of all news stories; less than 1 percent were based upon a reporter's own analysis. In addition, 90 percent of the stories were based on messages of key actors in the stories. Seldom do politicians speak for themselves. Reporters act as narrators and interpreters assessing the motives or consequences of political actors or events. And political realities are constructed to conform to the demands of the medium, demands that seem best satisfied by melodrama.

Regardless of the nature of the relationship between the press and the president, they desperately need each other. In the 1960s televised coverage of the presidency and political campaigns became a primary occupation of the news media. Since that time *image, audience share, targeting, packaging, teleprompter,* and a host of other such terms have become a part of the political lexicon. Ever since Theodore Roosevelt turned the White House into the "bully pulpit," presidents and potential presidents have needed to link their public persuasive efforts with the media. But today, the media equally need presidential "bits" of exposure and information to satisfy the public's curiosity and preoccupation with our chief executive. And the White House provides many services for the press. It offers background briefings, "off the record" comments, transcripts, and daily handouts and grants access and interviews.

The result of this symbiotic relationship is a constant battle of presidential access and control. To use a medium effectively implies control, planning, and proper execution. For presidents, each category is a chal-

lenge, a struggle, and a process of adaptation. Thus, public accountability of elected officials is lessened by the inequalities of power and
access to the medium of television. Broadcast journalists are now part
of the spectacle, less concerned with the quality of leadership than with
the latest Nielson ratings.

Information

In order for the public to make "good" decisions, they need "good"
information. Shanto Iyengar and Donald Kinder argue that television
news is "an educator virtually without peer, that it shapes the American
public's conception of political life in pervasive ways" (1987, 2). In their
original agenda-setting research, they found "those problems that receive prominent attention on the national news became the problems
the viewing public regards as the nation's most important" (1987, 16).
Successful politicians who can control the media can control the public's
perceptions. The more removed and less interested an individual is in
politics, the greater the influence of television (1987, 60). As the public
becomes even more reliant upon television as a source of political information and the medium increasingly simplifies the information, the
ability to recognize, perform, and appreciate complex social issues will
decline. The result, according to Jorol Manheim, "will be a continuing
qualitative reduction of the intellectual content of political discourse
among the mass of American citizens which may enable an elite which
preserves the requisite knowledge, skills, and resources more effectively
to manipulate the polity" (1984, 134).

It is not surprising there is some doubt whether television can provide
useful political information to the electorate. As early as 1967, Marshall
McLuhan observed that

The public, in the sense of a great consensus of separate and distinct viewpoints,
is finished. Today, the mass audience (the successor to the "public") can be
used as a creative participating force. It is, instead, merely given packages of
passive entertainment. (1967, 22)

The primary reason for this orientation is the requirements of the medium. David Altheide and Robert Snow posit that the media collectively
are a form of communication with a logic of its own. Media logic is the
interactive process through which media present and transmit information (1979, 9–10). Elements of the logic include organization, style of
presentation, focus on elements of behavior, and the grammar of the
media used. These elements impact social institutions such as politics,
religion, or sports to create a unique "media culture."

The major point is that when media are used to present the form and content of an institution, the very form and content of the institution are altered. A key part of this process is the audience's perception and interpretation of a particular medium's messages. As a technology, the modern media carry a connotation of rationality. Because of this, according to Altheide and Snow, both communicator and audience are oriented toward a "rational means-end" type of communication. Audiences view the information shared as accurate, objective, and current. As a society, we have become dependent upon the media. Pictures and visions make the world understandable and shape the environment. What is projected affects what is seen. People, of course, see things differently.

Television, as a medium, especially tends to reduce abstract or ideological principles to human, personal components. Political issues and actions are linked to individuals. We have choices not among policies but between actors. Victims, villains, and heroes are easier to identify and address than issues, causes, or ideas. Television is especially a "personalistic" medium. With television the presenter dominates. It is a medium for actors and animate objects. To some extent, the personalizing nature of the mass media has contributed to the decline and lack of interest in party organizations and smaller political jurisdictions.

It follows that the medium also impacts the content of politics. According to Dan Nimmo and James Combs, few people learn about politics from direct experience. They argue that political realities are mediated through mass and group communication. The result is the "creation, transmission, and adoption of political fantasies as realistic views of what takes place" (1983, xv). They define *fantasy* as

a credible picture of the world that is created when one interprets mediated experiences as the way things are and takes for granted the authenticity of the mediated reality without checking against alternative, perhaps contradictory, realities so long as the fantasy offers dramatic proof for one's expectations. (1983, 8)

McLuhan (1964) addressed this point years ago. He argued that television was too "cool" to properly handle hot issues and sharply defined controversial topics. "As a cool medium TV has, some feel, introduced a kind of *rigor mortis* into the body politic. It is the extraordinary degree of audience participation in the TV medium that explains its failure to tackle hot issues" (1964, 269). Thus, politics becomes an activity of style over substance, image over reality, melodrama over analysis, belief over knowing, awareness over understanding.

Of course candidates still talk about issues and policy, but there are media-created differences. For one, if you place a contemporary campaign speech beside one of the 1940s, you find that the contemporary speech is much shorter, probably only about one-third as long, and it is comprised of much shorter paragraphs (Jamieson 1988). The longer paragraphs of yesteryear contained arguments, attempts to convert the audience; contemporary short paragraphs contain assertions and conclusions, attempts to give the audience a position to identify with while simultaneously providing a 10- to 20-second pithy "bite" for the evening news.

Additionally, some contemporary campaign speeches are given purely to establish image. When a liberal gives an antiwar speech to the American Legion convention or a conservative attacks welfare programs at a meeting of the NAACP, neither expects to convert the audience. Rather, the speeches are given for image reasons, to prove their courage, to prove that the speakers can stand up to those opposed to their positions, to prove they are not "wishy-washy." Thus, while the messages of modern campaigners have not changed from issues to images, the structures of the messages and the motivations for them have. Electioneering politicians no longer try to convert through argumentation; rather, they attempt to say something we in the audience can identify with, to project an image by what they say, to communicate something about their personalities by the audiences they choose to address.

As the prime source of information for the public, the news on television is more believable, exciting, and dramatic than news in other media. Thus, the portrayal of the nightly news is the single most important element in impacting political cognitions in America.

From Nimmo and Combs's (1983) perspective, television news is storytelling and employs the elements of the dramatic narrative, utilizing verbal and nonverbal symbols, sound, and visual imagery. The key, then, is not so much in creating good, one-shot campaign ads as in learning the artful manipulation of television news. This act is what Martin Schram refers to as the greatest of "America's video games" (1987, 28).

Because of the demands of the medium, television journalism must be entertaining and highly visual. News crews, therefore, trim stories to support film and visual elements. The film footage no longer is used to *illustrate* stories but to *tell the story* (Altheide and Snow 1979, 109–10). This means that the footage stands alone, with little or no perspective or analysis. Peter Jennings, anchor for ABC's *World News Tonight*, states that "television is afraid of being dull . . . in television, you're obligated to write to the pictures" (Schram 1987, 58). Lane Vernardos, executive producer of *The CBS Evening News with Dan Rather*, builds news stories around exciting video rather than the strongest hard-news stories (Schram 1987, 51). Today, many news stories are prepared in advance. Producers develop a story angle and send reporters to capture the story on film. Because of economic factors, news crews don't want to waste footage and are more likely to stay near the Washington and New York areas.

The fact of the matter is that the news industry looks for and shares "news that wiggles." However, the more in-depth the coverage, the less "wiggle." Thus, the elements of action and movement are stressed over more cognitive elements. Stephen Wayne (1984, 228) reports that in 1980, CBS News spent only 20 to 25 percent of its presidential election coverage on issues. Emotional responses are the ones the public remembers, and they help define future reactions to people and events. On television, the news tends to be more political, personal, and critical than in other media. Television demands drama and a visual slice of life rather than comprehensive coverage of life, people, and events.

In addition to the quality of the news, there is also the constant attempt to control the news by politicians and incumbent officials. The president's press secretary is the immediate link with the press. Although the function of the press secretary is to serve as a conduit of information, he or she must attempt to control the agenda as well as what is said and what is not said. There are, of course, several ways a president can attempt to control or at least coordinate news coverage. News or information favorable to the president is released from the White House, whereas less favorable news is left unstated or is released from other departments. All interviews and statements are channeled through one source, thus ensuring control and consistency of content. Timing and managing of releases are also important techniques of news control. News items are often released in time to receive coverage on the evening news but not early enough to allow much time for full development or rebuttal. In addition, the release of two major stories on the same day is avoided. In a more active sense, presidents are always attempting to set the nation's agenda and goal priorities, creating "pseudo events," and taking every opportunity to "plug" administration accomplishments, thus infusing the news with self-serving commercials.

In truth, television is simply unreliable in providing sufficient and accurate political information for citizens to make electoral or policy decisions.

"The Free Marketplace of Ideas"

With the advent of cable television, the number of media outlets continues to increase but the diversity of programming does not, especially in terms of "hard" news and public affairs programming. There are both institutional and medium-specific factors that limit the free expression of ideas.

Perhaps the term *media effects* connotes too strong a deterministic notion, and *media influence* is more palatable. There is no doubt that the mass media collectively exert considerable influence in determining the agenda of topics for public discussion, debate, and action. However, there is a limit to the number of issues, topics, and so on that should or can receive public attention. In addition, the selection of specific concerns increasingly lies with the mass communication industries rather than with citizens or public officials. Actually, it is nearly impossible for politicians to initiate, establish, or maintain social agendas without the help and participation of the mass media. Politicians most often find themselves in the role of responder to rather than initiator of public concerns.

It should also be noted that the public "allows" media influence because of its dependence upon the media. We expect the media to investigate issues, ask candidates questions, and, in effect, keep public officials honest. If asked, I doubt many Americans would favor a mere "reporting" of information without synthesis, selection, and interpretation. At the same time, public officials and politicians use the media to convey ideas, share information, and attempt to solve social problems. Thus, because of the general lack of access and the competition for control, the media actually discourage the notion of an open and free marketplace of ideas.

The media give form and substance to world events. They construct our political realities, telling us who is good or bad, right or wrong, strong or weak, just or unjust. Media "snapshots" of the world become the "album" of both our knowledge and our memories of the outside world. In addition to telling us *what* to think about, the media also tell us *how* to think. With the reporting of the facts comes a subsequent judgment. There is always a conclusion, point, or reason for a presentation, but there is little or no time for synthesis or analysis. Awareness is valued more than understanding. Television demands a "perspective" and discourages ambiguity, innovation, and diversity.

It is important to remember the differences between news and politics. The mass media are first of all businesses. They require audiences in order to make money and turn a profit. Ratings are of great concern to news personalities, and news programming is very expensive. At best, news organizations are concerned about political values or issue dissemination. The product of journalism is not ideas but news (Entman 1989, 11). Politicians and journalists have separate and distinct motives, neither of which contributes to the genuine exchange of philosophies or ideas.

Television prefers action, drama, conflict, and immediacy over problems, approaches, issues, and ideas. Sophisticated programming requires sophisticated audiences, which are too small to be profitable. News journalists and politicians need each other. The result is an act of symbolic engagement. According to Christopher Arterton, it is like watching a tennis match without the benefit of actually playing the game (1984, 25). As spectators to the spectacle, we have lost access, control, and involvement in the process of democracy. This leads us to the final element of consideration.

Collective Deliberation

It is ironic that as the speed of communication and information increases, political delegation and representation become less satisfying. Citizens become directly involved in the day-to-day affairs of state by watching television news. The emphasis of citizen involvement has moved from action to reaction, from initiation to response. This new form of politics has resulted in the living room becoming the voting booth (McLuhan 1964, 22). But the privatization of politics has made us passive observers rather than active participants in the political process. Television has helped us to become politically lazy. We may watch debates but seldom engage in them. Our political discussions are most often confined to close, like-minded friends. After all, it's "not polite" to discuss sex, politics, or religion. As citizens, we no longer deliberate and debate. At best, through television we have established a "plebiscitary democracy" where mass public opinion is sovereign. But collective wisdom is not the same as collective opinion. The speeding up of counting votes and opinions does not address the quality of those votes and opinions.

Although television is highly involving, it does not encourage critical involvement of information. The medium literally reduces the message and prepares the viewer for its nearly automatic reception. This process is similar to consuming a great deal of food of little nutritional value. The meal is satisfying but critically deficient. As a personalizing medium, television presents a world of personalities who organize our reality and articulate our social agendas. Walter Cronkite's nightly statement ending his newscasts, "And that's the way it is," reinforced the certainty of his perception of the day's events. Humans fear isolation; television provides a pressure to conform, and responses become as predictable as those of Pavlov's dog. Television, then, is an *individual* medium that produces *mass* responses. The concern here is not so much election year campaigns as the day-to-day processes of government.

Bureaucracy and paternalism are enemies of democracy. A large government results in a lack of enthusiasm for the notion of self-rule. Individual action is lost in group action. The older the state, the more fixed and rigid it becomes. Dennis Thompson makes the point that liberty is counter to paternalism (1987, 148–177). Of course, with the complexity of modern society, the complete and unrestricted exercise of liberty is not possible. However, television reduces libertarianism as a mode of democratic expression. At best, paternalism constrains liberty for the purpose of mutual protection and social good. The issue is the degree of paternalism. Because of the personalizing nature of television, personal trust replaces personal involvement. Democracy is not founded on the deliberation of the few or the elite. It is founded on the duty and responsibility of all citizens to participate. Aristotle argued that the size of an ideal society should be limited in order to protect the proper interactions among the governors and the governed. He concluded that

both in order to give decisions in matters of disputed rights, and to distribute the offices of government according to the merit of candidates, the citizens of a state must know one another's characters. Where this is not the case, the distribution of offices and the giving of decisions suffer. (1970, 292)

THE PRIMETIME PRESIDENCY

The argument presented thus far is that we have entered a new age of presidential politics. Television has become the primary medium and tool of both campaigning and governing. But television, as a medium of communication, does not enhance the practice of democracy. In my opinion, the Reagan revolution, for example, was not so much in ideology or in programs as in instituting the primetime presidency (Denton 1988). There are three critical dimensions to the primetime presidency. First, the message must fit the medium in both form and content. Second, industry demands for news must be carefully crafted by the incumbent. Finally, today's president must be, if not an actor, at least a "media celebrity." A brief examination of the Reagan presidency illustrates the impact of television upon the quality of representational democracy.

Although less theoretically or philosophically stated than McLuhan (1964), the notion that "the medium is the message" recognizes the fact that a message must conform, in terms of content and structure, to a medium in order to maximize impact and effectiveness. Reagan's cool, informal style was perfect for television. Television rejects intense, "hot," and controversial material. Reagan was able to step through the television and join Americans in their living rooms in discussing the state of the nation. The consequence of this ability, according to Martin Schram, is that "Americans came to understand that if they were happy with Reagan's policies, the president deserved the credit, and if they were unhappy with them, the president was there with them, plainly disgusted too" (1987, 26).

The themes of the Reagan presidency were heroism, faith, and patriotism (Stuckey 1990). In Reagan's 1981 inauguration address, he set forth his beliefs that America has a special mission to the world, that individual action is superior to governmental action, and that governments threaten individual liberty. Reagan's primetime presidency offered positive and idealized images. As president, he identified and welcomed heroes, espoused faith in God and country, and surrounded himself with icons of patriotism. By the 1984 reelection campaign, the advertisers who had produced Pepsi commercials brought their skills to Reagan the product. The spots proclaimed, "It's morning again in America," showing a wedding, a family moving into a new home, fertile fields, and employed construction workers. In terms of the campaign, Dan Rather concluded that "the Reagan people saw the whole campaign as a movie . . . the Mondale people—at best—saw it as a series of quick sound bites" (Schram 1987, 59).

Roderick Hart's (1984) microscopic analysis of Reagan's rhetoric identifies three special characteristics. First, Reagan's rhetoric provided a sense of momentum—an emotional, take-charge, "can do" spirit of optimism that dealt with broad statements of philosophy rather than of policy. Second, Reagan's rhetoric identified a clear "sense of place" describing who we are, what's on our minds, and what we should do, and did so in short, crisp sentences with little embellishment. This allowed him to gloss over unpleasant facts, reduce complex issues, and create mass appeal. As Hart observes, "His words never force his listeners to imagine things they are incapable of imagining or require that they make a taxing intellectual association. . . . His language is drawn from life as it is lived most simply" (1984, 284). Finally, whereas Carter provided a sense of morality, Reagan provided a strong sense of tradition. His public addresses were national celebrations complete with appropriate national symbols and ceremonial settings.

Reagan's idealized images and cheerleader role were perfect for television. In his stories, Reagan changed reality to make it uplifting and positive. Once, for example, he told of a football game where the team won in the last 20 seconds, primarily because of his key block. In real life, he missed his block. Reagan turned real-life failure into success, which is much more dramatic and heroic for television (Rogin 1987, 14). In over 50 films, Reagan never played the heavy—a role that would be rejected on television. Film invites viewers to observe forbidden acts from a distance—a distance that keeps us "clean." Television, as a medium, does not allow a protective distance. Because of the interactive nature of television, we become partners in the sharing of bad news and events. To stay "clean," audiences must actively disassociate themselves from bad messages and reject the sources. Doomsayers are often tragic heroes in film but certainly are villains on television.

On the eve of his 1980 victory, when asked what the electorate saw in him, Reagan responded, "I think maybe they see themselves and that I'm one of them" (Rogin 1987, 12). His rhetorical style *was not* flamboyant but simple, and expressed the thoughts of common Americans. Reagan's speeches were written for the ear rather than for the eye, a reason why so many of his speeches sounded better than they read. This style, again, is best for television and increased his acceptance. Reagan made a virtue of acting as if he didn't know more than the voters. In our homes, he appeared as an informed equal, a reflection of us, rather than as a superior, star individual. Yet Garry Wills reports that "Reagan has often 'goofed' to look more natural—broken the grammar of sentences, feigned embarrassment, professionally avoided the appearance of being a professional. It is an important art in democratic politics" (1987, 163). On television, we relate to the human characters who are not perfect, are laid back, and show a sense of humor.

Reagan seldom acted in a substantive sense; others in his administration did that. But he shared much reaction to events, people, and issues. He could get angry when pushed too far; recognize a woman reporter at a press conference simply because she wore a red dress, Nancy's favorite color; or even berate Russia, but in the tone of voice of Marcus Welby telling a sick patient to "shape up or else." Reagan certainly would take a stand, but he did so with humility, righteousness, and anecdotes and quotes from letters written by children or common, everyday American heroes. As Joshua Meyrowitz observes:

If Nixon was thesis and Carter antithesis, then Reagan is synthesis. He is a man who says he will "talk Tough," but does so in a soft-spoken, folksy style. He seems comfortable in a full spectrum of costumes, from tuxedos to cowboy suits, and in a wide range of activities from ballroom dancing to gardening. He is part Nixon, part Carter, an "imperial" president who chops his own wood. Unlike Nixon, Reagan appears to be a sweet and likable person; unlike Carter, he offers a romantic notion of America's power and destiny. (1985, 301)

Not only was the content of Reagan's messages right for television; so was the structure or form of the messages. Even in Reagan's most straightforward addresses before Congress, he created a sense of drama through relating stories and parables. Although identified by name, the characters were often historic and symbolic, reflecting the values of family, patriotism, tradition, freedom, faith, and so on. A single hero mobilizes strong emotions. Even with real, genuine stories Reagan made complex operations the story of one person.

In addition to the personalized story, Reagan carefully controlled the settings and backdrops to heighten the dramatic effect. The perfect example is the June 6, 1984, ceremony commemorating D-Day. He reduced the invasion to one man, Private Zanatta, whose daughter had vowed to attend the ceremony in his absence. For Sam Donaldson, the ceremony was the epitome of theatrical news management. Reagan's performance included beautiful scenery (flags, bluff overlooking a beach, blue sea) and human emotion (aged heroes, tears). Donaldson, although recognizing the staging of the event, admits "I put three pounds of it in because it was a compelling, dramatic moment" (Schram 1987, 63). "By personifying his beliefs about good and evil in simply drawn men and women," Paul Erickson argues that the "president provides points of reference and points of view for his audience" (1985, 51). Thus, the characters were tools suited for the media. Garry Wills concurs by observing that Reagan "renews our past by resuming it. His approach is not discoursive, setting up sequences of time or thought, but associative; not a tracking shot, but montage. We make the connections" (1987, 4). Such an approach maximizes individual participation and interaction.

As already noted, television personalizes whenever it can, and Reagan perfected the "politics of individualism." Bert Rockman argues that there is a predisposition in America toward personalism in politics that is rooted in our history, culture, and institutions (1984, 177–78). Our political system promotes individual entrepreneurship where leadership, regardless of context, is an individual quest. Corporations are structured with the focus on individual rather than collective responsibility. Thus, by personalizing the office and issues, Reagan complemented the requirements of the form and content of the television medium.

Today, political competence encompasses not only performance but also the elements of personality, image, and style. Political rituals have replaced doctrine in American politics, and it has always been important to manage the medium of the era. Reagan's staff, as media professionals, recognized that the public has less and less of a historical memory. This required a daily concern rather than a long-term perspective for impression management. They also recognized that the mass media expected a steady and constant "din" from the White House. Finally, the staff knew that television could be managed because of what Gerald Pomper et al. refer to as its limitation: "Reporters can comment only in the context of a picture; the medium is impotent without 'photo opportunities' and cannot easily resist a story with good visual possibilities" (1985, 162).

As a result, Martin Schram argues that "night after night, Reagan had his way with the television news. He had succeeded in setting their agenda and framing their stories by posing for the cameras in one beautiful and compelling setting after another" (1987, 23). The key, therefore, was not to control what the news correspondents would be saying but to control what America was seeing.

Lesley Stahl, CBS News White House correspondent, was one of the first to attempt to tell the American people that Ronald Reagan's television access and presence was well orchestrated but actually contradicted policy positions. While presenting this viewpoint, the video showed Reagan with handicapped Special Olympians, at a senior citizen housing project, at home riding horses and cutting wood, in Normandy, at the Tomb of the Vietnam Unknown Soldier, and comforting families of dead marines. While the verbal report was critical and negative, the visual was positive and reinforced the values espoused by Reagan for years. A member of Reagan's staff was pleased with the piece. "We're in the middle of a campaign and you gave us four and a half minutes of great pictures of Ronald Reagan . . . and that's all the American people see" (Schram 1987, 26). The pictures tell the story more than the verbage. Television, as "cool," requires the viewer to participate in the generally positive "Americana" experiences. In effect, the viewers were sharing them (and in some cases sharing them for a second or third time) with Reagan.

The lesson is clear. Maintaining popular support means careful control over what is seen rather than what is said. To govern the nation means controlling the videos in the evening news.

Martin Kaplan, Mondale's speechwriter, said rather scornfully the day after the 1984 election that the only candidate who could have beaten "old actor Reagan" was another actor or a television anchorman, such as Robert Redford or Walter Cronkite (Reeves 1985, 93–94). But Reagan's success is more than just being an "old actor." Hart characterizes him as "combination orator-rhetorical-leader and performer"—a television performer (1984, 214).

It is important to remember that Reagan did not *use* television as much as he adapted to its essential requirements as a medium. In short, Reagan was a much better actor as president on television than he ever was in Hollywood. As an actor, his success was switching from the "big screen" of films to the "small screen" of television. Michael Rogin (1987, 38) best summarizes the argument by observing that failure in Hollywood succeeds in politics by breaking down the disjunction between image and life more effectively than the bigger-than-life stars of movies.

Reagan long favored and recognized the power of television as a medium. In *Where's the Rest of Me?* he claims to be "one of the first established motion picture stars deliberately to choose it for my own field at a time when everyone of stature in Hollywood was delicately holding their noses about it" (1981, 263). He writes, "I do not think [television] represents a new medium; it is, instead, simply a new kind of theatre. It is the proscenium arch in miniature brought into the home" (1981, 333). Movies, Reagan argues, offered an emotional experience once a week or so, but now television "is a knob within easy reach seven nights a week" (1981, 334).

Reagan's philosophy of acting is also well suited for the medium of television. Reagan claims an actor learns to see himself as others see him, from the outside in rather than from the inside out (Reagan 1981, 79). It is this audience perspective that is critical in successful television performances which result in audience participation and identification. Reagan believes that the basis of the dramatic form of entertainment is "the emotional catharsis experienced by the audience" (1981, 334). He was, to put it simply, a character actor who was comfortable within a defined (and controlled) context. Even in the 1980 presidential campaign it was a priority of the Reagan staff to make the candidate "stick to the script" (Germond and Witcover 1981, 210).

In television, the perfect technique is imperceptible. The medium provides techniques to make persuasion look nonpersuasive. For the camera, the scenes look unstaged, and Reagan acted as a nonactor—a very challenging role for any actor. Careful analysis provides several patterned responses of Reagan that evoke audience emotion. For example, Wills describes Reagan's "choreography of candor" as " 'Well'—eyes down, eyes up, smile, slight dip of head to the right, and begin . . . " (1987, 136).

For Ronald Reagan, the essence of his political success came from expressing how people felt—not by expressing what they thought. The personalizing medium of television allows the actor in the proper setting to engage us and become part of us in defining the world. Ronald Reagan the "great communicator" was really Ronald Reagan the "great television communicator." His persona, messages, and behavior fitted the medium's requirements in terms of form, content, and industry demands. Reagan, especially in the first term, surrounded himself with professionals of the modern communications technology. They made sure the settings were correct and the messages clear. Reagan as a television actor delivered the lines and gestures to ensure the desired response—agreement through empathy. Dramatic expressions mix reality with fantasy, who we think we are with whom we want to be, and the world as it is with the world as it should be. To lead is not to be led. To lead is not to manage. To lead is to mirror ourselves.

Through snapshots we validate who we are and what we have done. We construct the narratives, correct our wrongs, and celebrate the good times. Events we photograph, we control. Each photo we take has a purpose, a meaning. Reagan provided action photographs that were positive, optimistic, and even heroic. Television is a medium for social expression, not for social action.

CONCLUSION

Historically, modern presidents have had difficulty in gaining reelection and, if reelected, maintaining popular support throughout the second term. In the early 1970s, after the shock of Johnson and the reality of Nixon, George Reedy warned of "the twilight of the presidency," where the "institution provides camouflage for all that is petty and nasty in human beings, and enables a clown or a knave to pose as Galahad and be treated with deference. . . . As a device to lead us through the stresses of modern life, it is wholly inadequate" (1970, xv, xvii). Arthur Schlesinger described the problem as one of an all-powerful "imperial presidency": "We need a strong presidency—but a strong presidency within the constitution (1973, x). For James David Barber, it was simply a matter of "presidential character." We need to pick "active-positive" presidents—"a presidential character who can see beyond tomorrow— and smile—[and] might yet lead us out of the wilderness" (1972, 454). For some scholars, the answer was a stronger Congress. For others it was a matter of "more" and "better" citizen participation. By 1981, however, Terry Sanford warned of the "danger of democracy" where "we will use its name in vain, and in its name so unstructure our political institutions that nothing can be decided, or decided wisely" (1981, 100).

The world has always witnessed the struggle between republican and democratic principles of self-rule. Over the past 200 years, America has moved toward a more "inclusive" democracy: greater participation of women, minorities, and the young. Gradually, the people have been able to elect senators and help nominate presidential candidates. Yet, during this time of increased opportunity for participation, public interest, awareness, understanding, and participation have declined.

So what's wrong? Without being too deterministic, one can argue that television has changed the fundamental nature, structure, and function of American politics. The medium influences who runs, who is elected, the nature of democracy, and presidential leadership and the institution itself. Although it is difficult to predict the end product, there are alarming dimensions emerging that warrant serious consideration.

We are now at the point, as Schram observes, that "the instrument of television has taken control of the presidential-election process" (1987, 305). Television has taken control not in the sense of measuring candidates but as the instrument of the image makers. Campaigns today no longer reveal the depth of issue knowledge or understanding. Political debate is simply an exchange of predictable "sound bites." The background and experience of presidential candidates are less important than their ability to attract media support and public popularity. As professional politicians, our leaders no longer reflect the diversity of occupations and accompanying expertise of the general public. Gone are the true and mature laborers, businessmen, educators, and professionals who once comprised state and national legislators. Television has given birth to a new type of American politician and opened Washington to "outsiders."

In addition, issues have become less important as part of the public's evaluations of political candidates. Clearly the 1984 presidential election demonstrated that political issues and ideology matter little in selecting a president. The polls continually showed that voters favored Ronald Reagan based on elements of persona and charisma but disagreed with his issue positions. Rather than believing the public was somehow misinformed, Joan Carrigan of *NBC Nightly News* concluded "that if people were choosing Reagan even though they disagreed with him on the issues, then that must mean that issues do not matter—and so there is no need to better inform the public about them" (Schram 1987, 249).

Because of the intimate nature of television, voting for president is a personal thing—like endorsing a father or favorite aunt or uncle. It is easy to judge what we see (a very controlled image) and what we experience (television as a "cool" medium).

Television was once viewed as the ultimate instrument of democracy. Today, few would argue that it has increased the quantity or quality of democratic participation. Politicians use the medium to confirm rather than to challenge, to present rather than to engage the public. National audiences require generic appeals and predictable responses.

Theodore Lowi argues that today we have a "plebiscitary president." "The United States," he observes, "is the one major democracy without some kind of system of collective responsibility" (1985, 98). The presidency has become the center of responsibility and national government. This leads to what Lowi characterizes as the "second republic of the United States." The "plebiscitary president" implies rulers who govern on the basis of popular adoration. Lowi questions the real difference between Napoleon I and Ronald Reagan. "We have a virtual cult of personality revolving around the White House" (Lowi 1985, xi).

Television places greater importance on individualism which emphasizes the traits of warmth, articulateness, and style that results in personal popularity, prestige, and office legitimacy (Rockman 1984). Public opinion is more important than political persuasion. Image projection is more important than policy argumentation. Jeffrey Tulis charges that Reagan was a president

who often spent more of his day in photo opportunities and greeting dignitaries than in policy discussion, a president who rarely called staffers to probe or elaborate upon their very brief memos to him, a president who allegedly prepared for the Iceland summit by reading a novel. (1987, 190)

Presidential leadership today tends to be charismatic rather than programmatic. Does this leadership style of "presidentialism" help policy formation and execution? Can the primetime presidency support tax increases, strong measures to deal with the deficit, and so on? Probably not. One of the concerns of Rogin is the "false intimacy of the modern, personified state" (1987, 9). The media encourage us to look at the president in informal contexts and allows the president to demonstrate concern for citizens. This two-way mirror contributes little to the demands of leadership, governing, or program development. *We see our presidents more but know them less.*

The office is greater than the individual. It has a life of its own. The occupant either fits the mold or must "appear" to fit it. And television is the instrument of mass production. Just as each Barbie and Ken doll is the same in millions of households, so we all see the same manufactured president. The foundation of democracy is the notion of choice. Primarily because of television, presidents and presidential candidates will increasingly look the same, sound the same, and, unfortunately, act the same. The presidency has become a product, and the consumers were ready for Reagan's brand above all others.

One of the most important developments in American politics since 1980 has been the professionalization of political communication. Without doubt, the kingmakers of contemporary politics are the new breed of political and media consultants. Once limited to the continuing cycle of campaigns, they now find themselves on the permanent staffs of elected officials. These professional politicians have become the link between electoral politics and campaigns, leaders and the public.

For the incumbent, the professional staff must maintain public excitement and support that the president can translate into congressional votes and program implementation. Elements of management, planning, strategy, and image creation/reinforcement are as important in governing as in campaigning.

The presidency is a product that undergoes constant evaluation, and when support sags, advertising and public relations activities are used to recapture support. Professional political communicators and pollsters, as permanent members of the White House staff, are responsible for the president's public image. In marketing terms, they are responsible for brand identification, product life extension, and product adoption.

The argument presented here is certainly not new. The presidency is a product that is familiar to all Americans. To present a "new" and "improved" presidency is as risky and unwise as Coke's introduction of New Coke. Americans prefer the "classic presidency"—the one in history books that possesses the values and myths of Washington, Jefferson, Lincoln, Roosevelt, and Kennedy. In many ways, to govern and maintain support, the president must demonstrate that the product has not changed and fulfills citizen expectations. But to understand and to define the presidency properly is only part of the task. The next crucial step is to promote the product properly. To do so demands an understanding of the form and content of television.

The dangers are obvious. The presidency becomes more symbolic. The gap between issues and personality increases. Governing becomes more of a science than an art. Skills of public performance are more important than the skills of management. Some communication colleagues may take comfort in that fact—I do not.

Finally, television has contributed to the decline of political parties. Politicians can go straight to the people to build support and organization. It has increased the fragmentation of American society by becoming the instrument of special groups and causes. Television can join the "ears" of the nation but not necessarily its "hearts." It has created a "fishbowl" government that is largely paralyzed when it comes to taking decisive and reasoned actions.

It is usually at this point that one is supposed to offer brilliant insight and concrete suggestions for reform. Social analyses, however, should not always be compelled to adopt the format of a market research report or an engineer's memorandum. The processes of diagnosis and prescription are separate steps, each requiring careful preparation and analysis.

It is also true that academics tend to make simple notions rather complicated. To this I plead guilty. Television is the new opiate for the masses. It was supposed to take a largely uneducated, uninformed electorate and turn them into model democratic citizens. This, television cannot do. The responsibility belongs not to a medium designed, after all, as entertainment but to the citizens. Television allows us to focus the blame in the wrong places.

The central task is how to continue to cultivate an active, democratic citizenry in light of the heavy dependence upon television, an undemocratic medium. Perhaps discovering our illusions will at least serve as the first step toward discovering our problems.

We need, as Martin Levin (1980) argues, to return to a "politics of institutions, not men." This means a greater role and recognition of the other branches of government. Policy making is a collective affair rather than a competitive endeavor.

News needs to be a window rather than a mirror, providing more contextual stories. Perhaps more free air time will reduce the need for 30-second art. Greater labeling and segmenting of news would perhaps help our understanding of issues: presidential news, opposition news, interpretive news, and so on.

We also need to have a greater understanding of the role, function, and power of the media in our society. As social and scientific technologies rapidly increase, we must carefully plan for their usage within the context of democratic values. Walter Cronkite suggested in a speech at the University of South Dakota,

We could benefit by a journalism course for consumers. If we could teach people how to read a newspaper, how to listen to radio and watch television . . . we could create an understanding of media, of the individual strengths and weaknesses of each medium. We could lead them away from a dependence on television, back to good newspapers, magazines, and books. (1989, 7)

Finally, civic responsibility and initiative should once again become a keystone of social life that surely transcends the nature and use of any medium. Instead of viewing politics as talk, maybe we should view politics as people engaged in talk! It must be person to person. Jeffrey Abramson and his colleagues advocate a "communitarian conception of democracy" that would reverse the "centralization of politics and political communication" that has been the case with television (1988, 24–26). The goal is to use television and all the news media for the "common good" of the citizens. The key difference is interaction, community participation in debate at the local level. It is what they call the "electronic commonwealth," where the goals of the media are to inform and to empower the people.

In the end, it is probably not surprising that the real solution lies in the wisdom of Al Smith: "The only cure for the evils of democracy is more democracy."

REFERENCES

Abramson, Jeffrey, F. Christopher Arterton, and Gary Orren. 1988. *The Electronic Commonwealth*. New York: Basic Books.
Altheide, David, and Robert Snow. 1979. *Media Logic*. Beverly Hills, CA: Sage.
Aristotle. 1970. *Politics*. Edited and translated by Ernest Baker. New York: Oxford University Press.
Arterton, Christopher. 1984. *Media Politics*. Lexington, MA: Lexington Books.
Barber, B. J. 1984. *Strong Democracy: Participating Politics for a New Age*. Berkeley: University of California Press.
Barber, James David. 1972. *The Presidential Character: Predicting Performance in the White House*. Englewood Cliffs, NJ: Prentice-Hall.
Bennett, W. Lance. 1983. *News: The Politics of Illusion*. New York: Longman.
Bittner, John. 1986. *Mass Communication*. 4th ed. Englewood Cliffs, NJ: Prentice-Hall.
Cronkite, Walter. 1989. Acceptance Speech for the 1989 Allen H. Neuharth Award for Excellence in Journalism, October 27. University of South Dakota. Pamphlet.
Denton, Robert E., Jr. 1988. *The Primetime Presidency of Ronald Reagan*. New York: Praeger.
Elstain, Jean. 1982. "Democracy and the Qube Tube." *The Nation*, August 7, 108–10.
Entman, Robert. 1989. *Democracy Without Citizens*. New York: Oxford University Press.
Erickson, Paul. 1985. *Reagan Speaks*. New York: New York University Press.
German, Jack, and Jules Witcover. 1981. *Blue Smoke and Mirrors*. New York: Viking Press.

Hart, Roderick. 1984. *Verbal Style and the Presidency.* Orlando, FL: Academic Press.
———. 1987. *The Sound of Leadership.* Chicago: University of Chicago Press.
Hiebert, Ray, Donald Ungurait, and Thomas Bohn. 1988. *Mass Media V.* New York: Longman.
Innis, Harold. 1964. *The Bias of Communication.* Rev. ed. Toronto: University of Toronto Press.
———. 1972. *Empire and Communication.* Rev. ed. Toronto: University of Toronto Press.
Iyengar, Shanto, and Donald Kinder. 1987. *News That Matters.* Chicago: University of Chicago Press.
Jamieson, Kathleen Hall. 1988. *Eloquence in an Electronic Age: The Transformation of Political Speechmaking.* New York: Oxford University Press.
Jeffres, Leo. 1986. *Mass Media.* Prospect Heights, IL: Waveland Press.
Johannesen, Richard L. 1990. *Ethics in Human Communication.* 3rd ed. Prospect Heights, IL: Waveland Press.
Kaid, Lynda, and Dorthy Davidson. 1986. "Elements of Videostyle." In *New Perspectives on Political Advertising*, Lynda Kaid, Dan Nimmo, and Keith Sanders, eds. Carbondale: Southern Illinois University Press.
Kernell, Samuel. 1986. *Going Public.* Washington, D.C.: Congressional Quarterly Press.
Levin, Martin. 1980. "A Call for a Politics of Institutions, Not Men." In *The Post-Imperial Presidency*, Vincent Davis, ed. New York: Praeger.
Lowi, Theodore. 1985. *The Personal President.* Ithaca, NY: Cornell University Press.
Manheim, Jorol. 1984. "Can Democracy Survive Television?" In *Media Power in Politics*, Doris Graber, ed. Washington, D.C.: Congressional Quarterly Press.
McLuhan, Marshall. 1964. *Understanding Media.* New York: New American Library.
———. 1967. *The Medium Is the Message.* New York: Bantam Books.
Meyrowitz, Joshua. 1985. *No Sense of Place.* New York: Oxford University Press.
Miller, Arthur H., Martin P. Wattenberg, and Oksana Malanchuk, eds. 1985. "Cognitive Representations of Candidate Assessments." In *Political Communication Yearbook 1984*, Keith R. Sanders, Lynda Lee Kaid, and Dan Nimmo, eds. Carbondale: Southern Illinois University Press.
Naisbitt, John. 1982. *Megatrends.* New York: Warner Books.
Nimmo, Dan, and James Combs. 1983. *Mediated Political Realities.* New York: Longman.
Pomper, Gerald, Ross Baker, Charles Jacob, Scott Keeter, Wilson McWilliams, and Henry Plotkins. 1985. *The Election of 1984.* Chatham, NJ: Chatham House.
Reagan, Ronald, and Richard Huber. 1981. *Where's the Rest of Me?* New York: Dell.
Reedy, George. 1970. *The Twilight of the Presidency.* New York: World Publishing.
Reeves, Richard. 1985. *The Reagan Detour.* New York: Simon and Schuster.
Rockman, Bert. 1984. *The Leadership Question.* New York: Praeger.
Rogin, Michael. 1987. *Ronald Reagan, the Movie.* Berkeley: University of California Press.

Sanford, Terry. 1981. *A Danger of Democracy*. Boulder, CO: Westview Press.

Schlesinger, Arthur. 1973. *The Imperial Presidency*. Boston: Houghton Mifflin.

Schram, Martin. 1987. *The Great American Video Game*. New York: William Morrow.

Schwartz, Tony. 1973. *The Responsive Chord*. New York: Anchor Books.

Streitmatter, Rodger. 1985. "The Impact of Presidential Personality on News Coverage in Major Newspapers." *Journalism Quarterly* 62, 1 (Spring):66–73.

Stuckey, Mary. 1990. *Playing the Game: The Presidential Rhetoric of Ronald Reagan*. New York: Praeger.

Thompson, Dennis F. 1987. *Political Ethics and Public Office*. Cambridge, MA: Harvard University Press.

Toffler, Alvin. 1980. *The Third Wave*. New York: Bantam Books.

Tulis, Jeffrey. 1987. *The Rhetorical Presidency*. Princeton, NJ: Princeton University Press.

Wayne, Stephen. 1984. *The Road to the White House*. 2nd ed. New York: St. Martin's Press.

Wills, Garry. 1987. *Reagan's America*. New York: Doubleday.

Chapter Seven

Ghostwriting: Two Famous Ghosts Speak on Its Nature and Its Ethical Implications

Lois Einhorn

I've always thought of ghostwriting in terms of policy presentations. Here I strongly believe that ghostwriting is not only ethical, but is also indispensable. . . . A preacher using a canned sermon or ghostwriter seems no different than somebody using a canned love letter or ghostwriter to woo a girl.

—Robert T. Oliver

The public could handle knowing about the extensive use of ghostwriters. We tend to think the public is naive, but our job is to get the word out that ghostwriting goes on all the time. I don't think congregants, though, would approve of their local preacher using a canned sermon or a ghostwriter.

—Craig E. Smith

The practice of speechwriting dates back to antiquity and has proliferated through the ages. Almost every statement spoken today by major political, business, and academic leaders was written by someone else. Despite speechwriting's firm foundation in history, and despite its widespread use, we are only beginning to understand the process of one person writing a speech for another person to deliver and the ethical and critical implications of this practice.

In 1988, *Communication Quarterly* published an essay of mine on the views and practices of three ghostwriters: William Lee Miller, a professor and religious ethicist who served as a speechwriter for Adlai Stevenson's 1956 campaign for president; Robert Turner, a former professor of economics who was a key speechwriter for President Truman and who also contributed ideas for the speeches of President Kennedy; and Dorothy

Collins, who wrote speeches for three presidents and the chancellor of a large midwestern university. I asked all three the same questions, and thus was able to compare their answers. The essay contributed to the historical record about the practice of ghostwriting. Miller, Turner, and Collins became ghostwriters accidentally; they had, as it were, fallen into their assignments without professional training for such work and, hence, they worked intuitively.

There are, however, ghostwriters who have a thorough background in rhetorical theory and practice and, hence, bring a wealth of rhetorical knowledge to the process. I interviewed two such rhetorically trained ghostwriters. One was Robert T. Oliver, professor emeritus and former head of the Department of Speech Communication at The Pennsylvania State University, who from 1946 to 1960 was the primary professional speechwriter for President Syngman Rhee of Korea and who also wrote extensively for other Korean public figures, including Korean ambassadors to the United Nations, the United States, and France. The other was Craig R. Smith, professor of speech communication at California State University at Long Beach and president of the Freedom of Expression Foundation, who has been a staff writer for former President Gerald Ford, former Vice President George Bush, Senator Bob Packwood, and other political leaders. He was also a speechwriter for Lee Iacocca when Iacocca directed the Statue of Liberty campaign; for John Bryant of Consolidated Foods (now Sarah Lee); for Edward Orley, the chief executive officer of Michigan Health Care Corporation; and for other business leaders. Both men participated in college debate as undergraduates, and both hold doctorates in rhetoric. Professor Smith, in fact, was Professor Oliver's last Ph.D. student. Each has published significant scholarly books and articles, and has been or is a university professor of rhetoric.

This chapter investigates the views and practices of these two rhetorically trained ghostwriters. It is divided into four sections. The first section consists of excerpts from my personal interviews. In order to compare and contrast the interviewees' responses, I asked both the same questions. For the sake of clarity and coherence, I edited some of their responses in minor ways, such as removing vocalized pauses ("uh," "you know," and so forth). I tried not to alter their ideas or speaking styles. Professors Oliver and Smith have approved the edited transcripts and have given me permission to make their comments public.

The comments of Professors Oliver and Smith are especially interesting concerning the ethics of ghostwriting in general and especially the ethics of religious ghostwriting—members of the clergy using pulpit aids, canned sermons, and ghostwriters. Since I know of little research on the subject of ghostwriting for religious leaders, I interviewed eleven members of the clergy. In the second section of this chapter, I present my findings from those interviews.

The "Summary and Conclusions" section explains how the remarks of Professors Oliver and Smith fit into the general framework of our knowledge about ghostwriting. Since I asked them the same questions I had asked the "accidental" ghostwriters, I also discuss the similarities and differences between the rhetorically trained and the "accidental" ghostwriters.

Finally, I give a list of references so readers know where to look for additional information on ghostwriting. The references include not only works cited but also other works of importance to the study of ghostwriting.

EXCERPTS FROM THE INTERVIEWS

Join now in "listening" to Professors Oliver and Smith give a behind-the-scenes view of the practice of ghostwriting:

How did you first become involved in ghostwriting?

Oliver: I got involved with ghostwriting through meeting Syngman Rhee, who was the outstanding Korean independence leader exiled in the United States during the Japanese occupation of Korea. A mutual friend introduced us. He talked with great fervor and great feeling about the Korean people, the greatness of the Korean culture, the wrongs the Koreans had suffered under the Japanese, and efforts he had been making all his life to try to restore the independence of Korea. I was deeply moved by his earnestness and sincerity, and I was attracted by his intelligence and by the wonderful facility he had in presenting his story clearly and dramatically. I felt very much called to him.

Before December 1946, I wrote for him only a bit as a friend in my spare time. After the defeat of Japan, Rhee went back to Korea and became a very active leader in the independence movement there; he dealt with the American military government in trying to organize an election. During this time, we maintained a very active correspondence. In the letters we discussed in great detail the problems he was encountering inside Korea and the problems he was encountering dealing with the American authorities. In 1946, he invited me to Korea to give a series of lectures; during my summer there, we spent a lot of time talking about the problems. My most vital preparation for the ghostwriting I did for him came from our correspondence and talks and from my spending time in the country. I became increasingly familiar with the problems and policies of Korea.

Smith: I first became interested in speech communication through debate. I debated in high school and college. My first exposure to speechwriting was through Russell Windes's anecdotal stories. He had been a speechwriter for Adlai Stevenson's 1956 presidential campaign, and he chaired my master's thesis committee at Queens College. My Ph.D. degree is from Penn State. Robert Oliver chaired my dissertation committee and, as you know, he had done a lot of speechwriting.

My first full-time teaching job was at San Diego State. While teaching there, a Republican running for Congress asked me if I would write speeches for him and coach him on speech delivery. I had a lot of fun with it. That was my first ghostwriting experience.

Could you describe the process you used to ghostwrite speeches? Was the process the same or different for each speaker?

Oliver: I used different processes for the different speakers only to a minimal degree. Generally speaking, I used the same process for all of them, and my method of writing is a standardized method whether I'm ghostwriting for someone else or writing for myself. I think about the speaker, the goal of the speech, the audience, and the means that can best achieve this goal with this particular audience. After I have gone over all this in my mind, I sit down at the typewriter and write the speech, usually with considerable speed. My speeches typically go through one draft; after that, I make only minor changes. The draft for a 30-minute speech (10–12 pages) usually takes me about 1 or 2 hours to write. I write rapidly when I know what I want to say.

The speakers I wrote for gave me only minimal instructions. My relationship with Syngman Rhee was so close and so intimate that the ambassadors and ministers I wrote for took it for granted that I knew the kind of governmental policies he was espousing at least as well as they did, and perhaps even better. There was little need for instructions or discussion because I knew the subject and purpose very well.

I especially knew how to adapt the ideas to an American audience. It's a very interesting phenomenon. When you are in Korea, 6,000 to 8,000 miles away, you look at American-Korean relations from a Korean perspective, a perspective that becomes so dominant in your thinking that it is very hard to get out of. When you are in this country looking at the same problems, you think of them from an American perspective. I would go back and forth between Korea and the United States. I would spend two or three months in Korea in the summers; by the time I had been there for five or six weeks, the American perspective became dim and the Korean perspective became dominant. When I came back to the United States again, the Korean perspective became dim and I'd see the issues from an American viewpoint.

When in this country, President Rhee had an American perspective. He received his B.A. degree from George Washington University, his

M.A. degree from Harvard, and his Ph.D. from Princeton, and he was head of a school in Honolulu for about 15 years. But when Rhee was back in Korea and dealing with Korean problems on Korean terrain, he would forget how Americans viewed certain issues. So, when he was addressing American audiences, as he did sometimes in Korea, he needed me to present the material in a way that would make sense from an American perspective. When he spoke to international audiences, I tried to give him a global perspective.

Smith: The process I used to write speeches was different for the different speakers, although ironically I had very similar experiences with President Ford and Lee Iacocca. I had access to huge research divisions both at the White House and at Chrysler; anything I wanted was at my fingertips. A second similarity is that both made very few changes, so I could essentially draft a final product. Normally I met with President Ford or with Lee Iacocca, and they would tell me what they wanted. What they told me was general. For example, I would meet with President Ford about a particular speech. I would suggest he talk about certain things, and I would ask him, "What do you want to talk about?" He usually would say, "Yes, that's fine, but add this," or "I really think I ought to talk about defense." There was nothing much more specific than that. The same was true with Lee Iacocca. He would say something like "I want to push this product in the speech and then I want to get into economic concerns facing the country." He wasn't specific at all, except in one respect: Lee has a photographic memory. He would say, "In speech number two, three weeks ago, we said this. I liked that. Let's put it in this speech, too."

With George Bush, the ghostwriting process is different. I wrote for him most extensively in 1978 and 1979, when he was running for president, and since he has started up his campaign again [1988], I have written a few speeches for him. Bush gives me written notes that are usually one or two pages of talking points, almost a point outline. I write from that, and then he sits down and literally marks the draft up with me, changing small points or saying, "Well, we don't want to deal with strategic arms here." From what I have read about Nixon's speechwriting process and from what I know about this process from talking to some of Nixon's writers, Bush's approach seems similar to the Nixon approach. Bush participates in the speechwriting process.

Even though he participates in the *speechwriting* process, a problem with George Bush is that *speechmaking* is not a big deal to him. He usually doesn't rehearse, which causes a lot of trouble. I've talked to him until I am blue in the face about rehearsing. Lee Iacocca always rehearsed and rehearsed and rehearsed. When President Ford rehearsed, he was good; when he didn't rehearse, he wasn't so good. I have a feeling that

Bush feels it is unmanly to rehearse and, hence, won't often do it. He doesn't take the giving of a speech seriously; he thinks it is kind of a game and, for that reason, he is not as good a speaker as he could be. I have heard him give terrific speeches after he has rehearsed.

The ideal process would be an amalgam. I would like the participation of Bush, the access to White House research, and a speaker who really cares about speaking.

To what extent did you know the thinking and philosophy of the speakers for whom you wrote?

Oliver: Intimately. My relationship with Syngman Rhee was fairly similar, I think, to Ted Sorensen and John F. Kennedy's relationship. If President Rhee and I sat down for two hours of discussion, we would arrive at the same point I would arrive at without the discussion because we both knew the problems, available solutions, and policies.

It was very easy for me to understand Syngman Rhee's thinking. Although I was thirty-five years younger than he, we were very similar in temperament. We both had a keen interest in international affairs, we both were well educated, we both were idealists, and we both be-lieved that the good triumphs over evil in the end. We both also enjoyed jokes and social conversation. We really liked one another, and our personalities fit together well.

Over the years I got an ever-increasing sense of the Korean culture by talking to President Rhee. By spending every summer in Korea, I also became acquainted with many Koreans, and I made a real effort to develop a sympathetic understanding of Korean psychology, culture, history, social problems, and so forth.

Smith: Usually I knew the speakers' thinking and philosophy fairly well. When I went to the White House to work for Ford, I sat down for a full week and read his testimony when he was up for vice president to learn as much as I could about him. I've always been a conservative Republican, so I easily understood his philosophical position. The same is true with Bush. At the time I went to work for Lee Iacocca, he was a conservative Republican. He now says he is something else, but at the time he was a conservative Republican, so the general philosophy was easy.

In general, was the style you used your style or the speaker's style?

Oliver: I wrote in the speaker's style. Syngman Rhee was president, and I had a presidential mold when I wrote for him. Ambassador Ben Limb was informal, chatty, and social. He loved personal anecdotes, and so I tried to weave these aspects of his style in the speeches I wrote for him. Ambassador Soo Young Lee was a very sober-minded individual. He didn't make any pretense of philosophical acuteness. He liked to be serious, and so when I was writing for him, I tried to write in that style. When I wrote for people I didn't know very well, I didn't try to do much except straight exposition with a little bit of gracefulness in phraseology.

Smith: The style I use is the speaker's style, except that I try to maximize the strengths of the speaker's style and minimize the weaknesses. Gerald Ford wanted to talk the language of the common person. He had gone through several writers who tried to make him more eloquent than he was comfortable being. They wanted him to write in the "grand style." What I was able to do was find places where he was comfortable in the "grand style," such as in conclusions and transitions, but when he was discussing issues and facts, I used a plain style.

Lee Iacocca has what he calls a kind of macho style. He is not afraid of using a trite phrase. He likes to speak using tough, punchy, short words—which, by the way, is not the way he talks in private. He is very eloquent, and he has a very high vocabulary level. Once I understood the style he wanted, though, it was easy to write for him.

The people who are tough to write for are those who don't know what style they want. I think George Bush is such a person. He is well educated and comes out of an aristocratic background, and has a large vocabulary that, I think, frankly gets in his way. On the campaign trail, he wants to talk the language of the common person, and he gets mixed up between his vocabulary and the common person's vocabulary. In my opinion, he's still searching for a style. His campaign staff is debating this matter right now.

How do you determine a person's style?

Oliver: I determine their style by knowing them well. I know their personality and how they speak in conversation. Also, diplomatic speaking has its own characteristics that transcend the personality of the speaker, just as after-dinner speaking, political campaign speaking, and commemorative speaking all have their own demands.

Smith: To determine the style of different speakers, I look at past speeches and do a kind of stylistic analysis. I look for tropes and figures. I look particularly for analogies and metaphors to see if particular speakers are comfortable using them. I look for the colors they use. Do they use light metaphors? Do they use dark metaphors? For example, "the dark night of Nazism" is a dark metaphor. "The searing image of Hitler" is a fine metaphor, but it is a burning metaphor, not a dark metaphor.

I determine the kind of metaphor speakers use and then write using this type. I also look for descriptive levels. Are they comfortable with levels of description or do they talk in the abstract? For example, if they talk about inflation, do they talk about the price of lettuce or do they just talk about inflation? I look for their strengths and their weaknesses. So, to determine a person's style, you do a stylistic analysis of their speeches, you pick up this information in conversation with them, and you see what they are comfortable with when they rehearse their speeches.

Did you ever make visual aids for any of the speakers?

Oliver: Never. I didn't for myself, either. I don't like that sort of thing.

Smith: No. I don't like visual aids. The more you have, the more that can go wrong. I've done slide shows, and I've helped speakers with slide shows, but it's nerve-racking. Obviously Lee Iacocca had to use visual aids all the time, but I tried to minimize their use as much as possible.

Did you ever help any of the speakers prepare for question-and-answer periods?

Oliver: Never, and I never felt any need to. The speakers I wrote for had sharp minds, they were alert, they knew the subject matter, and they were very good at expressing themselves.

Smith: I was on the team that helped Bush prepare for his debate against Geraldine Ferraro, and I've helped some senators and other clients prepare for press conferences. This work mostly involves critiquing their delivery; I talk about controlling pace, eye contact, body language, and so forth.

You talked about an instance where speechwriting was a team effort. As you know, Ernest Bormann contends that group speechwriting encourages less risk-taking and a loss of color and style [Bormann 1960, 288]. Do Bormann's claims seem valid to you?

Oliver: Yes. I'm sure that when speeches are written by a committee, the speech becomes depersonalized. Even though individual ghostwriters try very hard to represent the personality of the speaker, their own personality gets into the speech somewhat, resulting in more of a personalization or an individualization of style. I agree with Bormann's claims completely.

Smith: In some ways, yes, because if other people are going to look at your product either before the client does or in front of the client, you can be criticized for taking a risk. You open yourself up to being eliminated from the team. And so there is a tendency to be more conservative in your writing style. On the other hand, if you are part of a team effort and you come up with a really good metaphor such as "the New Frontier," that will certainly help you advance within the group. So the competition of a team effort can produce better research, better arguments, and better style.

Do you think the process used to write an effective speech for another person to deliver is the same as that required to write an effective speech for yourself?

Oliver: Yes, except that when I write a speech for myself, I emphasize the use of evidence to support what I say, but when I was writing a speech for the people I mentioned, they themselves were the ultimate authorities. They didn't have to use lots of evidence, they didn't have to cite authorities, they could speak for the policy of the Korean government, they could represent the Korean position on international questions, and so on. So it was a lot easier for me to write for them than it is for me to write for myself.

Smith: Yes, except that, in a sense, you have to be two people when you're writing for somebody else, while you have to get your own style out when writing for yourself. One of the real keys of writing for somebody else or yourself is rewriting and rewriting and rewriting. As you rewrite for someone else, you see places where you say, "That's not the client, that's me there. I better take that out and put the client in." When rewriting for yourself, you can let yourself go, and develop and refine your own style.

Are there particular speeches you wrote that you would like to talk about?

Oliver: When Syngman Rhee was first elected president of the Republic of Korea, he asked me to ghostwrite his inaugural address. I was in Washington, D.C., at the time, and he was in Korea. I wrote the speech and sent it to him. He sent back a radiogram saying he approved the text except for such and such changes; he listed word changes for two or three sentences. Then he said I might release the text to the American press at the time of delivery in Korea. I delivered the speech to the press as he suggested, and I used the speech as an example in the book *Communicative Speech*. What makes this situation so interesting is that the speech was never delivered. When it came time for President Rhee to deliver the speech, he looked at the audience and decided he couldn't use a prepared text; instead, he talked very personally about Korea's struggles.

Smith: Because there were so many people who had suggestions for the six major speeches President Ford would give in the bicentennial period of 1976, Bob Hartman, who reported directly to President Ford, decided that the six speeches should be coordinated so each eventually could be a book chapter and then a book could be published in pamphlet form. He then said anyone who was interested in writing any speech for the president had to do an outline for all six speeches and show how the speeches would be integrated. Then President Ford was given the outlines with the authors' names deleted and told to choose the one he liked best. I was very lucky; he chose my outline out of all the ones submitted. It was a six-page outline, one page for each speech. So I got to coordinate the six speeches. For each speech I chose a primary writer and a secondary writer. They met with the president and discussed ideas he wanted to include. I took primary responsibility for the Valley Forge speech. I especially liked writing this speech because I was able to talk about something very physical: the encampment at Valley Forge, the bloody, ragged feet of the men, the coldness of the winter, and so on. For all the bicentennial speeches, I didn't want the president simply to talk about the past; I wanted him to use the speeches as an opportunity to project forward into our third century. This "forward cast" to the speeches is what sold my outline.

My questions so far have dealt with factual information about how you became involved in ghostwriting and the process you used in writing speeches for other people. I'd like now to learn about the role you think ghostwriters should play and about your views concerning the ethical and critical implications of ghostwriting. Do you think a ghostwriter should be a policymaker or a language craftsperson?

Oliver: Let's try to figure out what kind of ghostwriter we're talking about. If I open up a professional office, put an ad in the newspaper, and say I will ghostwrite for anybody who wishes to hire my services, I think I am nothing but a language craftsperson. In this case, I have no right, no interest, no desire, and no ability to formulate policy. If, on the other hand, I invest my life, reputation, feelings, convictions, and years of effort into understanding and being a part of a situation, as I did in Korea, then inevitably I'm interested in changing policy. In my work with the Koreans, I definitely tried to influence American policy toward Korea, Korean policy toward America, Korean policy toward Japan, and the Korean domestic policies of Syngman Rhee. I would not have wanted to work with the Koreans if I could not have affected policy.

Smith: Speechwriters should begin by being language craftspeople because really good speechwriters have to be generalists and, thus, will gain an expertise in various areas and will begin to see that policy can be shaped. Speechwriters can gain trust by writing a speech with a particularly striking metaphor or a style the client feels comfortable with. Once clients trust speechwriters, then the speechwriters can begin to make policy suggestions, and the suggestions have a certain credibility. One of the joys of speechwriting is when you gain that kind of trust and can put new policy ideas into a speech and the president says, "Yes, we'll go with that."

As you know, speech ghostwriters have not enjoyed a favorable reputation in the eyes of the public or even in the eyes of some people in the field of speech communication. Professor Ernest Bormann has compared ghostwriting to student plagiarism and has called the practice dishonest and unethical [Bormann 1961a, 263]. *Would you respond to these charges?*

Oliver: Of course I know full well that Ernie Bormann is an unusually brilliant person whose published works are a high credit to our profession. On this subject, though, I fear he is repeating a stereotype coined and used by people who know very little about ghostwriting. So I think the charges are stupid. Let's think for a moment about Michael Dukakis and his campaign staff. Wouldn't we consider Dukakis an idiot if he did not have a committee of people to give him advice and to help shape his policy-making? When we say, "Here is the Dukakis policy," we know it's not Dukakis's personal policy. Rather, it's the policy of Dukakis's committee. George Shultz [secretary of state at the time of the interview] is a very capable man, but he has to have a thousand people working with him to tell him what to think about Angola, and about Rhodesia, and what to do about India, Korea, and Italy. He needs all the advice he can get; he can't do *all* the thinking about *all* these issues himself. Ghostwriters are not only ghostwriters; they are also ghostthinkers. They help speakers gain the understanding, knowledge, and ideas they have to have. If speakers did not utilize ghostwriters, they would be jerks, they would be idiots, they couldn't operate.

If you're going to insist on not using ghostwriters, then you're going to have to insist on accepting executives who have a very narrow range of responsibility so they can understand all the issues and ideas they are dealing with. As soon as you extend those responsibilities, then executives must have the kind of help that speechwriters provide.

I wrote speeches for Syngman Rhee that made him sound better than he would have sounded if he had been speaking on the basis of his own knowledge only. Does that mean, then, that Syngman Rhee was being misrepresented as a greater man than he actually was? It doesn't mean that at all. It means he had enough sense to realize the responsibility of his position, and to get the kind of help he needed to clarify his positions and to allow him to operate in general. So I don't think there is anything unethical about ghostwriting.

Smith: I think Ernie [Bormann] assumes there is misrepresentation because the audience is naive, because they don't ask speakers if they have speechwriters, or because they don't try to find out. That's an audience problem rather than a speaker problem, unless the speaker is purposefully deceptive on this issue. There are a lot of things the American public doesn't question that I have real problems with. For example, the low quality of network programming is not the networks' fault; it's the audience's fault. If the audience wanted more, they would get more.

Like lawyers, speechwriters provide a service for clients, give voice to the arguments of clients, and help clients present their ideas in the marketplace in a competitive way. I see no ethical problem.

Have the people you've written for admitted you were their ghostwriter?

Oliver: President Rhee accepted me as his ghostwriter and very readily admitted that I was ghostwriting for him. He made no pretense, showed no concealment. He would introduce me to an audience in Korea, putting his arm around my shoulder, and say, "This is Dr. Oliver, who helps me to say what I want to say in a way that keeps people from getting mad at me."

On the other hand, the several Korean ambassadors and some other officials for whom I wrote speeches never told anyone that I wrote for them, and they would not want it known. Neither did they claim any personal credit for these speeches. They were "spokesmen" for their government, saying what they were authorized and expected to say. For obvious reasons, it would not have been helpful for it to be known that their speeches were authored by an American. Other than this, the authorship was wholly unimportant. It was not themselves they were representing but their government.

Smith: I never worked for anyone who hid the fact that I was the speechwriter. When I worked at the White House, the word "speechwriter" was on my door. By the way, Nixon started that tradition. Supposedly the most secretive president was the one who really opened things up for speechwriters and advanced the whole profession. And when I worked for Lee Iacocca, there was no secret about it; I traveled with him, and people knew that.

Do you think certain people have a legitimate right to use ghostwriters while other people do not? For example, you said the speakers you worked for did not hide your use, and given the status of these speakers, listeners probably assumed the use of speechwriters. What about local businesspeople or people in academia using ghostwriters when the audience does not know about their use? What about local preachers using canned sermons or ghostwriters when listeners probably assume that the only ghostwriter is God? Would you make distinctions?

Oliver: I've always thought of ghostwriting in terms of policy presentations. Here I strongly believe that ghostwriting is not only ethical but is also indispensable. I don't see how administrators could operate well without the use of ghostwriters.

On a local level, if the president of Penn State were speaking to the National Education Association about educational policy, he has the responsibility to speak as effectively as possible. He ought to consult with other people to see what kind of policy he should enunciate. Why not, then, also consult with experts in other skills to see how to present his policies in the most effective way?

I never really thought about local preachers using canned sermons or ghostwriters, but what if they do? Here's a preacher who does not have the ability to do the kind of speaking his position demands. What are his alternatives? Stop being a preacher? Resign from the pulpit? Get a job as a dock worker? Let's say he tells himself, "I want to be a preacher, and I want to be effective. Hiring someone to do some speechwriting for me will help me be an effective preacher." I wonder if God objects to that. I wouldn't think so. It's a religious message that's being presented; it comes out of the preacher's mouth, but it's a religious message. Actually, my younger son is a Presbyterian preacher. I'm sure when he utters his sermons, he believes he is transmitting God's message as best he can, not Dennis Oliver's message. Since the message is not his message anyway, if he needed some help in presenting it, I see no problem.

Take the minister of the Riverside Church in New York City, an enormously prestigious pulpit. He has a very important congregation in the sense that the congregation represents great wealth and power, so what the members think matters a great deal. I guess I would rather have the minister use canned sermons that were good and deliver them well than have him prepare and deliver bad sermons.

Smith: I hadn't thought about your question quite that way before. I know there are cases where churches distribute sermons; so the sermons are ghostwritten. When such a sermon is given, if the fact that it was ghostwritten is kept from the congregation and congregants are led to believe that this is an authentic sermon written by their preacher, it is misleading and, thus, unethical.

If the use of a speechwriter is hidden from the audience, then it's wrong. If someone who uses a ghostwriter denies it, then I believe the person is lying and acting unethically. In fact, if you look in Iacocca's book where he talks about speechwriting and speechmaking, he mentions Dale Carnegie, but does not mention using speechwriters. The book was itself ghostwritten by Bill Novak. I find this sort of thing ludicrous.

Do you think the public is prepared to know about a local preacher using a canned sermon or speechwriter?

Oliver: I'd have to think about that for a while. I'm not quite sure. What do I expect from a preacher? I expect him to elevate the moral character of his listeners, try to make them spiritually more comfortable, give them a better feeling about themselves and a higher sense of responsibility. If he can do these things better by asking his wife or second cousin or some secret ghostwriter to write the sermon for him, and the sermon helps the congregants, I'd have to scratch my head and wonder why I'd consider that unethical.

Whether the public is prepared to know about a preacher who doesn't write a sermon himself, whether I'm prepared to know—well, you caught me here. I'm not quite sure what I think. People want a preacher to be sincere, they want him to be honest, they want him to speak out of his experience. There's a very, very personal relationship here. A preacher using a canned sermon or ghostwriter seems no different than somebody using a canned love letter or ghostwriter to woo a girl. If I'm in love with a girl and wooing her, and I hire somebody to write love letters for me, I suspect that could be dangerous and, to an extent, unethical because there's an intimacy in the relationship. I'm pretending to her to be a different person than I really am, a better person than I really am. All this means a lot in terms of our future living together, and so on. So if somebody makes love to a girl in someone else's words and manner, that is not only unethical, but it is also stupid and unwise.

If I were a member of the Bethany Baptist Church here in Chestertown, Maryland—which I'm not, but if I were—and if the minister gave a sermon and I came home and said, "Gee, wasn't he wonderful today; what a fine man he is, and what insight he has," and then if somebody informed me that the sermon was taken from a book or written by a speechwriter, I would probably hastily withdraw from the Bethany Baptist Church and find another preacher. I would feel cheated because of the intimacy of the relationship. The minister would lose authority in my eyes and, I suspect, in the eyes of most congregants. But, you see, his functions are all very intimate things. Most ghostwriting situations do not involve an intimate, personal relationship. Most ghostwriting situations concern policy. So if the preacher communicated his ideas better and I didn't find out he had help in writing his sermon, I suppose the ghostwriting would be a good thing, but if I found out he had not written his sermon, I would think less of him. I never considered the ethics of ghostwriting before from this particular point of view. I didn't even imagine anyone would ghostwrite love letters for somebody or write sermons or parts of sermons for somebody.

Smith: The public could handle knowing about the extensive use of ghostwriters. We tend to think the public is naive, but our job is to get the word out that ghostwriting goes on all the time.

I don't think congregants, though, would approve of their local preacher using a canned sermon or a ghostwriter because they are taking care of the preacher and would probably wonder why he was spending his money on a speech. It may depend, of course, on how much collaboration is involved, but I still think the practice of ghostwriting is unethical if the speaker intentionally misleads the audience.

Do you think it is unethical for ghostwriters to write against their personal convictions?

Oliver: No. I think ghostwriters are like lawyers. Lawyers sometimes defend clients whom they think are guilty, but they feel these people are entitled to the best case that can be made for them.

There were lots of times when I wrote things that went against my convictions, but not in a vital way. For instance, if a speaker advocated a 50 percent reduction in import duties on Japanese automobiles and my own conviction was that the import duties ought to be eliminated entirely, I would be writing against my convictions. But my principle might convince me that political considerations were such that the best we could do was to get them reduced by 50 percent. Politics is the art of compromise, and many times you have to compromise what you would like to see achieved and do something only half as good or a third as good.

I'd resign rather than write against my basic and important convictions. If I felt something was morally repugnant or inimical to my own country or others, then I would resign.

I would not write against my basic convictions, but I don't think it's unethical for somebody to do so. A ghostwriter, for example, might write for a member of the American Nazi Party. I would view the speaker as unethical, not the ghostwriter. I wouldn't write myself for somebody who supported the Nazi Party, and I wouldn't like anybody who did, but my dislike would be based not on ethical grounds but on the grounds of human sensibility.

Smith: I personally will not write for someone with whom I disagree. If I disagree with somebody about a particular issue, I simply will not write a speech on that issue; the speaker will have to get somebody else to write that speech.

I don't think it's unethical, though, for other people to write against their personal convictions. A lawyer can defend a guilty person and help make sure justice is carried out. Likewise, a speechwriter can write for the other side of an issue perfectly fine just to make sure the idea gets fair play in the marketplace of ideas. I have no problem with that. I personally don't do it because I don't write as effectively when I'm writing about an idea I don't believe in.

All people, of course, possess certain idiosyncrasies. In what ways do you think your particular idiosyncrasies affected the speeches you wrote?

Oliver: Oh, I'm sure my idiosyncrasies affected my writing. For one thing, I'm an individualist rather than a committee person. I like to do things in my own way and at my own speed. For another thing, I have rather definite ideas about public affairs. I like to think of myself as a liberal. I like to think that morality ought to be supported and that trickery and Machiavellianism ought not to be encouraged. So I find it very difficult to do any ghostwriting that goes seriously against my convictions.

Smith: I believe in what I call triples, saying phrases like "I have a dream" three times and then moving to something else. In the speeches I've written, particularly for Ford, you'll see a lot of these triples. Another idiosyncrasy is exemplified in a speech George Bush gave at the United Nations. He said, "Of course, we are sorry about the death of these people, of course this, of course this." I don't know whether I picked up the use of "of course" from reading Franklin D. Roosevelt's speeches as a way to dismiss emotion and had put it in one of Bush's speeches. Bush likes it, though, and we may keep hearing "of course" from him. My idiosyncrasy is now his idiosyncrasy.

To understand a speech as fully as possible, do rhetorical critics need to investigate thoroughly who the speechwriters were and what their idiosyncrasies were?

Oliver: That depends on what you're looking for. Personally I don't care who did the writing because I'm interested in an historical situation, a problem that has to be solved, available solutions, why the speaker accepts a particular solution, how the speaker sells the idea to the audience that needs to be influenced, and to what extent it seems he succeeds. When the primary concern is the influence of a speech given by a speaker who represents an institution, it doesn't really matter who did the writing. If you were analyzing a personal, intimate type of rhetoric, knowing who the ghostwriters were and what their idiosyncrasies were might matter.

Smith: I'm not sure investigating speechwriters and their idiosyncrasies is really relevant. When a speaker delivers a speech, he or she takes responsibility for it.

Of course, whether you should investigate who the speechwriters were depends on the kind of rhetorical analysis you're doing. If you're doing a textual analysis, I don't see the need for investigating the speechwriters. If you're looking at how the style works to move an idea or you're looking at the lines of an argument, I don't think you would need to make such an examination. If, however, you're looking for the inventive process and want to get into intentionality, then it would help to research the speechwriters and their idiosyncrasies.

If I wanted to conduct such an investigation, how would I go about it? How, especially, can we locate ghostwriters for speakers who are deceased?

Oliver: If I wanted to know who was writing speeches for Senator Hatch, I probably wouldn't ask him directly. I would try to get acquainted with one of a half-dozen top aides in his office. I would explain in a serious way that I write books about how speechwriting is done and I need to know how it's done in senatorial circles. I would make it clear that I do not have any political motivation whatsoever either for or against Senator Hatch, and I'm not trying to spy on him or to get his secrets and tell them. I would ask a question like "Would you say that what Senator Hatch does is typical of what other senators do?" rather than ask, "How does he do it?" After the discussion gets going and the aide sees that I'm really seeking academic information, the person usually will speak more freely. I think this approach would work more successfully than asking at the outset how speechwriting is done in Senator Hatch's office.

Smith: If possible, I would interview the writer, and I would also look at the training of the writer. You can't always identify the writer, of course, and many times the writers won't talk to you. The Nixon writers tended to be reluctant to talk. Democratic writers, in my opinion, tend to be more self-promoting and easier to get interviews with than Republican writers are.

Locating the ghostwriters for speakers who are deceased is, of course, even more difficult. You look at letters and see if you can find evidence. For example, Edward Everett edited Daniel Webster's 1850 Compromise speech for the pamphlet version. You look at why Everett was selected, what his biases were, and how much of a role he played.

You have to remember, too, that speechwriters often distort things, and you have to examine those distortions. For example, as best as we can tell, Sam Rosenman, one of Franklin D. Roosevelt's speechwriters, took much more credit than he deserved for writing some of Roosevelt's speeches.

I once had an experience where I wrote a speech for President Ford to present to the Southern Baptist Convention in 1976 in Norfolk, Virginia. Ford wanted me to talk to the southern preacher so I could remove or alter anything that might offend Baptists. I showed the preacher the draft for the speech, and he found nothing offensive. Ford gave the speech, and it was received well. Two days later, I read in the *Washington Star* that this preacher claimed he had written the speech. So it is very difficult to weed through and find out who really wrote something, who's taking credit for what, and how the whole speechwriting process actually occurred.

You are obviously more aware than the average person that many politicians and businesspeople do not write their own speeches. How does this knowledge affect your interpretation of a speech by someone who probably did not write it?

Oliver: I tend to think of the presidency more as an institution than as an individual. If the institutional president is saying something sensible that represents a good solid policy position, then I respect him. I couldn't care less whether he wrote it himself or hired somebody to write it for him.

Below the level of president, we need to think about whether the person is speaking to represent a policy position of an institution. For example, AT&T's president or AT&T's third-level manager speaks for the institution of AT&T.

Smith: Knowing that many politicians and businesspeople do not write their own speeches affects me in two ways. First, I become kind of an art critic and say, "Isn't that neat." The more we know about certain subjects, the more we become fascinated with them. For example, it has been shown that the more we know about television technology, the more fascinated we become with the medium, and the more we know about music, the more we appreciate it. Being a speechwriter and knowing other speechwriters makes me look at the art of a speech and examine how the speech was created. Second, I eliminate all that and just listen to the speech to understand the main ideas.

Why do you think so few speechwriters come from the field of speech?

Oliver: I think so few speechwriters come from the field of speech because many professors of speech don't do speechwriting themselves, and if you don't do something, you want a reason for not doing it. An obvious reason is to say, "It's not that I lack the skill, it's not that I don't get opportunities; instead, it's because I disapprove of it. I'm ethically superior to that sort of thing."

I also think many professors of speech coming out of the rhetorical tradition honestly believe that speech is the person, that style is the person, and that ethos [an individual's character and credibility] is the most persuasive appeal a speaker can use. Viewed this way, the rhetorical tradition goes against the idea of ghostwriting.

Paradoxically, if I ask professors of speech, "Do you expect the president of the United States to write a speech for the Boy Scouts?" they would probably say, "Oh, no, that's different; that's trivial and standardized. These speeches don't really matter." If I ask, "Do you expect the president of the United States to write a speech to Congress on the state of the union?" I don't know how professors of speech would respond. They might say, "Sure, the president ought to write this type of important speech." If they give this answer, though, they are speaking out of a vast morass of ignorance about the enormous responsibilities of the presidency and about how the country is better served when the president employs a group of speechwriters.

Smith: I don't think the field of speech has done a very good job of marketing the people who are most qualified to become speechwriters. I haven't noticed, though, that it's a reticence on our part for ethical reasons. I may be wrong.

Our discipline should do more to train students to become speechwriters. Every speech or communication department should have a course on ghostwriting.

If you were to teach a course on ghostwriting, how would you design it? What topics and issues would you consider most important to cover?

Oliver: I think a course in ghostwriting ought to stress the need to study sociology, political science, and economics. Teachers of courses in ghostwriting ought to tell students that if they want to be a ghostwriter, they better have their mind packed with information and ideas. They're going to need information and ideas a lot more than they're going to need to know about different sentence structures. Students should know also how to do research, how to use the library, and how to get information quickly. Then students should practice writing so they can write clearly and dramatically and so they can learn how to think about audience reaction. In other words, to teach people to be a ghostwriter in general, you need to teach the general principles of good writing and good speaking and more. Francis Bacon said it very well. I might paraphrase him by advising: "Learn all you can and, as a speaker, learn to bring it together into focus."

Smith: I'd use Aristotle's *Rhetoric* as the basic text, because Aristotle asked all the right questions. He didn't always give the right answers for our society but, even here, he was pretty close. He gave us a set of questions that will generate a speech, and that's what you really need as a generalist speechwriter.

[Kenneth] Burke's dramatistic approach adds some dimension to the fundamental basis that Aristotle provided. I don't find the pentad very useful in speechwriting, but I do find this dramatistic approach helpful and inventive; it gives you a little more freedom than Aristotle does in the stylistic area.

I would have students read the King James Bible and study the way language is used there; it's beautiful. I would also cover the way Shakespeare used style to advance plot and depict character. When I teach rhetorical criticism, I have students look at the speeches of Brutus and Mark Anthony as good examples of two different kinds of style and as good examples of how style can depict a character. I also think it's very important to master tropes and figures. Style is very important in speechwriting.

In our field, we tend to spend more time on invention than style. Invention is kind of automatic in speechwriting. Perhaps I feel this way because the structure of the argument of a speech comes so automatically to me from my training in debate and argumentation. It should come automatically to everybody in speech. They should have that foundation. One of the reasons why so many rhetorically trained speechwriters came out of debate is because invention is easy for them. Because the construction and organization of evidence is automatic, they can focus on the stylistic area, which is what really sells you as a speechwriter. And if you can also help speakers with delivery, then everything works. So I would make sure students were well rounded in argument, particularly the forensic kind of argument. By that I mean competitive debate, because competitive debate involves the stock questions for handling policy issues that are critical if you're working for a politician. You'll also be writing ceremonial speeches that should have high stylistic qualities. So I would also focus on style in a speechwriting course.

Did you find ghostwriting rewarding?

Oliver: Ghostwriting was rewarding to me. I find any writing rewarding. I like to spin out of my mind something I can put down on paper.

I enjoyed ghostwriting for President Rhee and the various ambassadors because they treated me so well. They were gracious and they were grateful, and I felt I was doing something that needed to be done for good people.

Smith: Most of the time I find ghostwriting rewarding. I prefer ghost-writing as a consulting job rather than as a full-time job. You get burned out pretty fast when doing it full-time. I also think full-time you have dead periods; this happens especially when speakers want a speech without giving you enough time. A speech is like bread; it has to sit for twenty-four hours. Then you come back to it and find that stuff that sounded wonderful to you one day sounds awful the next. You have to let it sit and redo it, and then redo it again. As you get the big errors out, you see the smaller errors. When you have the time and when you're writing about something interesting, ghostwriting is very rewarding, especially as a consultant.

I would like to take the specific aspects of your background one at a time and ask in what ways your speechwriting experiences have related to these aspects. First, in what ways have your speechwriting experiences related to what you studied in speech communication?

Oliver: A great deal. I think I'm a pretty good speaker myself. It's hard to be a good speechwriter if you're not a good speaker. Having knowledge about how to go about getting the information you need and having the ability to give speeches effectively definitely help in speechwriting.

Smith: My speechwriting experiences relate a great deal to what I studied in speech communication. I could not do speechwriting without the training I've had. There is a sense that you have a much bigger arsenal than you will ever use. For example, George Bush does not like a lot of organizational language. By organizational language, I mean previews and organizing things in a consistent way: "I'm going to look at causes, I'm going to look at effects, the first cause is," and that kind of thing. You can't get clients to do that very often. They think it's pedantic, or they just don't want to bother with it, or they think the audience can see what's on the paper. They don't understand that what's oral is invisible, and that organizational language gives the audience a sense of security and increases their own credibility as a speaker. Basically, you are driven back to a lot of very fundamental things that you have learned in basic speech courses. You don't always get a chance to use Burkean style or a particular stylistic ploy in a speech. It's too high-falutin for some speakers. Some speakers don't like metaphors or don't feel comfortable with highly stylized language. But it's important to have the training that you get in rhetoric and public address, in speech criticism, and in speech in general because the training gives you confidence. You know you have this arsenal of strategies and tactics available, even if you don't always use them. You know you can write a good speech.

In what ways have your speechwriting experiences related to your participation in debate?

Oliver: There were no speech courses in the high school I attended, so the only speech training I got was in debate. In college there were speech courses and I took them, but debate seemed more realistic. I remember that I didn't take my speech courses very seriously; I prepared a speech on the way to class and that sort of thing. But I took debate very seriously. In debate I had to win a vote from the audience or from judges. I really put my heart into it because I knew I was in competition.

Smith: My speechwriting experiences have related to my debate *a lot*! The stock questions in debate give you a way of generating a good speech. Is there a need? Is the need significant? Is it physical? Is it psychological? Is it inherent? Do the laws have to be changed? All these questions are important. Does the plan fit the need? Do you need to trim the need back to fit the plan? Does the plan have advantages? Is the plan workable? Is it practical? All these questions are extremely helpful in writing a deliberative speech, and that's mainly the kind of speech I've written. Also, many times you do the research for a speech or you tell people the kind of evidence they should get; debate helps you know how many examples you need and what kinds of examples you need to support particular arguments. So I think debate training is absolutely vital!

My experience in coaching debate has helped in terms of my helping clients understand how much evidence is needed to make a certain point and in terms of helping clients with delivery. My coaching experience certainly has been helpful when I've worked on presidential debates, which I've done with Ford and which I've done with Bush and Quayle. In Bush's case, I worked in 1984 with his vice presidential debate. In October 1988, I coached Quayle in preparation for his vice presidential debate; Bob Packwood played the role of Lloyd Bentsen. Coaching debate has helped me also show people in press conferences how to handle questions, how to turn a question into something that has a stylized answer to it, hopefully three-pointed. Also, coaching helps me in assessing the strengths and weaknesses of particular clients as speakers. You do that with debaters. You have to decide what they're good at and what they're bad at. Should they be a first speaker or a second speaker?

Are they better on the affirmative or the negative? Experience in coaching debate gets you in a frame of mind for looking at a client and saying, "Well, maybe you ought to do press conferences; just make statements and leave. Have your staff take care of questions, because you're bad in that format." Or "You ought to sit down and talk with one reporter, one at a time. You're better at that than standing up and speaking to a large group."

In what ways have your speechwriting experiences related to your teaching of speech communication?

Oliver: Very closely! I try to teach what I know, and what I know is mostly from what I read in books and what I know from my own experience. Of course, all this goes together. I've done a lot of speaking as well as a lot of listening; my convictions arise out of experience and observation. So I bring into the classroom what I have done outside and take from the classroom into what I'm doing outside. The two are the same; when they're not, it's because the teaching is removed from the real world.

A lot of college professors of speech are poor writers; one of the curious things to me is that they do not apply to themselves the same principles they demand of their freshman students. For instance, in class they say, "You have to have a theme, you have to have a purpose, you have to have concrete illustrations, you have to have facts, you have to make them interesting, you have to make them convincing, you have to prepare for a specific audience and adapt to that audience." Then, when it comes time for them to write an article, they forget all these things. So many of them say to me, "Oh, gosh, I just can't write. I wish I could write like you do. I just can't write." What would they say to a freshman in their class who said, "I just can't give a speech?" They probably would say, "Get a theme, get a purpose, write an introduction, and so forth." If they applied these same principles to their own writing, they could write, because the principles that make somebody a good speaker are the same principles that make somebody a good writer and a good speechwriter.

Smith: There's a real synergy between my speechwriting experiences and my teaching speech communication. For instance, when I talk about tropes and figures in the classroom, that frankly sounds pretty dead. I talk about Quintilian or about the Roman second sophistic and nobody's awake. But when I talk about the fact that Ronald Reagan or George Bush or Lee Iacocca used something from these tropes and figures, and here it is in a speech or here it is on videotape or audiotape, suddenly students come alive. They begin to see the relevance of understanding something as dry as tropes and figures. So my speechwriting experiences give me credibility as a teacher and enliven the classroom.

In the field of composition, there is an ongoing debate about whether one becomes a good writer through intuition or through formal training and practice. As you know, most ghostwriters become ghostwriters accidentally; hence, they work intuitively rather than with the rhetorical knowledge and art that you bring to the practice. Do you think there are differences in the process used by accidental ghostwriters and rhetorically trained ghostwriters?

Oliver: Yes. You have to learn the skills. In piano playing or speechwriting, you have to learn the skills. Just as it helps to have a piano instructor to teach you the skills, it helps to have a speech instructor to teach you the skills. Basketball players, golfers, and other athletes always talk about the importance of confidence. If you have confidence, you play a much better game of basketball or golf. If you have confidence, you also play a much better game of writing.

There is nothing mysterious about writing. When I fail as a writer, when I sit at my desk upstairs and cannot write, I don't tell myself, "Oh, I just can't write." Instead, I tell myself, "I just can't think." Anybody can come downstairs and say to his wife, "Well, I just didn't have inspiration today. This was not a writing kind of day for me." They're not ashamed of that; it's an excuse they readily accept. But how can they look at themselves in the mirror or face their wife and say, "I just couldn't think today"? They can't. So I tell myself the trouble is I'm not thinking, and I make my mind work. Once I've figured out what I want to say and learn what I need to know, then putting the words down on paper is easy and speaking the words is easy.

A person with a really good ear and a willingness to do an awful lot of hard, penetrating work can learn to play the piano or play basketball without any teacher. It's harder, but the person can do it. In the same way, a person can learn to be a good speaker, writer, or speechwriter without any teacher, but it's harder to do. It definitely helps if you know basic rhetorical skills, such as how to research thoroughly, organize coherently, and communicate clearly.

Smith: There definitely is a difference in the process used by accidental ghosts and rhetorically trained ghosts. The rhetorically trained ghost can put out a much better product. What you get with an accidental ghostwriter is just that. So many accidental ghostwriters do not "make it" and get left by the wayside. Accidental ghostwriters who do succeed have the talent to write effectively. If they have this talent, though, they would be even better at ghostwriting if they had rhetorical training. I believe in Isocrates's model: People have talent; if you add training and the art, the three go together. In speech communication we learn methodologies than can help make the writing process much more efficient and much more effective. In the *Wall Street Journal*, I read an interview with Lee Iacocca's current writer, Mike Morrison, who said an Iacocca speech goes through 22 drafts. If he wasn't joking, he's got a big problem! I can see maybe 8 drafts, given the subject matter, but if he's going through 22 drafts, rhetorical training would save him a lot of time. I never did more than 6 or 7.

Many speech ghostwriters and literary ghostwriters come from journalism; they are *prose* writers. For example, when Jimmy Carter became president, his first speechwriter was a novelist, and it showed. Carter's speeches were prosaic, very long, and not very effective. If the writer had received rhetorical training, he would have been much better. Not surprisingly, he did not last very long as head writer.

Accidental writers either don't make it or they learn the process and improve as they go along. Sorensen was the first person who really knew how to write in John Kennedy's style, but even he learned more and more about writing as he went along. At least five people were involved with Kennedy's Inaugural Address. One of these people, Arthur Schlesinger, still says the worst thing he did to the Inaugural was to put in the line about he who rides on the back of the tiger might wind up in his stomach. He says the line is totally out of character with the rest of the speech. So, even in 1961, Sorensen did not have complete control over the writing process, and a lot of people who were not rhetorically trained wrote the speech. While the address is full of balances, I don't think it holds up very well if you examine it carefully.

Do you think there are differences in the quality of the final product between accidental and rhetorically trained ghostwriters?

Oliver: Yes. At the basic level of just good organization, having been taught how to organize obviously helps a great deal. When speakers get to what I call a higher level of how to get an audience to respond, I think the speaker's basic personality is involved more. Unfortunately, some students have been overly trained on how to stand "correctly," and how to gesture "correctly," and how to manipulate their voice "correctly." They sound as though they are performing, not as though they are communicating. In these cases, academic training actually hurts the quality of the speech, but, of course, it has been stupid academic training. Good rhetorical training can help speakers deliver their message effectively and adapt to their audience.

Smith: Accidental and rhetorically trained ghostwriters definitely differ not only in efficiency but also in the quality of the speech. You'll see a difference in construction. Accidental speechwriters often write speeches that meander in places, that are inductive as opposed to deductive, and that have less organizational structure. Speeches written by people who are rhetorically trained, particularly debaters, usually use a first affirmative structure, clear organizational signals, and a deductive structure—state the case and prove it.

"HOLY GHOSTING"

Not surprisingly, the issue of religious ghostwriting (members of the clergy using pulpit aids, canned sermons, and ghostwriters) is even more delicate and supercharged than the normal ethical considerations of ghostwriting. Whereas the public is becoming increasingly aware of the use of ghostwriters by political and business leaders, most congregants assume all members of the clergy write their sermons themselves; the only possible ghostwriter is God or perhaps the Holy Ghost! Before discussing Professor Oliver's and Professor Smith's thoughts about the topic, I will provide some background information about "holy ghosting."

Little research has been done on the topic of ghostwriting for the parsonage. To gain knowledge on the subject, I personally interviewed 11 clergymen, most of whom wished to remain anonymous. I chose clergymen from several different religious denominations. None of the 11 clergymen with whom I spoke knew of an instance of a member of the clergy hiring a ghostwriter, but all knew of many instances of clergymen who presented the ideas of others as their own and, in fact, eight of them admitted they themselves had used the words of others for an illustration or an entire sermon.

Members of the clergy speak the equivalent of the 400-page book a year, just in sermons (Beckelhymer 1974, 139). Many sermon aids exist to help them. Some churches publish a lectionary each year, offering specific biblical passages, sample sermon outlines, and anecdotes to use with particular passages. Commentaries on the Scripture exist in numerous forms; some give several interpretations of a particular passage. *Pulpit Digest* reprints entire sermons, and *Pulpit Resource* contains sermon outlines; both publications are available by subscription. Many libraries contain books of entire sermons. Literature from Bible colleges often includes free sermons, and prewritten sermons can be purchased in paper form, on floppy disks, or on cassette. A sermon cassette costs about eight dollars. One reverend told me, "I have had prewritten sermons sent to me in a generic-style brown wrapper. It was like receiving a 'free sample' or 'trial-size' sermon. Someone is using them, because there are an awful lot of them out there." Clearly resources are available for ministers, priests, and rabbis to use or not use, as they choose.

Three people I interviewed argued that using sermon aids is blasphemous. They contended that in the clergy, faith in the speaker is an integral part of ethos; members of a congregation put their trust in the person who is guiding their faith. We look to the clergy because they are specifically trained to interpret the Bible, the Torah, or whatever their religion follows. When ministers of the Word use someone else's words, one minister asked, "How can they be credible?" Another argued vehemently that using canned sermons is deceptive: "My congregants expect to hear my own words. How can I let them down? Being deceptive is wrong in any occupation," he continued, "but it is especially wrong in the ministry." All three agreed that the covert identity of a ghost adds to the delusion of the listeners.

The other eight clergymen with whom I spoke, however, found nothing unethical about using pulpit aids. Some used commentaries to clarify and verify their personal understandings. "I check my understanding," one minister explained, "against other writers so I don't become a maverick. I want to get a broad range of opinions. I always check one or two sources, especially on a sensitive topic."

Other clergymen spoke about how they used pulpit aids as sources of insight, interpretation, and inspiration. Before incorporating ideas from a pulpit aid into their own sermons, they adapted the ideas to their own preaching style and to their congregations. One explained, "I wrestle with the ideas, sometimes for long periods of time, before accepting them, and then I adapt the ideas to make them my own."

Several of the interviewees edited the ideas of others before using them. This editing ranged from making very minor changes to making major changes so the ideas became, in a sense, the person's own. One leader of a nondenominational Christian group makes a recorded telephone message every day. Rather than using his own words, he reads a passage from the *Daily Word*, a publication from United Village in Missouri. He assured me that he makes "significant changes" in the passages. When I asked him how, he explained that he substitutes "you" for "we," in order to make the passages relate more directly to listeners. To me, minor pronoun substitutions do not constitute "significant changes."

Over half of the clergymen I interviewed found nothing unethical about using entire sermons. They argued that, like other public leaders, it is unreasonable to expect leaders of congregations to write every word of every sermon afresh. One minister said, only half in jest, "The only alternatives are to change congregations every few years and repeat your sermons or to neglect all the other responsibilities of your ministry." Another remarked, "This job would be great if it weren't for weekends!" One priest argued, "I'm trying to reach a large group of people, and I want them to gain something. If I can't give them this, then I need to get some help." Another explained, "Clergymen are a conduit for God's word. If someone else can express a point better than they can, then they have a right to use this help." A third pastor justified using canned sermons by saying, "What is important is that I feed my sheep a well-balanced meal."

One minister told the story of a preacher who before every sermon would bow to the left of the congregation with hands outstretched, arms parallel to each other. After every sermon he would repeat the action, this time bowing to the right. The congregation was long puzzled by this strange blessing. Finally, at the preacher's retirement dinner, they asked him about it. "Blessing? Heavens no," he replied. "Those were quotation marks." The real irony is that the pastor does not remember where he had heard the story.

Borrowing in preaching is an age-old practice, and "feeding my sheep a well-balanced meal" is a justification of long historical and homiletical standing. Early in the fifth century, St. Augustine endorsed this view:

Certainly there are some men who can speak well but who cannot think out what they are to say. If they can take something which has been wisely and eloquently written by other people, commit it to memory and speak it out publicly, they are not acting dishonestly, that is if they do not conceal the part they are playing. For this is the way many people become preachers of the truth, and it is a good thing that it should be so. . . . People who steal are taking what belongs to someone else, but the word of God is the property of all who obey it. (1959, 340)

A point St. Augustine makes here that some of the clergymen I interviewed did not discuss is whether it is incumbent on preachers to tell their auditors that they are presenting someone else's ideas.

SUMMARY AND CONCLUSIONS

The fact that many listeners are surprised to learn about pulpit aids and canned sermons is demonstrated in the interviews with Professors Oliver and Smith. These two renowned ghostwriters had not thought before about religious ghosting. Professor Oliver defends the practice if the congregation does not know, but indicates he personally thinks a preacher using a canned sermon or a ghostwriter is no different from someone using a canned love letter or a ghostwriter to woo a girl. Interestingly, Walter Lippmann also equated not writing one's own speeches with not writing one's own love letters (quoted in Safire 1968, 414). Professor Smith consistently argued that if speakers do not deceive listeners, then ghostwriting is ethical; if speakers do deceive listeners, then ghostwriting is unethical. When asked if most listeners were ready to learn about some member of the clergy using the words of others without giving credit, he answered, "No."

Most of the responses by Professors Oliver and Smith concerning the process of ghostwriting are consistent with the findings from my interviews with people who became involved in ghostwriting accidentally (Einhorn 1988). This consistency underscores the importance of certain rhetorical principles, whether the principles come from training or from intuition. Both Professor Oliver and Professor Smith made it clear, however, that rhetorically trained ghostwriters have a clear edge over "accidental" ghosts. Professor Oliver said in summary, "A person can learn to be a good speaker, writer, or speechwriter without any teacher, but it's harder to do. It definitely helps if you know basic rhetorical skills such as how to research thoroughly, organize coherently, and communicate clearly." Professor Smith argued that "accidental ghostwriters who do succeed . . . would be even better at ghostwriting if they had rhetorical training also." Both strongly believe that training in rhetoric makes the process of ghostwriting much more efficient and makes the quality of the speech much more effective.

REFERENCES

Augustine, Saint. 1969. *De Doctrina Christiana*, Book 4. In *St. Augustine on Education*, trans. George Howie. Gateways edition, South Bend, IN: Henry Regnery, 1969.

Beckelhymer, Hunter. 1974. "No Posturing in Borrowed Plumes." *Christian Century* (February 6): 138–42.

Bormann, Ernest G. 1960. "Ghostwriting and the Rhetorical Critic." *Quarterly Journal of Speech* 46:287–88.

———. 1961a. "Ethics of Ghostwritten Speeches." *Quarterly Journal of Speech* 47:262–67.

———. 1961b. "Ghostwriting Speeches—A Reply." *Quarterly Journal of Speech* 47:420–21.

Brigance, W. Norwood. 1956. "Ghostwriting Before Franklin D. Roosevelt and the Radio." *Today's Speech* 4:10–12.

Devlin, L. Patrick. 1974. "The Influences of Ghostwriting on Rhetorical Criticism." *Today's Speech* 22:7–12.

Duffy, Bernard K., and Mark Royden Winchell. 1989. " 'Speak the Speech I Pray You.' The Practice and Perils of Literary and Oratorical Ghostwriting." *The Southern Speech Communication Journal* 55:102–15.

Einhorn, Lois J. 1982. "The Ghosts Unmasked: A Review of Literature on Speechwriting." *Communication Quarterly* 30:41–47.

———. 1988. "The Ghosts Talk: Personal Interviews with Three Former Speechwriters." *Communication Quarterly* 36:94–108.

McGlon, Charles A. 1954. "How I Prepare My Sermons: A Symposium." *Quarterly Journal of Speech* 40:49–62.

Medhurst, Martin J. 1987. "Ghostwritten Speeches: Ethics Isn't the Only Lesson." *Communication Education* 36:241–49.

Nichols, Marie Hochmuth. 1963. "Ghost Writing: Implications for Public Address." In *Rhetoric and Criticism*, pp. 135–48. Baton Rouge: Louisiana State University Press.

Noonan, Peggy. 1990. *What I Saw at the Revolution: A Political Life in the Reagan Era*. New York: Random House.

Oliver, Robert T. 1962. "Syngman Rhee: A Case Study in Transnational Oratory." *Quarterly Journal of Speech* 48:115–27.

Safire, William. 1968. *The New Language of Politics*. New York: Random House.

Segar, Matthew W. 1985. "Ghostbusting: Exorcising the Great Man Spirit from the Speechwriting Debate." *Communication Education* 34:353–58.

Smith, Craig R. 1976. "Contemporary Political Speech Writing." *The Southern Speech Communication Journal* 42:52–67.

———. 1977. "Appendum to 'Contemporary Political Speech Writing.' " *The Southern Speech Communication Journal* 43:191–94.

Smith, Donald K. 1961. "Ghostwritten Speech." *Quarterly Journal of Speech* 47:416–20.

Tarver, Jerry. 1982. *Professional Speech Writing*. Richmond, VA: The Effective Speech Writing Institute.

Chapter Eight

Ethical Dimensions of Political Advertising

Lynda Lee Kaid

A lie can travel half way around the world while the truth is putting on its shoes.

—Mark Twain

Modern technology has given Mark Twain's statement a literal meaning and raised considerable concern about the ethics of political advertising. Certainly, politics has always been a forum in which exchanges about truth and falsity, hyperbole, oversimplification, and distortion have reigned; but the growth of television as the dominant medium for political advertising has definitely heightened concern about ethics. Several factors account for this increased salience of ethical issues, including the high cost of buying television time, the wide and instantaneous reach of television messages, the possible inherent predisposition of television to the dramatic and the visual, and the seeming ability of technology to alter reality. The purpose of this chapter is to explore the ethical issues raised by political advertising in all forms, with particularly emphasis on television. Following this exploration, some attention is devoted to regulation and monitoring of abuses, and some suggestions for improving adherence to ethical standards are provided.

COMMUNICATION ETHICS AND THE RATIONAL DEMOCRATIC PROCESS

As Johannesen (1990) has suggested, ethical concerns about human communication usually revolve around judgments of what is right or wrong behavior, the potential effects of such behavior, and the manner in which means/ends choices are consciously made. More specifically, "standards such as honesty, promise-keeping, truthfulness, fairness, and humaneness" (Johannesen 1990, 1) would be easily acknowledged by most as important ethical goals.

In politics much of the concern about ethics turns on adherence to classical beliefs about the rationality of man and the ideal democratic process (Kelley 1960; Regan 1986). In this vein, Franklyn Haiman (1958) has argued that communication should encourage the human ability to reason logically, a perspective that is clearly consistent with Kelley's (1960) presumption that the goal of all political communication should be to create an "informed electorate." If voters are to make rational choices about leaders and policy issues, they must have access to information that is true and accurate, unambiguous, unclouded by emotion, and, therefore, enhances, rather than undermines, the decision-making process. For many political observers, political advertising is inherently unable to meet the tests of communication necessary to create good decision making. For instance, Spero has charged that political advertising "is without peer as the most deceptive, misleading, unfair, and untruthful of all advertising" (1980, 3). Considering what most people think about advertising in general, this is indeed a damning indictment.

MAJOR ETHICAL CONCERNS

This section concentrates on examining the major issues that have been raised about the ethics of political advertising. In considering these topics, it is important to acknowledge at the outset that a major test of ethical conduct, truth vs. falsity, is not inherently present or absent in any given communication format or medium.

Buying Access to Voters

Concerns about the clearly unethical practice of "buying votes" has in the twentieth century given way to concerns about the ethicality of buying access to promulgate a point of view. Electronic advertising is viewed as the major culprit since the largest part of campaign expenditures in major electoral contests now goes to produce and air political commercials (Patterson 1983). Thus, political consultant Charles Guggenheim estimates that political television ads in the form of 30- and 60-second spots account for up to "70 percent of what Americans hear and see in a political campaign today" (Committee on Commerce, Science, and Transportation 1985, 54).

There is no denying that political campaigns today are costly endeavors. In 1988 candidates Bush and Dukakis and their respective national parties spent a combined total of over $79 million on television advertising during the presidential campaign (Devlin 1989). The average U.S. senator elected in 1988 spent $3.7 million on his entire campaign, and the winning U.S. House campaign averaged $393,000, much of it going to electronic advertising (Berke 1990). A recent mail survey concluded that 88.9 percent of Senate candidates and 87.2 percent of House candidates rely on television more than on any other medium (Hoff and Bernstein 1988).

Beyond these factually true statements, it is not clear why some people see it as unethical to use money to communicate with voters. The most compelling arguments for regulating the relationship of money to politics, potential corruption and undue influence, have already been recognized. In the 1970s the United States adopted stringent campaign contribution limits and reporting and disclosure requirements. The Supreme Court in its landmark *Buckley v. Valeo* (1976) decision allowing contribution limits and disclosure requirements also ruled that it was an unconstitutional violation of free speech to limit expenditures (unless tied to public financing). The court clearly equated the right to spend to express political views with the right to free expression (Jones and Kaid 1976).

The only viable argument against the expenditure of money to buy television advertising time seems to be that free expression rights must be set aside to eliminate the possibility that well-financed voices may drown out the underfinanced viewpoints. Many legal scholars are skeptical that such arguments could ever be successfully balanced against free expression. "Any legislative effort to forbid or regulate speech from a particular source because it may be expected to dominate a debate or be overpersuasive, misguided, or misleading, causes severe constitutional problems and probably would not survive court scrutiny" (Fox 1978–79, 101).

Furthermore, there is no justification for concluding that televised political advertising is unethical just because campaigns in general and ads in particular cost a lot of money. In fact, Diamond and Marin have maintained that if a campaign is supposed to educate voters, "then perhaps we should ask whether *enough* money is being spent in the U.S." (1989, 387). Penniman (1985) has even suggested that, compared with other democracies on a per voter basis, U.S. elections are a "bargain."

Issues or Images/Logic or Emotion

One of the most enduring criticisms of political advertising has been that it concentrates more on "images" than on "issues." Related to this concern, and in some ways a presumption of it, is the view that image concerns are inherently "emotional" in contrast with issues, which are "logical." Rational voter decision making is presumed to be linked to logical, and thus issue-oriented, information. Thus, the ethical concern here is twofold: Do spots detract from "rational" decision making by concentrating on images instead of issues, resulting in emotional, not logical, vote choices? Is it inherently irrational to consider image or other emotional information in making vote choices? Neither question lends itself to a clear-cut answer.

However, before considering these two components of the issue-image dichotomy, a caveat is in order about the distinction between images and issues. Image and issue are not necessarily dichotomous concepts. These concepts are inextricably entwined in political advertising (Louden 1990). For purposes of considering the ethical concerns in this area, however, this discussion will adopt the common distinction that *image* applies to candidate personality or qualifications, while *issue* refers to information about policy positions or topics of public concern (Garramone 1986; Kaid and Sanders 1978).

The concern that spot ads on television emphasize images over issues has no shortage of advocates. Even the political consultants who often create the ads are willing to admit that they believe the best way to appeal to voters is through the use of emotional constructs in ads (Kaid and Davidson 1986; Kern 1989; Perloff and Kinsey 1990; Sabato 1981; Schwartz 1973). No observer of televised political advertising would deny that consultants put this belief to work. Many political ads do concentrate on eliciting emotions from viewers rather than on communicating solid policy information on issue stances. President Ford's 1976 "Feeling Good about America" ads with their upbeat music and Reagan's 1984 warm and fuzzy "Morning in America" commercials are good examples of ads that seem to concentrate more on emotional images than on issue stances. Yet the argument that such ads are the exception and not the rule is a persuasive one. Diamond and Bates believe that while many ads do appeal to emotions, they often make "serious, issue-oriented points" (1984, 311).

Content analysis research has further demonstrated that, overall, substantial percentages of television ads in political campaigns contain issue information (Joslyn 1980). Kern (1989) quantifies this by showing that 89 percent of ads in a recent sample had issue information. Although some would argue that such issue mentions are not the same as detailed issue presentations, researchers have demonstrated that voters do actually encode a great deal of issue information from such ads (Patterson and McClure 1976). In contrast with the poor record of issue coverage in the news media (Diamond and Marin 1989; Kern 1989; Patterson and McClure 1976), televised political advertising provides a wealth of issue-oriented information for voters. Whether this issue information is sufficient to satisfy "rational" voting models or whether it leads voters to make the "right" decisions is, of course, a matter for relative judgments, but it is not a matter of ethicality.

The second concern about the issue-image question is whether it is wrong for voters to consider image information when making voting decision. As noted above, it is clear that not all political advertising focuses on issues; some tries to elicit emotional responses or concentrates on information about the candidate's personality or "image." This concern raises much more difficult questions and calls for a distinction between "image" and "emotion," which often are erroneously considered synonymous in the context of political ads.

It is easy to condemn the gratuitous use of emotion in political advertising. When emotion is used for no purpose other than to elicit fear or to create unthinking allegiance, it has no defensible place in a democratic society. Examples of such usage in political ads abound. The 1964 Johnson ad that used scenes and statements from the Ku Klux Klan to create fears about Barry Goldwater provided voters with no important policy issue information. As Haiman has said, the use of emotional arguments is often designed to stir listeners or viewers "to set aside reason," and in that case their use is a "violation of democratic ethics" (1958, 388). There may, however, be times when valid issues have strong emotional content, and the melding of emotion with issue content in such cases is not necessarily unethical.

The other aspect of the image controversy is whether political advertising serves any democratic principle by focusing on the character and qualifications of political candidates. While it is not an explicit part of the rational voter model, it is not unreasonable to consider candidate image as a valid part of voter decision making (Andersen 1989; Miller, Wattenberg, and Malanchuk 1985). As with emotional issues in general, few could defend personal concerns based on race, sex, ethnic origin, or personal habits; yet it is possible to argue that many so-called character concerns have a place in voter consideration of a candidate's fitness for office. Whether a candidate is honest, moral, and competent, and related issues, often have a clear bearing on his or her ability to govern. How could it be unethical to consider the ethics of a candidate in making voting decisions?

Oversimplification of Political Argumentation

Another major criticism of political advertising is that spot commercials tend to oversimplify political issues, debasing and trivializing the democratic process (Oreskes with Toner 1990). News reporters have argued that 30-second spots "invite a debate that will wallow in shallowness, distortion, half-truth and false inferences" (Taylor 1989, A14). One can, of course, make the same indictment of network television news. Jamieson (1988) suggests that in the past, political argument consisted of "statement and proof," whereas political ads consist of statement alone. Appeals to reason may get lost in such a process. The concern here is primarily with the *length* of political ads. Opponents argue that 30- and 60-second spots are just too short to contain useful voter information, and thus do not contribute to the goal of an informed electorate. Others argue that the problem is even more troubling, in that the modern tendency used to produce information in short segments that are unconnected and unrelated has reduced the ability of the public to reason logically or complexly on any topic (Mitroff and Bennis 1989).

It is difficult, however, to lay the blame entirely on the length of the ads or to endorse longer television time blocks as a panacea for the ills facing democracy. Research noted above has already demonstrated that such spots do, in fact, contain substantial issue information. As Patterson has pointed out, brevity "does not preclude informative communication" (1983, 44), and the fact that few voters might choose to watch longer programs would actually reduce voter information levels rather than increase them. Longer political programs may get a 6 percent share (Patterson 1983), whereas a short spot seen within a regular television program might be seen by five to six times as many voters each time it is shown.

The length of a commercial also has nothing to do with whether it encompasses good democratic values. Political advertising can communicate ideas that are true or false in 10 seconds or 30 minutes. A politician can come straight to the point easily in 30 seconds, or one can dance around a point for 30 minutes. Political consultant Tony Schwartz derives the ultimate irony from this concern when he says that earlier in the twentieth century radio "was hailed as a means to shorten the longwindedness of politicians" because many felt that political speakers were "deceiving the public through long circumlocutions" (1973, 90).

Another reason for rejecting the belief that short spots are inherently wrong is to consider the possibility that voters may, in fact, be rational by relying on an information source that does not require them to expend additional time and cost to acquire (Goodin 1980), a perspective that is somewhat consistent with Downs's (1957) economic theory of rational voting. Finally, on the oversimplification question, observers would do well to remember that any individual political television commercial does not have to carry the weight of the candidate's entire campaign policy program. Any individual 30- or 60-second spot is usually one of many spots and many communication formats. The sufficiency and depth of a candidate's communication with the electorate should be judged on the totality of messages in all formats through all media.

Failure to Disclose Information

One of the most difficult aspects of ethical communication requirements is the judgment of how far a source must go in disclosing information to the receiver, even if the information is not in the best interest of the source or the source's persuasive end. This problem manifests itself in many ways in political advertising, but three of the most common deal with (1) disclosure of the source of a communication, (2) providing adequate or complete information, and (3) ambiguity and/or inconsistency of political messages. The ability to determine the source of a message is an important consideration in evaluating its worth and objectivity. The determination of a source is particularly crucial in advertising, since it is by its very nature advocacy, lacking neutrality or objectivity (Crichton 1980). Two ethical issues have dominated the presentation of sources in political advertising.

First has been the question of anonymous sources of campaign literature, a technique often used to make attacks on an opposing candidate without having to take the open responsibility for having done so. Although the courts have occasionally ruled that some types of political literature should be guaranteed anonymity so as to avoid the "chilling" of free speech (*Talley v. California* 1959), this is not a great problem in modern campaign advertising because anonymous sources are often viewed with suspicion and because federal law (Federal Election Campaign Act 1971) and many state statutes (Gardner 1984) have made disclosure of the source of campaign materials mandatory. In addition, of course, the Federal Communications Commission has mandatory disclosure requirements for broadcast political advertising.

Of far greater concern has been the ability to identify the "true" source of advertisements sponsored by third parties in political campaigns. The period since 1970 has seen a tremendous increase in the amount of political advertising sponsored by third-party groups in favor of both specific candidates and particular positions on referenda. Even when the ostensible source of such advertisements is identified, it is not always easy for the voter to discern the ties or political agendas of such groups (or occasionally individuals). A section later in this chapter will address the general problem of political action committee, corporate, and independent spending of this kind, but the basic problem of disclosure is a serious one in itself. A good example of the problem is the group of anti-McGovern ads sponsored by the Democrats for Nixon in 1972. Considered by many to be the most effective ads of the 1972 campaign, the spots appeared to come from an independent third-party group headed by Democrat John Connally, but actually the ads were conceived, produced, and financed by the Nixon reelection team (Jamieson 1984). Many voters undoubtedly believed this to be an independent, and thus more credible, source than the campaign itself and were misled by the fact that the advertising did not disclose its true source. The courts have not offered much hope for solving this kind of problem, since they have tended to rule that broadcasters have no excessive affirmative duty to investigate and disclosure the "true source" of political messages (Marylander 1985).

The second ethical problem with failure to disclose information is the judgment of the extent to which a communicator should disclose complete or even unfavorable information about his own position or that of an opponent. Suppose a candidate produces an ad telling voters that he or she favors abortion but fails to mention the qualification that he or she favors it only in cases of rape, incest, or danger to the mother. Or suppose candidate A attacks candidate B for voting against an increase in Social Security benefits in a particular bill, while knowing that candidate B actually voted against the bill in order to preserve even higher benefits and has voted for other increases in the past. Another question might arise if a candidate releases financial information in conformity with legal standards but without disclosing detailed sources of some income.

Have these three candidates been unethical by failing to disclose complete information? In none of these cases is a strict truth/falsity standard helpful. Two other standards might be used. Is the missing information necessary for an informed electorate to make a rational decision, and was it intentionally withheld to create a false or misleading impression? In the first two instances, the answer to both questions might easily be "yes." In the last instance, the electorate would need the missing income information only if it indicated some potential corporate or special interest group tie and such circumstances would then create some evidence for judging intent. If there was no potentially conflict-creating aspect to the missing income, then its absence should not necessarily be judged as an intentional attempt to mislead.

A final aspect of information disclosure involves the use of ambiguous or inconsistent messages. Many communicators find it advantageous to couch their messages in vague or ambiguous terms, leaving receivers free to "hear what they want to hear" and the communicator free to claim misunderstanding or a different interpretation if confronted later. Again truth/falsity is not a useful standard. As Johannesen (1990) has explained, intentional ambiguity is usually judged to be unethical in situations where accurate information transmission is a goal, although some circumstances may justify the use of this technique. The question of consistency relates to information disclosure in terms of the ethicality of communicating one set of positions to one audience and another set of positions to another audience. The classic example of this type of unethical behavior in political communication would be to advocate the death penalty before one group and to oppose it before another, depending on the known predispositions of each group. Fortunately, this is one area in which the pervasiveness of television has had a positive effect. Because it is such a general medium, transmitted simultaneously to so many people in so many locations, and the chance of exposure of inconsistency is now so great, television advertising greatly restricts the ability of candidates to take inconsistent positions without detection (Patterson 1983).

Tricks of Technology

Concern about the use of technology to create false or misleading impressions has been a legitimate ethical problem for political advertising in all mass media channels. In the print media, photographs taken from certain angles, cropped in certain ways, or resulting from deliberate superimpositions or fakery have been used to create political ads that leave false impressions with voters. In the audio channel, voice editing can easily give an erroneous impression, and voice compression can alter the sound of a candidate's or an opponent's voice for use in either audio or video commercials. The latter technique is particularly effective in making a candidate with a slow, halting delivery sound forceful and dynamic.

Today most concerns in this area center on television's capabilities for altering or enhancing reality. Among the most common concerns about use of television technology are (1) editing techniques, (2) special effects, (3) visual imagery/dramatizations (4) computerized alteration techniques, and (5) subliminal techniques. Each has the potential to interfere with the ability of an informed electorate to make rational choices.

The use of video editing techniques to create a false impression is not difficult to conceive (Diamond and Bates 1984; Sabato 1981). An often cited example is the 1968 Nixon ad that interspersed scenes of a laughing Hubert Humphrey with horrifying Vietnam war footage. Many observers also have difficulty with spots that are designed to fool the viewer into thinking they are actual news reports or bulletins, particularly when they are aired during actual news broadcasts, a practice that used to be explicitly decried by the National Association of Broadcasters' now-defunct Television and Radio Codes.

The use of special effects takes many forms in televised political matter. In the first Eisenhower campaign, the Walt Disney studios produced the well-known "I like Ike" animated ad, complete with catchy music and classic cel animation techniques. Subsequently, politicians and their media advisers have utilized every technique from cutout animation to slow motion and backward motion to computerized 'Star Wars' sequences. Some observers decry such special effects for their inherent inability to contribute to the political reasoning process, maintaining that the use of special effects in political ads does "not seem to amplify or to expand upon a point already made, but rather to evade the requirement of rational argumentation altogether" (Winsbro 1987, 915–16).

Similar concerns are raised by those who see television's predisposition toward drama and visual imagery as inherently bad and thus contributing to unethical political advertising outcomes. While some observers find nothing positive for the democratic system in talking cows (which appeared in a famous ad for Montana's Senator Melcher) or a fish puppet (a protagonist in an ad during Nelson Rockefeller's 1966 New York gubernatorial reelection campaign), others would argue that such dramatizations are not harmful in any way but merely serve to focus voter attention on important issues or candidate qualifications.

The first three of these television technology concerns (editing, special effects, and dramatization) can easily be viewed as techniques whose ethicality is dependent upon the nature of the usage, the *intent* of the source, and the degree of misperception and harm caused. After all, political speech has always employed whatever technology was currently available to it, from classical times to the present, from posters and billboards to satellite distribution. Television did not invent unreasoned political discourse (Shannon 1990). However, the next two concerns raise much clearer ethical questions. New computerized video technologies, such as Scitex, now make it possible to alter real moving video images (Sheridan 1990). Not only can a candidate's actual visual image be changed, but all types of alterations can be made in live video footage and its components. As long as candidates make live or news-covered appearances, concerns about make-up, hair color, and smile brilliance are not likely to give way to computerized solutions, but the ability to manufacture and alter "live" video will create new questions for ethical concern. The ability to make "undetectably false pictures" (Sheridan 1990, 6) is a technology twist that politicians must leave to entertainment and fantasy programming; it has no place in politics.

It would be equally impossible to defend the use of subliminal techniques in political advertising. Such techniques, possible on an audio or a video level, allow the creation of messages that are designed to implant persuasive ideas below the level of human consciousness. While it has been argued that such techniques can have a positive social value in a commercial environment (such as deterring crime or shoplifting), these techniques work to short-circuit the reasoning process and are easily seen as unethical, "nondemocratic practice" (Haiman 1958).

Independent and Noncandidate Advertising

In many ways the ethical concerns about independent and noncandidate advertising are tied directly to questions about money and politics. There is a long-standing concern in the American political system that corporations, political action committees, and independent individuals and organizations can spend large sums of money on advertising to influence the election of political candidates or the outcome of policy choices on public issues.

The growth of "corporate advocacy advertising" has been clear over the past several decades. Such advertising refers to the process by which corporations or similar entities speak out on public issues in an attempt to influence public opinion or, in some cases, specific policy outcomes (Sethi 1977). Advocacy advertising became particularly salient during the energy crisis of the mid–1970s, when the oil industry attempted to correct what it thought were misleading accusations about windfall profits and artificial shortages. Since then major corporations such as Mobil Oil, AT&T, Phillips Petroleum, Union Carbide, and Weyerhaeuser have spent millions in advertising on various causes, although many print and broadcast media outlets refuse to accept such advertising (Sethi 1977). Some observers believe that such ads have been used by corporations to convey false information to the public, as Dionisopoulos (1986) argues in his analysis of the fallacies and interpretive problems in the ads run by Commonwealth Edison concerning the Three Mile Island nuclear plant incident.

Corporations have also been active advertisers in noncandidate campaigns. For instance, the insurance industry has spent millions on no-fault insurance ballot referenda in some states (Rosenthal 1988). Not only have corporations spent vast sums to influence the outcome of ballot issues, but there is strong correlational evidence that such spending gets results (Garrison 1989). In both advocacy advertising and support of referendum issues, the ethical concern raised by most observers is often centered on the accusation that corporate spending can muffle the voices of the majority by allowing those with the most money (corporations) to overshadow the debate (Shaw, Hurd, and Bader 1984).

As with many other questions where free speech may be at issue, the Supreme Court has tended to rule that open debate must not be restricted, regardless of who is paying the bill. In the landmark *Bellotti* decision regarding corporate rights to support referendum positions, the court concluded that "it is the type of speech indispensable to decision-making in a democracy, and this is no less true because the speech comes from a corporation rather than an individual" (*First National Bank of Boston v. Bellotti* 1978, 1416). Although corporations are prohibited from contributing to political candidates because of potential corruption, the courts have generally felt that the risk of such problems (exchanging money for later politician support) is absent from referendum elections when the advertising/expenditure is directed to the public at large (Fox 1978–79).

Far more controversial than corporate advocacy or referendum support has been the contribution of independent, third-party entities to political advertising. This type of advertising is officially known as "independent expenditure," defined by the Federal Election Campaign Act (1971) as any expenditure "expressly advocating the election or defeat of a clearly identified candidate which is made without cooperation or consultation" with the candidate or his or her official committee. The *Buckley v. Valeo* case (1976), in which it was ruled that independent expenditures could not be regulated on First Amendment grounds, opened up a new era for political advertising of this kind. Although broadcasters and print media do not have to accept ads from independent spenders, the growth of independent campaign activity in the aftermath of the *Buckley* decision "has been staggering" (Oldaker and Picard 1983). Political action committees (PACs) have received the most attention for their independent expenditures. Although few of the thousands of current PACs actually engage in independent advertising expenditures (only 4 percent of multicandidate PACs did so in 1981–82), the total amount of money is significant, amounting to $13.7 million in the 1980 presidential election and $5.75 million in the 1982 U.S. Senate and House elections (Sabato 1984).

The major complaint against independent advertising is that it has been basically negative in nature and often misleading or false. Critics point to such well-known examples as the many negative ads used in the early 1980s by the National Conservative Political Action Committee (NCPAC) to target liberal congressmen and the U.S. Senate race in Illinois in which California businessman Michael Goland spent over $1 million to unseat Senator Charles Percy (Clinger 1987). It was also an independent group (not the Bush campaign itself) that sponsored the infamous "Willie Horton" ad in the 1988 presidential campaign (Feeney 1989), an ad that drew virulent criticism for its racial overtones as well as for its selectivity, use of emotional and fear appeals, and generally misleading content.

Like many of the concerns discussed above, it is difficult to conclude that there is anything inherently unethical about corporate, PAC, or other independent expenditures. As long as the courts equate the right to expend money for advertising with free speech rights, it is in the interests of a well-informed electorate to open the forum of public debate on candidate (independent) and ballot decisions. While some believe that this is a "romantic view of the First Amendment" unsupported by the realities of modern mass-communication systems (Clinger 1987), it remains in the interests of democracy that all voices have a chance to be heard in public debate. The alternative is worse; not to allow spending dooms voters to even less information than is now available. Who could support reduced availability of information as a guide to responsible voter decision making? However, to the extent that such expenditures result in advertising which has unethical characteristics (false, misleading, inadequate disclosure, technological misuse, etc.), condemnation is appropriate.

Negative Ads and Negative Campaigning

No aspect of modern political advertising has drawn more critical fire than the use of negative television commercials. While there is no shortage of examples of "dirty politics" or advertising abuses in past campaigns (Felknor 1966; Jonas 1970), the news media seemed to have discovered negative campaigning on a grand scale in the 1988 presidential contest. Political reporters decried the use of smear tactics in negative ads and often considered the negative ads the only things worth talking about in the campaign (Grove 1988; Martz with Warner, Fineman, Clift, and Starr 1988; Taylor 1989).

There is no universally accepted definition of negative advertisements, but most would agree that they basically are opponent-focused rather than candidate-focused. That is, negative ads concentrate on what is wrong with the opponent, either personally or in terms of issue or policy stances. Many of the arguments raised against negative ads are actually variants of the concerns already discussed above (costly, image-oriented/ nonissue content, emotional, oversimplified, misleading or inadequate disclosure, technologically tricky), but these concerns have reached such a high level of salience in recent years that the application of these ideas to negative ads as a class deserves special attention. This is especially true in light of many recent legislative proposals to curb or regulate negative ads.

It is often difficult to isolate the reasons why many find negative ads inherently unethical. There does seem to be an underlying assumption in the criticism of negative ads by the press and other political observers that somehow it is prima facie unethical to engage in negative campaigning or negative advertising. If the goal of campaigns is to create an informed electorate, nothing could be farther from the truth. Most political consultants are probably right to view negative ads as legitimate forms of voter information, a way of telling the public about the positions or characteristics of the opponent (Baukus, Payne and Reisler 1985; Orlik 1990). Consultants often label these ads "comparative" or "contrast" ads, and suggest that they help voters assess the strengths and weaknesses of the candidates (Toner 1990b; Slater 1990). Others, such as pollster Lance Tarrance (1980), are quick to distinguish negative campaigning with its "rational" underpinnings from mudslinging or *ad hominem* attacks.

This latter distinction may provide an important way of understanding the difference between useful, legitimate negative ads, which point up policy or performance failings of the opponent, and personal, nonsubstantive attacks. Many researchers have documented that negative advertising can provide voters with solid information that can be useful in decision making (Garramone et al. 1990; Joslyn 1986; Surlin and Gordon 1976). Such ads are also more effective. Roddy and Garramone (1988) have found that negative ads which focus on issues are more effective than those which focus on personal (image) attacks. It is difficult to understand, then, what is so wrong about providing voters with useful information. As political commentator Jeff Greenfield has noted, the "really outrageous aspect of the debate over 'negative' politics is the automatic response of 'outrage' to perfectly legitimate questions" (1990, 31A).

If one acknowledges that knowing the issue positions and even some types of personal qualifications and performance information about an opponent is not all bad, what are the arguments against negative advertising? As mentioned above, some would argue that, more than positive ads, negative ads contain false, misleading, distorted, or incomplete information. Again, examples of *opinions* on ads that may do this are in ample supply. For instance, Devlin (1989) believes that in the 1988 Bush "revolving door" prison furlough ad the visuals and the words combine to create a misleading impression, and Spero (1980) can find something that is "not quite right" by his own political predispositions in almost every television ad used by every campaign since 1952. So much of the interpretation of what is right or wrong, true or false, in such situations is perceptual.

Another argument that has been particularly salient in negative ad attacks has been the concern that voters do not know who has sponsored an ad (and therefore whom to blame if they do not like the sentiment or the style). Proposals such as those in the Danforth-Hollings Clean Campaign Act would remedy this by requiring the candidate to make attacks in person, believing that "voters should be able to see the candidate's dirty hands" (Will 1989, 92).

Finally, in regard to negative ads, there has been a recent outcry that negative campaigning and negative ads are decreasing voter turnout. The basic argument, exemplified by the position of Curtis Gans, head of the Committee for the Study of the American Electorate, is that as people get turned off by negative campaigning, they tune out of the electoral process, choosing not to vote at all (Much Ado 1985). Media consultant Tony Schwartz sees a different side to this as he suggests that television "has made millions feel that they can influence government and public affairs *without participating in politics . . . without voting*" (1983, 117). There is absolutely no causal evidence to support this notion. It is even possible to argue on the opposite side that negative campaigning stimulates voter interest in campaigns and enhances turnout (Nugent 1987). In fact, recent empirical research has demonstrated that negative commercials, compared with positive ones, do not have a significant negative impact on political involvement, on political communication behaviors (such as attention to news, debates, or interpersonal discussion), or on voter turnout (Garramone et al. 1990).

SAFEGUARDS IN THE CURRENT SYSTEM

There should be no question, after the above discussion, that while political advertising may not be inherently evil or unethical, there are many opportunities for abuse. It is important, therefore, to consider what possibilities exist within the current political and legal system for dealing with misuse when it does occur. Four basic areas are considered here: (1) laws and regulations, (2) voluntary codes, (3) news media scrutiny, and (4) popular judgment or backlash.

Laws and Regulations

The courts have already, as discussed above, upheld on free speech grounds the right to use money for advertising as a way of communicating with voters. Court rulings and FCC regulations have also provided safeguards relating to disclosure of the source of political advertisements. Beyond these areas, the greatest contribution of the legal system to ethical abuses in political advertising probably lies in the ability to prosecute offenders who sponsor advertisements that can proven to be *false*.

A candidate who is unfairly attacked in a political advertisement can sue the attacker for libel. However, the courts set rigorous standards for proving libel of public figures. The attacked candidate must prove that the charge made against him or her was indeed malicious (knowingly false or with reckless disregard for the truth) in order to win such a suit (Albert 1986). While such procedures offer legal remedies for extreme cases where the stringent burden of proof can be met, the judicial system is generally a slow and cumbersome remedy, the outcome of which cannot be expected in time to affect directly the outcome of electoral contests (Albert 1986; Winsbro 1987).

Many states have laws that prohibit candidates from making false or deceptive claims. Some state laws offer protection against false affirmative claims by a candidate as well as false accusations against an opponent. Ohio has a detailed code that prohibits false claims of incumbency, untruthful qualifications (such as earned degrees or occupations), false endorsements, and false statements about voting records (Winsbro 1987).

Such state regulations may offer a candidate's best hope of combating falsehood through the legal system. While there will always be difficulty in distinguishing between truth and falsity (partly because of the difficulty in differentiating fact and opinion), the courts at all levels have usually been contemptuous of anyone who attempts to argue that false claims must be heard on free speech grounds. For instance, in *Gertz v. Robert Welch, Inc.* (1974) the court said, "There is no constitutional value in false statements of fact." There is, of course, no democratic system value either.

One final possibility might exist under federal law for combating false advertising claims, and that is to file a false advertising complaint in federal court. To date, this approach has not been widely used, but precedent for it exists in the application of these regulations to political advertising in the case of *Tomei v. Finley* (1981). The advantage of such a procedure, if upheld in other federal districts, is that it could be used to grant immediate injunctive relief to a disadvantaged candidate (Albert 1986). The expansion of such efforts in the courts could lead to political commercials being subjected to some or all of the types of standards now required by FTC regulations of product commercials, as Spero (1980) has proposed.

Voluntary Codes

Professional codes of ethics for advertising and media professionals have often been touted as methods of controlling abuses in political advertising. The American Association of Advertising Agencies has a general code that condemns the use of visual or verbal falsehoods, misleading or false claims, or any claim not backed by solid evidence; it has also developed a specific Code of Ethics for Political Campaign Advertising (Johannesen 1990). The American Association of Political Consultants (AAPC 1990) also has a Code of Professional Ethics that asks members to refrain from appeals which are based on racism or discrimination and to eschew false or misleading attacks. However, columnist David Broder (1989a) points out, the AAPC has never disciplined any member for violation of its code.

Some scholars have suggested that campaign messages be subjected to content analysis by impartial judges who would evaluate ethicality on the basis of predetermined "cues" (Caywood and Laczniak 1985). Such an approach, however, would be impractical in modern campaigns with the demands for quick responses.

Some have argued that the voluntary professional code approach could work if it were administered by an independent body. At one time the Fair Campaign Practices Committee (FCPC) had the potential to serve such a function. The FCPC Code, to which candidates were asked to subscribe voluntarily, condemned misleading tactics, distortions, appeals to race, and other dishonest and unethical practices (Archibald 1971). Although no longer a functioning entity and lacking legal clout or punitive measures, the FCPC was tremendously good for the political system in monitoring ethics in political campaigning (Tucker and Heller 1987).

News Media Scrutiny

Many political observers now believe that one of the best hopes for containment of unethical practices in political advertising is the intense scrutiny provided by the news media. David Broder (1989b) has called for the press to take a much more active role in pointing out the truth, falsity, and general accuracy of political ads. By analyzing ads the media can serve as watchdogs for the public during election cycles (Dessauer 1990). Some reporters even argue that such scrutiny not only points up inaccuracies but also serves as a deterrent against blatant abuses (Taylor 1989; Toner 1990a).

Two problems have been raised about the viability of this approach to monitoring ethics in political ads. First, there is the persistent doubt about whether the news media are, in fact, neutral adjudicators in such situations, which raises the classic cry "Who will watch the watchdogs?" Second, there remains a kind of symbiotic relationship between news reporters and the political consultants upon whom they depend for inside information about campaigns. This mutual relationship may reduce the likelihood that reporters will choose to expose unethical practices (Sabato 1981).

Popular Judgment and Backlash

The most effective of all current safeguards may be the good judgment of an informed electorate. Research has certainly shown that negative advertising may result in voter backlash (Garramone 1984; Hill 1989; Merritt 1984). During its operation the FCPC documented many examples of situations where those perpetrating ethically offensive advertising lost the election, thereby demonstrating the good judgment of the electorate (Archibald 1971).

This type of backfiring or backlash has been seen in many recent campaigns. No example is better than the anti-Sasser ad in Tennessee that used a fake "Castro" to indict the incumbent senator. That ad backfired primarily because media scrutiny combined with voter judgment to label the ad "outrageous" and false (Thorson 1989). Given access to competing information in the marketplace of ideas, the American public can be trusted to evaluate political advertising, not only for what it actually says about an opponent but also, perhaps, for what it tells about the person who has sponsored it.

SUGGESTIONS FOR REFORM

The recent outcry about the high cost of political advertising, along with concerns about negative advertising, has spawned several reform proposals. This section discusses some recent congressional initiatives and concludes with some recommendations for coping with ethical problems in political advertising.

Congressional Reform Initiatives

The 1980s witnessed a spate of legislative proposals aimed at controlling campaign processes and expenditures. The prospective legislation has covered many avenues of concern, but high priority has been given (1) to controlling independent or PAC contributions and expenditures, and (2) to regulating advertising in a way that would reduce or defuse negative advertising. Detailed discussion of all of the proposals introduced in the past few years is beyond the scope of this chapter, but a few examples will suffice.

At the time this chapter was written, both the House and the Senate had passed (in July and August 1990) new campaign spending bills that would place expenditure limits on House and Senate races, further limit PAC contributions, provide some public financing for House and Senate races, increase the amount of candidate appearance/identification in television ads, and provide some free television advertising time to federal candidates (House Approves 1990). This legislation has been referred to a conference committee for resolution of differences in the House and Senate versions but faces the threat of a presidential veto.

Other proposals, such as the Danforth-Hollings "Clean Campaign Act," have gotten some attention in recent years. This legislation proposed sweeping changes that would have included guarantees of free response time for candidates opposed by "independent expenditures" or by negative ads in which the sponsoring candidate did not appear (Hoff and Bernstein 1988; Clinger 1987). Other proposals have suggested that candidates be given free blocks of time in lengths of at least five minutes (Hoff and Bernstein 1988), would require candidates to appear and address the camera for the duration of their ads (S.340 1989; S.577 1987), or would require that when negative attacks are made, the candidate must make the attacks in person (S.2 1987).

Many of these proposed changes would seem to be obviously unconstitutional (Clinger 1987), but there are many viable arguments on both sides of these issues. Some contend these regulations affect only the format of ads and thus meet the constitutional test of being "content-neutral" regulations (Dugan 1989). However, the visual aspects of a television ad (its format, techniques, style, etc.) are just as much "content" as words are. It seems equally certain that any attempt to regulate based on negativity in ads would itself be a content-based regulation and not likely to withstand constitutional tests. Despite disclaimer and source disclosure laws, the courts have not been particularly sympathetic to attempts to outlaw the right to anonymity in making attacks (Clinger 1987; Jones and Kaid 1976), calling into question even the constitutionality of "talking head"/candidate appearance restrictions.

Proponents have some hope of surviving such challenges if the restrictions are made a condition for receipt of public funding, since the *Buckley* decision allowed spending limits only when presidential candidates accept public financing (Hoff and Bernstein 1988). The extension of this position to regulation of actual content of commercials, however, may not find as much judicial sympathy as did the notion of simple adherence to an overall spending limit.

Beyond constitutional problems, there is a very real concern about the wisdom of allowing incumbents to legislate procedures that clearly would enhance their own electability at the expense of challengers. Incumbents must find the notion that they could outlaw, diminish, or severely restrict the amount, nature, and format of attacks that challengers could mount regarding their performance extremely attractive. Even the ability to restrict the amount of affirmative communication with voters surely enhances incumbent prospects.

Recommendations

A free and unfettered marketplace of ideas is ultimately the best guarantee of an informed electorate and a stable, healthy democratic system. The difficulty in separating perceptual and partisan interpretations and opinions from actual falsehoods and distortions makes it imprudent to yield substantial power over political speech to governmental legislation or judicial oversight. However, given that there are clearly some types of ethical abuses in political ads for which the current remedies are either nonexistent or too little too late, there is merit in considering some changes that might enhance the morality of political advertising without endangering free expression rights.

First, the government should enact a process calling for the allocation of limited amounts of *free time* to qualified candidates for major office. For pragmatic reasons, some limitations on this requirement would have to be made so as not to burden broad outlets unduly. Such time blocks, say of five or ten minutes, could be provided near the end of the campaign, giving candidates a chance to communicate with voters on affirmative, negative, or attack-response items. This system would serve as a supplement to current advertising, not a substitute for the candidate's free-speech right to buy time and control its content. Such a system would enhance voter information opportunities and guarantee response potential for candidates who had been attacked but lacked the money or the opportunity to respond.

Second, state regulations against corrupt campaign practices should be strengthened. If all states adopted somewhat uniform laws outlawing unethical campaign practices, both affirmative and negative abuses, candidates would have a clear path for legal remedies. Such laws should specify stiff penalties for violation (including office forfeiture) and injunctive relief to permit immediate cessation of the airing of unethical ads. In addition, all states should set up a process for constituting special courts during campaigns, within a very short time, for legal action to commence and end so that candidates do not find themselves hampered by traditional time delays in overcrowded court systems.

Third, a federal campaign commission should be established to hear complaints about ethical abuses in campaign communication, particularly advertising. This commission could function much like the defunct Fair Campaign Practices Committee, promulgating a code of ethics in campaign advertising and hearing complaints about abuses. The components of such a code should include condemnation of false advertising claims, insufficient proof of claims, distortions, unreasonable appeals to emotion, false endorsements or source attributions, subliminal techniques, misleading alterations in live video or audio events, and similar techniques. With sufficient visibility, clout, and media attention, it would probably be possible to pressure all candidates into voluntary adherence and submission to scrutiny. The existence of such an entity, coupled with the consequences of adverse media publicity upon exposure of abuses, would undoubtedly serve as a powerful deterrent. In addition, the commission might be given some legal remedies, including (1) injunctive relief, (2) fines and penalties, (3) a budget for publicizing abuses, and (4) perhaps the power to order "corrective advertising," as the FTC has done in product advertising situations.

CONCLUSION

In order to ensure rational decision making, an informed electorate requires exposure to a wide spectrum of political information. Political advertising, particularly on television, is a major component of such information for today's electorate. While there is much potential for ethical abuse in political advertising, there is little about television advertising that is inherently unethical. The knee-jerk opposition to negative advertising, which actually performs legitimate voter information functions, is particularly troublesome. However, there should be no easy acceptance of outright falsehoods and distortions, as long as one is meticulous in the objectivity of such judgments. Too often accusations of negativity and falsehood are based on political predispositions and subjective interpretations.

For situations in which there are clear abuses, there are some safeguards in the present system. It is clearly not sufficient to equate legality with ethics, but the legal system does offer some remedies, as does media scrutiny.

In conclusion, those concerned about ethics in political advertising would do well to consider Kenneth Andersen's (1984) suggestions about one of the frequently overlooked aspects of communication ethics, the responsibilities of the audience/receiver. The audiences for political advertising have some obligations as ethical receivers, as well as rights to receive and judge for themselves all relevant information. As Smith has pointed out, "Those who would manage *political* content . . . are anti-democratic because they do not trust citizens to decide issues or select communication materials for themselves"(1989, 219).

REFERENCES

Albert, J. A. 1986. The remedies available to candidates who are defamed by television or radio commercials of opponents. *Vermont Law Review* 11:33–73.

American Association of Political Consultants. 1990. *Code of professional ethics.* Washington, DC: AAPC.

Andersen, K. E. 1984. Communication ethics: The non-participant's role. *Southern Speech Communication Journal* 49:219–28.

———. 1989. The politics of ethics and the ethics of politics. *American Behavioral Scientist* 32:479–92.

Archibald, S. J., ed. 1971. *The pollution of politics.* Washington, DC: Public Affairs Press.

Baukus, R. A., J. G. Payne, and M. S. Reisler. 1985. Negative polispots. In *Argument and social practice: Proceedings of the fourth SCA/AFA conference on argumentation,* eds. J. R. Cox, M. O. Sillars, and G. B. Walker, 236–52. Annandale, VA: SCA.

Berke, R. L. 1990. An edge for incumbents: Loopholes that pay off. *New York Times,* 20 March, A1, A10.

Broder, D. A. 1989a. Politicians, advertisers agonize over negative campaigning. *Washington Post,* 19 January, A1, A22.

———. 1989b. Should news media police accuracy of ads? *Washington Post,* 19 January, A22.

Buckley v. Valeo. 1976. 424 U.S. 1, 60–84.

Caywood, C. L., and G. R. Laczniak. 1985. Unethical political advertising: Decision considerations for policy and evaluation. In *Marketing communications—theory and research*, ed. M. J. Houston and R. J. Lutz, 37–41. Chicago: American Marketing Association.

Clinger, J. H. 1987. The Clean Campaign Act of 1985: A rational solution to negative campaign advertising which the One Hundredth Congress should reconsider. *Journal of Law and Politics* 3, 4 (Spring 1987): 727–48.

Committee on Commerce, Science, and Transportation, U.S. Senate. 1985. *Clean Campaign Act of 1985* (Hearings). Washington, DC: U.S. Government Printing Office.

Committee on Rules and Administration, U.S. Senate. 1987. *Senate Campaign Finance Proposals of 1987* (Hearings). Washington, DC: U.S. Government Printing Office.

Crichton, J. 1980. Morals and ethics in advertising. In *Ethics, morality and the media*, ed. L. Thayer, 105–15. New York: Hastings House.

Dessauer, C. 1990. *Washington Post* staffs up with watchdogs. *Campaigns & Elections* 11 (April/May):11.

Devlin, L. P. 1989. Contrasts in presidential campaign commercials of 1988. *American Behavioral Scientist* 32:389–414.

Diamond, E., and S. Bates. 1984. *The Spot*. Cambridge, MA: MIT Press.

Diamond, E., and A. Marin. 1989. Spots. *American Behavioral Scientist* 32:382–88.

Dionisopoulos, G. 1986. Corporate advocacy advertising. In *New perspectives on political advertising*, ed. L. L. Kaid, D. Nimmo, and K. R. Sanders, 82–106. Carbondale: Southern Illinois University Press.

Downs, A. 1957. *An economic theory of democracy*. New York: Harper.

Dugan, J. R. 1989. Secondary effects and political speech: Intimations of broader governmental regulatory power. *Villanova Law Review* 34:995–1033.

Federal Election Campaign Act. 1971. 2 U.S.C. §§441(d)(1982).

Feeney, S. 1989. Limits on negative ads in campaigns studied. *Dallas Morning News*, 20 July, 5A.

Felknor, B. 1966. *Dirty politics*. New York: W. W. Norton.

First National Bank of Boston v. Bellotti. 1978. 98 S.Ct. 1407.

Fox, F. H. 1978–79. Corporate political speech: The effect of *First National Bank of Boston v. Bellotti* upon statutory limitations on corporate referendum spending. *Kentucky Law Journal* 67:75–101.

Gardner, J. A. 1984. Protecting the rationality of electoral outcomes: A challenge to First Amendment doctrine. *The University of Chicago Law Review* 51:892–943.

Garramone, G. M. 1984. Voter responses to negative political advertising. *Journalism Quarterly* 61:250–59.

———. 1986. Candidate image formation: The role of information processing. In *New perspectives on political advertising*, ed. L. L. Kaid, D. Nimmo, and K. R. Sanders, 235–67. Carbondale: Southern Illinois University Press.

Garramone, G. M., C. K. Atkin, B. Pinkleton, and R. T. Cole. 1990. Effects of negative political advertising on the political process. *Journal of Broadcasting and Electronic Media* 34:299–311.

Garrison, M. J. 1989. Corporate political speech, campaign spending, and First Amendment doctrine. *American Business Law Journal* 27:163–213.

Gertz v. Robert Welch, Inc. 1974. 418 U.S. 323, 339–40.

Goodin, R. E. 1980. *Manipulatory politics.* New Haven: Yale University Press.

Greenfield, J. 1990. Negative campaign or legitimate question? *Dallas Morning News,* 21 April, 31A.

Grove, L. 1988. Attack ads trickled up from state races. *Washington Post,* 13 November, A1, A18, A19.

Haiman, F. S. 1958. Democratic ethics and the hidden persuaders. *Quarterly Journal of Speech* 44:385–92.

Hill, R. P. 1989. An exploration of voter responses to political advertisements. *Journal of Advertising* 18(4):14–22.

Hoff, Paul S., and K. Bernstein. 1988. *Congress and the media: Beyond the 30-second spot: Enhancing the media's role in congressional campaigns.* Washington, DC: Center for Responsive Politics.

House approves bill limiting political campaign spending. 1990. *Dallas Morning News,* 4 August, 3A.

Jamieson, K. H. 1984. *Packaging the presidency.* New York: Oxford University Press.

———. 1988. *Eloquence in an electronic age.* New York: Oxford University Press.

Johannesen, R. L. 1990. *Ethics in human communication,* 3rd ed. Prospect Heights, IL: Waveland Press.

Jonas, F. H., ed. 1970. *Political dynamiting.* Salt Lake City: University of Utah Press.

Jones, C. A., and L. L. Kaid. 1976. Constitutional law: Political campaign regulation and the Constitution. *Oklahoma Law Review* 29:684–711.

Josyln, R. A. 1980. The content of political spot ads. *Journalism Quarterly* 57:92–98.

———. 1986. Political advertising and the meaning of elections. In *New perspectives on political advertising,* ed. L. L. Kaid, D. Nimmo, and K. R. Sanders, 139–83. Carbondale: Southern Illinois University Press.

Kaid, L. L., and D. Davidson. 1986. Elements of videostyle: Candidate presentation through television advertising. In *New perspectives on political advertising,* ed. L. L. Kaid, D. Nimmo, and K. R. Sanders, 184–209. Carbondale: Southern Illinois University Press.

Kaid, L. L., and K. R. Sanders. 1978. Political television commercials: An experimental study of type and length. *Communication Research* 5:57–70.

Kelley, S., Jr. 1960. *Political campaigning: Problems in creating an informed electorate.* Washington, DC: Brookings Institution.

Kern, M. 1989. *30-second politics.* New York: Praeger.

Louden, A. D. 1990. Transformation of issue to image and presence: Eliciting character evaluations in negative spot advertising. Paper presented at the International Communication Association convention, Dublin, Ireland.

Martz, L., with M. G. Warner, H. Fineman, E. Clift, and M. Starr. 1988. The smear campaign. *Newsweek,* 31 October, 16–19.

Marylander, G. 1985. Sponsor identification: When must a broadcaster disclose who really pays for those political advertisements? *Loyola Entertainment Law Journal* 5:211–17.

Merritt, S. 1984. Negative political advertising: Some empirical findings. *Journal of Advertising* 13:27–38.

Miller, W. E., M. P. Wattenberg, and O. Malanchuk. 1985. Cognitive represen-
    tations of candidate assessments. In *Political communication yearbook 1984*,
    ed. K. R. Sanders, L. L. Kaid, and D. Nimmo. Carbondale: Southern
    Illinois University Press.
Mitroff, I., and W. Bennis. 1989. *The unreality industry*. New York: Carol Pub-
    lishing Group.
Much ado about ads knocking candidates. 1985. *Broadcasting*, 16 September, 64–
    72.
Nugent, J. F. 1987. Positively negative. *Campaigns & Elections* 7(6):47–49.
Oldaker, W. C., and D. S. Picard. 1983. Broadcasters' rights: Whether to air
    independent political action committee advertisements. *Hastings Consti-
    tutional Law Quarterly* 10:649–77.
Oreskes, M., with R. Toner. 1990. Swamp of political abuse spurs a new con-
    stituency, for change. *New York Times*, 21 March, A1, A12.
Orlik, P. 1990. Negative political commercials: 1988 snapshot. *Feedback* 33 (Win-
    ter):2–7.
Patterson, T. E. 1983. Money rather than TV ads "root cause" of election cost-
    liness. *Radio/Television Age* 44 (28 March):130, 132.
Patterson, T. E., and R. D. McClure. 1976. *The unseeing eye*. New York: G. P.
    Putnam.
Penniman, H. R. 1985. U.S. elections: Really a bargain? In *The mass media in
    campaign '84*, ed. M. J. Robinson and A. Ranney. Washington, DC: Amer-
    ican Enterprise Institute for Public Policy Research.
Perloff, R. M., and D. Kinsey. 1990. The consultants look at advertising: Beliefs
    about political advertising effects. Paper presented at the Association for
    Education in Journalism and Mass Communication convention, Minne-
    apolis.
Regan, R. J., Jr. 1986. *The moral dimensions of politics*. New York: Oxford University
    Press.
Roddy, B. L., and G. M. Garramone. 1988. Appeals and strategies of negative
    political advertising. *Journal of Broadcasting and Electronic Media* 32:415–427.
Rosenthal, A. M. 1988. Quest for ideal campaign: No tears, no monkey business,
    no candidate. *New York Times*, 15 May, 11.
S.577. 1987. *Congressional Record*—Senate, 23 February, S2389.
S.2. 1987. *Congressional Record*—Senate, 3 June, S7526–65.
S.340. 1989. *Congressional Record*—Senate, 2 February, S1093.
Sabato, L. J. 1981. *The rise of political consultants*. New York: Basic Books.
———. 1984. *PAC power*. New York: W. W. Norton.
Schwartz, T. 1973. *The responsive chord*. New York: Anchor Books/Doubleday.
———. 1983. *Media: The second God*. New York: Anchor Books/Doubleday.
Sethi, S. P. 1977. *Advocacy advertising and large corporations*. Lexington, MA: Lex-
    ington Books.
Shannon, M. R. 1990. Glass houses for sale—cheap. *Campaigns & Elections* 10
    (February/March):18.
Shaw, B., S. N. Hurd, and M. B. Bader. 1984. Corporate political speech and
    the First Amendment. *Oklahoma City University Law Review* 9:271–90.
Sheridan, D. 1990. The trouble with Harry: High technology can now alter a
    moving video image. *Columbia Journalism Review* 28(5):4–6.

Slater, W. 1990. Negative ads becoming dominant campaign force. *Dallas Morning News*, 20 June, A1, A28–29.

Smith, C. R. 1989. *Freedom of expression and partisan politics*. Columbia: University of South Carolina Press.

Spero, R. 1980. *The duping of the American voter*. New York: Lippincott & Crowell.

Surlin, S., and T. Gordon. 1976. Selective exposure and retention of political advertising. *Journal of Advertising Research* 5:32–44.

Talley v. California. 1959. 362 U.S. 60.

Tarrance, V. L. 1980. *Negative campaigns and negative votes*. Washington, DC: Free Congress Research and Education Foundation.

Taylor, P. 1989. Consultants rise via the low road. *Washington Post*, 17 January, A1, A14.

Thorson, E., ed. 1989. *Advertising Age: The principles of advertising at work*. Lincolnwood, IL: NTC Business Books.

Tomei v. Finley. 1981. 512 F.Supp. 695 (N.D. Ill.).

Toner, R. 1990a. 90's politics seem rough as ever despite criticism of negative ads. *New York Times*, 9 September, 1, 18.

Toner, R. 1990b. "Wars" wound candidates and the process. *New York Times*, 19 March, A1, A14.

Tucker, L. A., and D. J. Heller. 1987. Putting ethics into practice. *Campaigns & Elections* 7 (March/April):42–46.

Will, G. 1989. The pollution of politics. *Newsweek*, 6 November, 92.

Winsbro, J. 1987. Misrepresentation in political advertising: The role of legal sanctions. *Emory Law Journal* 36:853–916.

Chapter Nine

Polls and Computer Technologies: Ethical Considerations

Gary W. Selnow

Technology and political communications are no strangers. Early whistle-stop tours in the nineteenth century gave candidates time to see and be seen by more voters, shake more hands, and visit more districts than they could by riding on dusty buckboards. The telegraph compressed time and space, connecting campaigns to faraway districts once accessible only by tireless riders of the pony express. Telephones gave a human voice to the dots and dashes. Radio brought the candidate into American living rooms. Television gave voters everything but the flesh and blood of a candidate. Technology has shrunk the distances, reduced the delays, focused the energies, and streamlined the efficiency of political campaigns.

Clearly, at the heart, political campaigns are communication campaigns. Bagging the vote is the bottom line of politics, and in our political system this is achieved through good communications. Polling, the tools and techniques of audience analysis, and all the computer technologies that streamline, focus, and make communication more efficient serve the ends of political campaigns. Campaigns today are more targeted, more responsive to audience information needs, and better able to deal immediately with spontaneous events.

OVERVIEW

This chapter is about some of the latest technological advances in political communication and about the ethical problems that have risen in their wake. We will examine the application of polling technology that has been used in political campaigns since the early 1940s but only recently has been honed to a razor-sharp political tool. We will look at the increasing use of computer technology. In the 1980s the power and capacity of personal computers have reached proportions unimaginable just a few years earlier. This sophisticated technology, once confined to well-financed national races, now is available for Mom and Pop campaigns. Computers level the playing field among candidates. They have become the great equalizers.

Political consultants, polling flacks, and computer gurus sing the praises of the new technologies, but there are sour notes we cannot ignore. Campaigns have profited from recent developments, yet there is a cost to voters and to the political system. There are side effects of these technologies, and problems that resonate long after the campaign songs are over.

For instance, political operatives today know more than ever about the personal lives of voters. The new data bases essential to targeted communication hold intimate details, usually without voters' consent or even their knowledge. The maintenance of so much personal data by so many campaigns raises questions about privacy abuses and about the violation of a citizen's wish to remain anonymous.

One of the great dangers of the new technologies is voter manipulation. Persuasive strategies that play less to reason and more to emotional and visceral reactions are plied best on small, homogeneous groups. The new technologies cultivate micro strategies designed to exploit the vulnerabilities of individual voters.

Technology has enabled political campaigns to promote different sets of issues and agendas with different voter groups, and thereby contributes to the growth of single-issue politics. The practice divides voters and perpetuates political factionalism. Some believe focused preoccupations with personal concerns render a voting population indifferent to global problems. Divide-and-conquer politics is a growing problem.

New technologies facilitate "Lone Ranger" campaigns characterized by their alienation from party mechanisms. This creates a climate for political extremism that deepens in the absence of party discipline, which traditionally has moderated such positions.

The new information technologies have implications beyond the campaign. Candidates who make decisions by public rating rather than by reasoned deliberations carry their bad habits into office with them. This results in governance of the polls, by the polls, and for the polls. Officials elected by cadres of narrow voter groups are forced to govern under the scrutiny of what later become narrow constituent groups. Each has been led to expect action on specific issues; the polls never allow the officeholder to forget an early pledge.

POLITICAL RESPONSIBILITY

Theodore Tronchin once said that the sins of commission were mortal and the sins of omission venial. Both are sins, but one is worse than the other. We should make such a distinction of magnitude in our discussions by noting the differences between what political candidates *mean to bring about* and what they *actually bring about*. Let's be clear. There is no evidence that anyone in the political arena wishes the disturbing side effects of the new technologies. Most of them probably don't even recognize what is happening on the downside. Tronchin could find no mortal offenses.

Still, there is the matter of the victims: the voters, the political system, the operations of government. Can harmful ends be derived from noble intentions? Of course. Most of us drive an automobile because it serves our daily transportation needs. The environment suffers nonetheless from these joint decisions. Individually we indulge in innocent practices that collectively deplete the ozone, erode the soil, and foul the waters. One need not wish to harm for the ends to be harmful. Even candidates who recognize developing problems with the technologies thus may find peace in the innocence of their own intentions. There is an offense, but no one feels the blame.

The "diffusion of responsibility" rationale also can salve a conscience. If everyone is guilty, then each of us is innocent. When we collectively pollute the environment, we disperse the blame and the guilt among millions of offenders. Everyone pollutes. Where is the personal guilt for the collective violation?

Such thinking figures in many discussions of political ethics. It is particularly evident in considerations of the new technologies. In the 1990s candidates must accept the high-tech campaign tools. If they choose to join the political battle, they must accept the political swords and shields.

Thus form the resolution of dissonance and the dispersion of guilt. Intentions are noble. The ends justify the means. Ill effects are the fault not of any individual but of all candidates collectively.

In the final frame we will be left with this frustrating irony: polling and computer technologies, so helpful to a political campaign, are damaging the political system and menacing the voters. At the same time, few political candidates may see the problem. Of those who do, most escape a sense of personal guilt through soothing rationalizations.

This chapter will describe the new technologies and examine the ethical concerns they raise. While we cannot resolve the problem, we may better understand the issues.

TRENDS IN POLITICAL COMMUNICATION

The use of polls and computer technologies is not unique to political campaigns. During the 1980s there was a conspicuous movement in all communication fields toward the use of targeted techniques. Electronic technologies expanded the number of channels and the means to use them. Both audiences and communicators are separating into ever more refined and narrow subgroups.

Targeting appears to be a natural phenomenon. New media (for instance, radio from the 1920s to the 1940s and television in the 1950s and 1960s) begin with general material for all users. They serve undifferentiated, heterogeneous audiences containing members of virtually all demographic and ideological descriptions. And because, by definition, mass audiences include members with such an assortment of characteristics, they typically are large.

But as nature abhors a vacuum, the nature of mass media abhors a heterogeneous audience. During the early stages of media development, large numbers of users demonstrate public support and acceptance, thereby holding out the carrot of future rewards for hungry media entrepreneurs. Early media outlets become victims of their own success, over time having to face growing numbers of competitors whose market entry they have helped to inspire.

Media outlets evolving later stake their success on smaller, homogeneous audience subsets budded from the larger group. Cable stations, for instance, have been going after special-interest audiences. Radio stations have been comfortable with small portions of the audience pie since the mid–1950s. Narrow audiences are parochial and uniform. They are identified by the demographic and ideological similarities of their members.

And so, historically, a medium starts with a few channels serving large audiences with general programming and evolves into many channels serving smaller audiences with specific programming. This is the media trend.

Communicator strategies have followed. As channels have provided the opportunity to reach ever narrower audience subgroups, communicators have rushed to segment their messages. It has long been known that personalized communications are the most effective. Door-to-door sales, popular during the first half of the twentieth century, were remarkably successful. One-on-one campaigning has always been viewed as the best way to amass the vote. But as changing life-styles and values have rendered such face-to-face techniques less viable, the media have provided a new way through the front door. Cable television and refinements in direct mail and telephone communications have become the new tools for interpersonal contact.

The new media, in concert with polling information and computers, have revolutionized communications. Media deliver segmented, homogeneous audiences. Polls and computers pinpoint the audiences and identify their special characteristics. While targeting techniques have been around for years, only during the 1980s were they sophisticated and incisive enough to excite political operatives. As we proceed through the 1990s, when these technologies grow beyond their infancy, we will come to recognize the real implications of targeted communication and campaigning. Our concerns for political ethics will grow with the precision and power of the communication tools.

THE USE OF POLLING

Information is power. In politics, information is the power to read the minds of voters: to know what they know, to know what they feel, to know how they are likely to behave in the voting booth. Information can make the difference between the success and the failure of a campaign.

Polls are the eyes and ears. They tell about the voter population and, more important, they tell about differences among voter subgroups. "In a sense, the polls provide the script for the politician by indicating which issues to emphasize or 'low key' and which positions or themes are most likely to provide a majority coalition" (Berkman and Kitch 1985, 151).

In terms of communication theory, polls provide feedback data. They produce the ongoing information necessary for the maintenance of a dialogue. Feedback in an interpersonal conversation keeps two people talking. Without it discussion stops. No less is true of a conversation between a candidate and the voters. To be successful in conveying a persuasive or informational message, a candidate needs to assess the views, reactions, values, and expectations of the audience. The more information available on which to act, the more successful a candidate-communicator is likely to be. Information is power: the power to anticipate concerns and expectations, needs, and susceptibilities; the power to persuade.

In current political applications, information also is the power to distinguish among voter groups. Voter clusters are defined by discriminating characteristics: demographics, ideologies, predispositions on issues. There is likely to be, within each group, a different set of views that require different persuasive strategies. Polls reveal these differences and thus provide a basis on which to develop separate plans. Lynn Pounian, president of Reese Communications says, "You can't drop your B–52 message down into the crowd anymore. . . . Ronald Reagan understood that and moved away from those mass appeals" (quoted in Brower 1988, 158). Staying with Pounian's hawkish metaphor, the preference today is for precision strikes. The field equipment necessary for such tactics is becoming widely available. Polls are providing the reconnaissance information; computers are breaking down and then reassembling the data for selective targeting.

In the 1988 presidential election, both political parties used computer-manipulated polling data to sort voter populations. They polled daily, following subgroup threads that spun the cloth of public opinion. Through use of computer matching techniques described in the next section, voters were analyzed, grouped, and parceled for separate treatment. The polling data told the candidates where to tiptoe and where to march. It told them where to challenge commitments and where to confirm them. This election demonstrated the importance of polling. "Winning elections has become a business, a big business . . . where volunteers have been replaced by computer-assisted polling" (Oreskes 1990, 22).

Thumbnail Sketch of Polling Processes

We will examine the computer manipulation of polling data and database building in the next section, but it will be helpful first to present a brief sketch of the polling process. Many data-gathering techniques have been called polls. Most legitimate approaches involve four elements: sampling, questionnaire design, methods, and analysis.

Sampling. Sampling is the process of selecting people to interview. Since researchers identify only a handful of respondents to represent an entire population, the choice of whom to include is no small matter. A biased sample, or one not representative of the larger group, can waste time and money. Worse, it can send candidates off in the wrong direction, and even aid an opponent's efforts.

At the heart of all representative samples is a random selection process that ensures everyone in the target population an equal chance of being chosen for participation. It may be hard to accept at first that polls are based on chance selections, but over time Lady Luck has proven to be an excellent judge of respondents.

Questionnaire. The questionnaire serves to guide the data-collection process. It provides the exact wording and the order of questions, and it gives instructions to interviewers.

When polls are challenged, usually it is question wording that comes under attack. Critics say phraseology can sway a respondent. They are right. For instance, a recent *New York Times*/CBS News poll looked at abortion in two ways. First it asked, "Should there be a constitutional amendment prohibiting abortions?" The majority said "no." A page later it asked, "Should there be an amendment protecting the life of the unborn child?" Twenty percent of those who had answered "no" to the first question switched their position and said "yes" (Brower 1988, 146).

Methods. This discussion examines two aspects of polling methods: the techniques of data collection and the kinds of polls typically used in a political campaign.

There are several common data collection techniques. The most popular today is the *telephone survey.* It usually is easy to assemble and comparatively inexpensive. Computer-assisted telephone interviewing (CATI) equipment allows easy survey administration and instant data entry.

The *door-to-door survey* once was the method of choice, if only because the choices were limited. Today, there must be compelling reasons to consider this technique. A population must be inaccessible by phone or the topic must require special props (e.g., "Select from this chart your favorite shade of green."). Door-to-door surveys are expensive, they have logistical difficulties, and they introduce peripheral problems that confound the results.

There are various other survey techniques, most of which do not allow a representative sample and, therefore, are of little use in providing comprehensive population data. *Mail surveys, clip-and-return newspaper and magazine coupons,* and *dial–900 surveys* are little more than cotton candy techniques. They may have the illusion of substance, but they offer little of value other than perhaps some public relations hype. Such approaches rarely figure into campaign polling schemes.

Finally, *focus groups* have been of some use in recent campaigns. These techniques do not provide the thorough, representative data bases that figure so prominently in new campaign technologies, but they do offer a source of information on which to make some important campaign decisions. For instance, it was a focus group in Cook County, Illinois, that assured Lee Atwater, President Bush's campaign director, of the strength of the antitax theme. Focus groups provide a first blush response to new concepts. They also serve as a precursor to general telephone surveys and sometimes can provide visible and convincing evidence that the big polls really are right.

Berkman and Kitch (1985) outline five categories of polls that serve political campaigns. First, a *benchmark poll* assesses voters before a campaign is launched. It takes a broad sweep of the issues and of the potential candidates. This omnibus survey often is lengthy and encompassing as it attempts to paint a picture of the political landscape before strategies take shape.

Follow-up surveys pick up on dominant themes, many of which may have evolved from the benchmark survey, and track them through a campaign. These surveys are shorter and more focused than the benchmark poll but, like the larger study, they seek a develop a data base that permits rigorous analysis for targeting purposes. Much of the information used in computer manipulations is derived from follow-up surveys.

Panel Surveys, viewed with skepticism by some researchers, monitor voters' movement through a campaign by returning periodically to the same respondents. Advocates say the panel survey shows how people with certain starting positions are likely to evolve. Many see a problem in the limited projection of panel members' experiences. Ironically, the participants' involvement taints them. Their participation renders them unlike the population they are chosen to represent. Data from such studies may help identify looming problems, but panels are not a reliable source of detailed information for general planning.

Tracking polls are conducted daily among small samples to sense emerging problems or helpful trends that may become significant factors in a campaign. A "moving average" system collapses new data with data from the previous few days. Trend comparisons reveal population shifts and help a campaign staff become aware of patterns before they reach compelling proportions.

Data Analyses can range from simple counts of responses to more sophisticated statistical manipulations. We will review some of the common techniques when we examine computer applications.

Some Problems with Polls

Several problems inherent in the polling process have implications not only for the technological accuracy of the results but also for the interpretation of their meaning. When examining these problems it becomes particularly important to distinguish between the two general applications of polling information. First, polls may be used in ways that preoccupy discussions in this chapter: for campaign guidance, insights, and strategies. In these applications, flaws can hurt a campaign. The candidate needs accurate information—the good, the bad, and the ugly—anything less can interfere with appropriate decisions.

The second application of polling results involves the public release of data. Candidates often use selected poll results to establish public concurrence with a position or to verify viability of a candidacy. Most such uses are completely legitimate. Flawed polling procedures, however (defined as honest mistakes or conscious procedural distortions), can provide misleading information by endowing a candidate's personal positions with the appearance of public endorsement.

Candidate Bush frequently cited survey data as evidence of his mainstream environmental stands. It would have been helpful to know the survey details confirming the validity of those claims. Both sides in the endless abortion debate are quick to cite polling data that confirm public support. Which better reflects true public opinion depends on how the survey was conducted. As we have seen, question wording and other technical features can readily affect the results.

Technical details must be viewed differently, depending on whether the results are to be used exclusively for internal strategic planning or are to be released for public consumption. In the first case, misleading information can injure only the candidate. In the second, it can mislead the public and so becomes an ethical matter.

For many reasons poll results may not accurately reflect public views. Several stand out. First, as we have noted, questions may be worded to prompt a desirable response. Obviously, respondents will answer a question about "killing unborn babies" differently than they would one about "a woman's right to choose." Still, both may be presented as confirmation of a candidate's views on abortion regulation.

Not only question wording but also question placement within a survey may affect the results. For instance, a question asking about military spending may be seen differently if it follows a series of items about conflict in the Middle East than if it follows items about funding shortfalls in infant care subsidies and inoculation programs. Lead-in questions predispose respondents' views. A survey may encourage desired results not only through question wording but also through question placement.

Sampling can be a problem. The public does not understand the difference between a representative and a nonrepresentative sample. Results of focus groups, dial–900 surveys, clip-and-mail coupons, and other "pop" poll techniques sound as authoritative as findings from legitimate studies. Outcomes of such exercises can deceive voters and unfairly manipulate public perceptions. During the mid–1980s the Moral Majority was known to conduct postcard surveys of its members on various issues. Without discussion of methods, the group would distribute the results to the press. These findings came across as legitimate soundings of the U.S. population. Publication of the outcomes left unsuspecting newspaper readers with the impression that the country was considerably more right-wing, more conservative, and more militant than honest polls suggested.

Another deceptive practice is the failure to reveal statistical limitations. Every survey has margins of error and confidence levels that delineate the accuracy of results. When numbers are close, it is particularly difficult to conclude that real differences exist in public views. Yet campaigns often release such information without cautions. This is a small point, but the practice can suggest unwarranted conclusions.

If the misuse of polling data in public forums is a problem, the fault is not a candidate's alone. Clearly the press has a responsibility to ensure that the public is aware of limitations. It is common for newspapers and broadcast media to reveal the strength of an information source. They routinely explain whether news story information is hearsay or firsthand knowledge. They reveal qualifications of an expert source and often discuss the means by which information was obtained. The same standards should apply to the coverage of campaign polling results. Not only should news organizations discuss features of their own polls, but they should describe limitations of polls conducted by candidates. At a minimum, they should publish the text of a question, describe the sample, and review the implications of error margins.[1]

Political surveying became more sophisticated in the 1980s. Polls today do more than chart voter perceptions. They yield information that is integrated with other facts and figures to form detailed voter data bases.

Polling data changed character and function when computers became common campaign appliances. Computers uncapped the full power of polling data to describe populations, subgroups, and individuals. While polling techniques have not changed much, polling data are being put to new and effective uses. Computers perform the magic. The real questions of political ethics arise when computers go to work.

THE USE OF COMPUTERS

Computer involvement in political campaigns, as in most other applications, has been a function of equipment cost and size. In the early 1980s, when personal computer power was measured by only dozens of megabytes, enthusiasts would relate the capacity of their machines according to 1950 computer dimensions: "In the fifties it would take a computer as big as the Sistine Chapel to do what this 48-megabyte baby can do." Today, nobody bothers with such comparisons. They would require references to geological formations.

Not only have computers shrunk to desktop proportions, but their cost has dropped to discount store prices. In the 1980s powerful computers became readily affordable even to neighborhood campaigns. Republican fund raiser and direct-mail pioneer Richard Viguerie said, "Anybody with a PC now can be a political force in their community, state, or the country" (quoted in Frenkel 1989a, 101).

Benefits of computer technology, once confined to the largest and best-endowed campaigns, now are available to everyone. And this is just the beginning. Computer applications will expand with the sophistication of the equipment. The ethical concerns now emerging likely will grow as well.

In this section we will discuss some of the campaign applications of computer technology, most of which have come into existence only during the past few years. Throughout these discussions it will be helpful to keep in mind that most developments improve targeted communication. They seek to identify the correct information for the correct group at the correct time. The strategies demonstrate the unyielding belief by political communicators in the concept of audience focusing. At heart, a political campaign, after all, is a communication campaign.

So what can computers do? Software already in the field provides a variety of integrated functions. At the simplest level computers allow a candidate to sort, label, and classify voters. They automate mailings, phonings, and door-to-door contacts. They develop lists of who votes absentee, who drives to the polling station, and who is likely not to drive at all (and thus may need a ride to the polls). They say who is a dyed-in-the-wool Republican or Democrat, and who sits on the fence. The programs are flexible enough to allow candidates to create lists that meet any local need.

Software packages also serve a variety of campaign management functions. For instance, they coordinate direct mail activities, prompt press relation strategies, schedule speaking engagements for campaign workers and the candidate, and assist with fund raisers. When the campaign staff conducts its own polls, these packages draw random samples, format questions, analyze data, and prepare tables and charts to help interpret results.

Thus far in this description, the application of computer technology is simply an automation of procedures that have been, or at least could have been, accomplished by hand, albeit with some effort. With the increasing power and proliferation of computers, a new generation of applications is evolving.

Data-base merging, the most rapidly growing computer application, compiles ever greater amounts of voter information. Consider the political uses of magazine subscription lists, for example. Magazines are recognized as the most targeted mass medium. They enjoy the narrowest, most focused, most homogeneous audiences of any nonpersonalized medium. Like the company you keep, you are known by the magazines you read. Consequently, subscription lists reveal subscriber characteristics.

It is now a simple task to combine (concatenate) voter registration lists with magazine subscription lists. The result is a highly personalized, detailed voter profile. Voter registration data bases provide addresses, age, gender, perhaps party affiliation, and other personal facts. Magazine subscription lists add details about special interests, hobbies, perhaps even political views, personal philosophies, and other, often sensitive, information. John Phillips, owner of Aristotle Industries, a campaign management and software firm, offers an example. "If someone subscribes to *Guns and Animal Magazine*, it's a pretty good bet that he's a gun-control opponent. . . . We rent lists, match names against the voter file, and create a list of gun owners" (quoted in Frenkel 1989a, 103). In the process, Phillips and other concatenators have classified entire voter registration lists according to special interests revealed by magazine subscriptions. This is just the beginning.

Within a year of completing the 1990 census, the U.S. Census Bureau is planning to make available an extensive data base that, joined with available population demographic data, will yield information revealing voter profiles, house by house, for most cities and towns across the United States.[2] The information, released on CD-ROM disks,[3] will provide a powerful refinement tool for targeted data bases. The software is ready and waiting for this avalanche of new data.

Even without this information, campaign personnel are amassing deep piles of personal data. The process involves computer matching and sorting, not with just two data bases, but with multiple files from many sources. The resulting record is a highly refined, deeply personal account of voters' lives.

Political consultant and campaign computer guru Joseph L. Cowart has been developing data-base applications since 1981 and is among the leading innovators and advocates of computer techniques. He recently has been working on a more complex statistical protocol that weights selected voter characteristics. "You run a regression analysis that nails people against the polling data, combining geography and demographics" (quoted in Frenkel 1989a, 110). Through this procedure Cowart can pinpoint voters by income, age, educational background, and more, then weight the characteristics appropriately to disclose the most effective voter appeal. The end result is "a very finely targeted list of excellent voter prospects. Such a list could be specific enough to include the locations of potential supporters who agree with the candidate on certain issues" (quoted in Frenkel 1989a, 110). As a result, campaign staffers who contact these voters by phone, by mail, or in person will have access to a detailed voter dossier from which to assemble a highly individualized message.

Another application of campaign computer technology involves the integration of voter registration information with mapping programs. The procedure is new and requires a powerful PC, but software is readily available and well within the budgets of most campaigns.

Here is how it works. Graphic mapping programs, similar to those used by government foresters and land use specialists, are selected for the appropriate geographic region. These programs provide images of streets, neighborhoods, divisions, or larger areas, depending on a user's need. With a key stroke the computer operator can zoom in and out and across a region.

Next, a voter registration list or other data base containing rich, voter-specific information is merged with the mapping program. The result is an integrated cartographic data base capable of producing color-coded maps of any desired perspective. They can show concentrations of registered voters identified by any characteristic that helps the candidate recognize voter patterns. They can display information that shows at a glance regions in need of additional canvassing, mailing, billboard placement, or other special attention. Furthermore, the maps can identify individual houses and therefore mark friends, foes, and fence sitters as campaign workers canvass the precincts.

Very soon mapping programs will accommodate more elaborate, compound data bases that will enable a candidate to combine and recombine a multitude of voter features for instant graphic display. Where is the concentration of middle-aged, yacht-owning Presbyterians in this neighborhood? Where are the Republican households with people 55 to 65 years of age and incomes over $90,000? A few commands will cause the computer screen to illuminate images of homes that meet any desired set of characteristics.

Here is an important afterthought. Computers have been involved in most political campaigns for only a decade, and only since the mid–1980s have the power and costs of PCs permitted their use in local campaigns. Think about the developments in data base-building and voter targeting during this short period and imagine the refinements likely during the decade ahead. Wider and deeper computer involvement in campaigns is inevitable. Consultant Cowart sees computer technology as an expanding campaign tool of great importance: "Already, people can't remember campaigns without computers. It gets easier and easier" (cited in Frenkel 1989b, 210).

ETHICAL ISSUES

It should be evident that polling and computer technologies are interrelated conceptually and physically. Audience targeting and persuasion are the fundamental functions of any political campaign, and through the years practices that have improved communication operations have improved the effectiveness of political campaigns. Polling and computer technologies have been enhancing message intimacy and relevance, focus and placement, timing and precision.

Consequently, when we discuss ethical implications of the new technologies, it is appropriate to look at the integrated functions rather than at individual components. Polls without computers provide superficial population descriptions. Computers are hollow shells without data bases. Disjointed data bases are nothing more than scattered lists. The combination and integration of these, however, yields a powerful resource heretofore unknown to political campaigns. Joining them offers blessings and curses. The curses now concern us.

Ethical concerns, like the technologies that drive them, are interrelated and mutually defined. For our discussion it is possible to identify five categories.

Individual Concerns

• Privacy issues
• Voter manipulations

System Concerns

• Single-issue politics
• Lone Ranger campaigns
• Implications for governing

Privacy Issues

Privacy is a casualty of an open society. Even so, the political use of personal information has taken the assault on privacy to new dimensions. Never before has so much information about so many people been available on such a wholesale level. For pocket change a candidate can rent a stack of lists, concatenate them with voter registration information and other data, and, for every individual in a region, amass a substantial personal dossier. Without an individual's permission or even awareness, often intimate details about him or her are bartered and traded among list brokers and political operatives. There are no practical limitations to these information flea markets, nor are there adequate safeguards to govern the use of personal data.

What does it mean when scattered information is assembled into a unified data base? Do bits and pieces of data joined into a single frame reveal an image that people have a right to keep secret? These questions are neither trivial nor academic. They tap our fundamental right to privacy and the privilege to be known only by those we choose to know us. Where does the unbounded acquisition and compilation of personal information fit into these protections? Does the need to improve political communication justify this violation?

Years before computer technology was known, Ayn Rand wrote, "Civilization is the progress toward a society of privacy. The savage's whole existence is public, ruled by the laws of his tribe. Civilization is the process of setting man free from men" (Rand 1943, 1). Clearly, the unregulated use of computers does not suggest a civilization's progression toward privacy. In an effort to improve the efficiency and effectiveness of political campaigns, the people who write the laws are involved in a process that challenges the security of private citizens. Whether the process chips away at the foundations of civilization envisioned by Ayn Rand is another matter. In less than a decade the technologies have reached an alarming level of sophistication, and they are rapidly evolving.

The first ethical concern about personal privacy is for the data-collection process itself. It asks these questions: Should political campaigns be permitted to collect, aggregate, and act on the growing volumes of data now becoming available? At what point does the activity intrude on the right to privacy? When does a data base become so complete that it poses an unacceptable threat?

The second concern deals with the public's knowledge of such activities. Do people know their dossiers are being assembled in order to render them better targets of political messages? Would they choose to have their voting records, purchasing activities, life-style characteristics, and demographic data concatenated, then mapped, charted, and outlined for campaign workers and persuasion strategists? Should they be given a choice?

The first step in dealing with both ethical concerns is to raise the issue for public discussion. Very little has been written about the topic in the popular press, which suggests most people have no information about their unwitting participation. The recipient of a political letter, phone call, or visit is unlikely to understand what complex technology has made it possible for the communication to be so extraordinarily convincing and precise. Before new developments permit further refinement and improvement of targeted persuasion techniques, it is time to let the public in on the process. Voters should be told about the data bases, their origins, contents, and application. They should understand that important features of their lives are being used to make them more susceptible to campaign merchandising.

Notification will require legislation, since it is unlikely that any political candidate would choose to inform voters about such activities without assurances of similar disclosure by opponents. It may be necessary to require bona fide candidates to inform potential subjects about a plan to compile and manipulate personal data. This may be accomplished by direct mail, newspaper notices, or some other recognized public communication technique.

At some point it also may become necessary to consider legislation governing the assembly and use of aggregated data bases. There must be some determination of what constitutes a critical mass of personal information. Then, accordingly, campaigns (and commercial interests, for that matter) should be limited in the amount of personal information they may collect and use in communication activities. This may curtail the effectiveness of targeted strategies, but the violation of personal privacy is no small matter and is worth strong measures.

It is difficult to predict the chances of such legislation. At this time there is no public outcry (because there is little public knowledge) about privacy invasions, and it is unlikely that motivations will rise from within the institutions whose members are the primary beneficiaries of the technologies. But as computers accommodate larger and more intrusive data bases, public pressures are likely to increase. The unknown at this point is the tolerance level of a population growing more accustomed to and comfortable with institutional maintenance of personal information. Again the race is on between the advances of technology and the human tolerance of technology's effects.

Voter Manipulation

Voter manipulation is a product of political agenda setting. When we set the agenda—when we tell people what to think *about*—we direct attention to an issue of our choosing. Two things happen. First, we fix attention on our topic. This commits audience energy and involvement. Second, given that two ideas, like two stones, cannot be in the same place at the same time, we divert audience attention from other topics. Agenda setting is an important component of the persuasion process because it both focuses and distracts the attention, and thereby affects the priorities.

Manipulation occurs when a political campaign sets different agendas for different voter subgroups, directing the attention of some groups to one set of issues, and of other groups to different issues. Targeting techniques, refined by polling and computer technologies, expand the opportunities for such strategies. For instance, a candidate may identify his or her anti-abortion stand with concurring voter groups. Campaign letters, phone calls, and media messages can prominently identify the candidate's abortion position for kindred thinkers. This is good targeting.

At the same time, voters unlikely to agree with the candidate on abortion will be treated to a different set of issues. Their letters, phone calls, and media messages may deal with such carefully selected topics as the candidate's more agreeable position on environmental matters, or veterans' concerns, or the savings and loan bailout, whichever demonstrates a convenient alignment of views. Again this is good targeting. It directs the most effective issue at each group. It focuses, aims, and shoots the right bullet at the right bull's-eye with pinpoint accuracy.

Here is the problem with such manipulations. An officeholder does not deal with one or two issues. Mayors, state legislators, members of Congress, and presidents must deal with a host of issues. Yet through the pigeonholing techniques of targeted communication, voters are led away from issues on which they may oppose the candidate. Different agendas are set for different groups. Candidates direct voters' attention to one or two issues and divert attention from the rest. When the net effects of these divide-and-conquer strategies are measured, the candidate will have been successful in reaching isolated groups with congruent images while concealing the total picture from all groups. Voters thus are manipulated by the agenda-setting process. Each group has a vision of the candidate. Few have the full view.

There is yet another character of targeted strategies that permits voter manipulations: It is easier to practice psychological strategies on well-defined, homogeneous groups than on heterogeneous mass audiences. For example, in targeted mailings during the 1980s, the Moral Majority used its customary fire and brimstone to inspire the faithful. The letters and fliers mentioned godless Communists, menacing liberals, and murderers of unborn children. These references, bolstered by appropriate rhetoric and pictures, made a compelling pitch for contributions and political action. They worked their psychological magic on many recipients. The tactics would have had little effect on broader audiences, but they pulled the right strings for this special group. Moral Majority coffers swelled and elected officials felt the pressure.

Similar manipulations directed to targeted groups are used by supporters of environmental positions, abortion choice advocates, and others. There are no monopolies on the tactics, right or left. The point is, when groups or candidates wish to persuade a narrow voter segment through targeted channels, there is considerable opportunity to exploit persuasive techniques calculated to have maximum impact on target group biases and views. Polling and computer techniques expand the opportunity for, and improve the effectiveness of, targeted communications.

Thus far we have considered how voters are open to manipulation by the targeting technologies. While individuals may be victims, perhaps a larger casualty is the political system. We will explore this next.

Single-Issue Politics

The identity of this nation is derived from two views held by its citizens. First, there is the parochial view in which people identify with one or more subgroups. They may see themselves as Africans, Europeans, Asians, Latins; Catholics, Jews, Protestants, Muslims, Buddhists; Republicans, Democrats; pro-choicers, pro-lifers; conservatives or liberals. By our history and our philosophy we are a nation of segments. We value our individuality and our eclecticism. We revel in the freedom to associate with racial, ethnic, and ideological factions, all of which exist individually but at the same time are part of the total mosaic.

The second view is of that mosaic. From this larger perspective we see ourselves as part of the nation. We are Americans. We have a common government, a common set of laws, common national problems and fortunes. Natural disasters, economic difficulties, threats to one portion of the country affect the rest.

We have always held dual visions of membership, in narrow groups and in the wider collective. The delicate balance enjoyed in this country has not been achieved everywhere. Radical factionalism in many countries has eroded a sense of national unity and created dangerous conflicts. The Soviet Union offers a prime example. Ireland, Canada, South Africa, and Honduras provide a few more.

In light of the workable stability achieved in this country (which has the greatest representation of subgroups anywhere on earth), it is worth asking about the possible effects of divide-and-conquer politics. Do strategies that seek to identify, isolate, and prosper from the differences among groups yield a perilous cumulative effect?

Political campaigns benefit from exaggerated voter differences. Voters have an innate attraction to dichotomous issues where distinctions are clearly drawn and camps are clearly formed. People like clear choices. They like to know who are the good guys and the bad guys. It is easier that way to pick an issue and choose a side. Targeting strategies amplify differences between the sides and establish clear factions. Private communications with different camps allow campaigns to play off the distinctions, further separate the views, and build distinctive coalitions.

Although political campaigns have always engaged in such tactics, only during the 1980s did the new technologies give candidates the capacity to dissect the population with such precision. It is easier today to sort the voters into sides. We have a good idea that these tactics help campaigns, but as the targeting capacity grows, we must ask what they will do to the political system and to the society.

Over a decade ago *Washington Post* columnist and syndicated writer Meg Greenfield envisioned such problems. She said these approaches "put a premium on identifying yourself with the special subgroup and help to thin, if not destroy, whatever feelings of larger national loyalty various citizens might have" (Greenfield 1978, A13). Greenfield's concern is for the second view, the unified perspective of a nation bound by common elements. Will the result of repeated drumming for parochial issues strain the bonds of national loyalty and thus of national unity? Such an outcome would imperil the society and the functioning of government. Special-interest agendas will blind voters to larger needs. Legislation will become more difficult to develop. For instance, budget debates during the upcoming lean years will be increasingly more contentious, each group fighting for its own allotment, with diminishing regard for collective needs.

This may be an unduly pessimistic view. The appeal to ever narrower voter subgroups may not have the unhappy effects we have described. Yet the consequences are so severe that the possibility cannot be overlooked. This is a matter of political ethics ripe for public consideration. Political professionals should not be allowed to dodge this ethical implication of their technologically enhanced campaigns. The impact poses a tangible threat and deserves open discussion.

Lone Ranger Campaigns

Paraphrasing an old expression, it could be said that the person who controls communications, controls the campaign. Before the mid–1950s, parties exercised substantial control over campaigns largely because they controlled campaign resources and communications. With the advent of television, candidates were able to circumvent the party apparatus by appealing directly to the voters. Through the 1950s and 1960s the direction continued away from the parties as television and other media came under more direct candidate control. Perhaps the best-known demonstration of media inroads into a party came in 1976 when Jimmy Carter (for a while known as "Jimmy Who?") entered the national limelight through his surprising victory in the New Hampshire primary.

Since then, however, the media have become more plentiful and more targeted, and with the increasing opportunity for channel selection and effective message development, the candidate wields yet greater control. The country only recently has become webbed by cable systems that have increased channel availability to more than 33 stations for the average household. This has expanded voter targeting opportunities. At the same time, as we have seen, candidates have invested heavily in computers and elaborate software that enable them to exploit the new targeted outlets. High-tech, targeted direct mail and telephone techniques add to the communication repertoire.

This convergence of communication technologies has changed the character of political campaigns. Most notably, the parties have become less relevant. Their heavy influence on campaigns at all levels, once an accepted force, now has eroded measurably. House Minority Whip Newt Gingrich bemoaned the loss of his Republican Party's input when he complained that the party was losing its grip at the local level (Edsall 1990). He argued for greater strategic planning and coordination by the party to channel the efforts of local candidates. Despite Gingrich's appeals, the trend clearly is away from such party leverage.

What is the problem? Why should anyone lament the decline of political parties? Not long ago critics complained about political bosses who cut unholy deals in smoke-filled back rooms. Wasn't this corruption of the democratic process as offensive as anything that may occur in the party's absence?

There are several responses. First, despite the apparent reduction of political party influence, deal making continues. Parties may have institutionalized such activity, but it is naive to think back-room politics does not go on—with strong party bosses or without them. Second, and more to the point of this discussion, the loss of party influence affects the stability and cohesion within political structures. Berkman and Kitch describe some of the problems.

Without parties to provide political focus or forge alliances among the multiple, overlapping, and conflicting interests that characterize the American political scene, the electorate has been fragmented into little pockets of single interest groups. These small narrowly-focused, single interest groups promote a politics of selfishness, intolerance, and zealotry. This kind of politics reopens old wounds, separates rather than unites, and poses a mighty threat to the principles of democracy. (Berkman and Kitch 1985, 320)

Such a forlorn view may be justified. The Lone Ranger campaign, unrestrained by the balance and discipline of party influence, finds little motivation for cohesive, mainstream strategies. The natural result is a set of disjointed political campaigns in pursuit of hot-button issues among disparate voter groups. The process began with the advent of television and has assumed new dimensions with the arrival of advanced information technologies.

Causes and effects become muddled. The relationships among computer-directed, targeted strategies, the decline of parties, and the formation of isolated voter groups are reciprocal. Technology permits the identification and segmentation of groups, which diminishes party influence, which in turn promotes the use of individual targeted strategies. The circle is complete and contracting.

The campaign of a former Ku Klux Klansman, David Duke, in Louisiana provides a good example of party irrelevance. Although this state legislator is nominally a Republican, the national Republican Party has publicly disavowed him and has exercised no recognizable influence on his U.S. senatorial campaign. Duke ran for the state house using targeting strategies among narrow subgroups receptive to his racist philosophies. He adopted a similar approach in his senatorial campaign, using focused communication techniques to deal with issues involving affirmative action, "parasitic welfare recipients and programs for minority contractors" (Newsweek 1990, 37). This campaign is, perhaps, one of the most visible examples of party influence run aground. Duke's maverick white supremacist campaign would have little chance within traditional party structures.

Promises of continued technological developments will only encourage the further decline of party influence. Lone Ranger candidacies likely will become commonplace.

Implications for Governing

One of the most serious concerns over the use of polls and other targeting technologies in a political campaign is that they don't stop with the political campaign. The weak single-issue support system constructed during a campaign ensures that the techniques of candidacy become the techniques of governance. Large numbers of voters support a candidate not because they subscribe to a comprehensive platform but because they have been motivated by focused appeals on a single topic. More pigeonholing and less party influence cultivate a thin, single-view constituency. People vote for candidates because of unidimensional thinking on abortion, the death penalty, the environment, military buildup, taxes, or some other impassioned issue. Uncommitted and unaligned voters are romanced by special appeals. Each voter, in turn, understandably expects the officeholder to fulfill expectations generated during the campaign. The official now must address the seductive, hot-button issues separately, not as part of a larger package. "No new taxes" voters want no new taxes, no matter what happens with the economy. Pro-environment voters want no development despite the impact on jobs and industry. Pro-development voters want economic growth despite the destruction of natural resources. It's everyone for his or her special interest, with little regard for the larger context. Campaigns foster these selfish views.

Berkman and Kitch have noted the troubling evolution of politics and governance: "Modern governing has become a permanent campaign. Once elected, politicians must continually seek public approval for support of their policies. Techniques used to get the vote are now necessary to maintain public approval" (1985, 147).

Public approval is paramount. The Bush administration has become known for its loyalty to the polls. Bush's candidacy took full advantage of the targeting technologies, segmenting audiences and directing messages of particular appeal to ideological, demographic, and geographic subgroups. Now his presidency is known for its Pavlovian responses to the polls and public opinion.

This mindset was clear in the White House's immediate reaction to the Middle East crisis in 1990. Iraq invaded Kuwait just as President Bush was about to embark on his midsummer vacation in Kennebunkport, Maine. Among the casualties of war was a peaceful presidential holiday. Public perception became a problem for the president and his political advisers: Should the president sit in Washington to direct the U.S. Middle East operation, or should he continue with his vacation to avoid being seen as a hostage to the crisis? Jimmy Carter became absorbed by the 1979 Iranian takeover of the U.S. Embassy in Tehran. His preoccupations contributed to the loss of his second bid for the presidency. Public opinion assaults on Carter taught Bush a lesson. The presidential vacation set the stage for some interesting public relations posturing.

White House spokesman Marlin Fitzwater publicly explained Bush's careful balance. The *Washington Post* quoted Fitzwater:

The president thinks it's good for *Americans to "see* that he is able to continue carrying on the business of government at the same time worrying about this situation in the Gulf. . . . He carries on the work of the White House wherever he goes, and it's important for the *American people to see* that he's not holed up in the White House, as has happened in the past. So we're comfortable with the *American people seeing* that he's combining his work and his vacation." (quoted in Balz 1990, A15; emphasis added)

It is interesting that the president's pollster and political strategist, Robert Teeter, was prominent throughout this delicate public relations episode. The *Post* said:

But Robert Teeter . . . argued today that it is only journalists who are upset with the idea of Bush vacationing while the gulf crisis deepens. . . . Teeter insisted that the *public supports the president's policy* and does not begrudge him some time for relaxation. (Balz 1990, A15; emphasis added)

The Congress is no less immune to the grip of public reaction. They draw from the same well of technologies and so are similarly afflicted. *New York Times* writer Michael Oreskes notes some of the maladies:

In the past, when a President failed to seize the initiative, Congress often tried to. But now both ends of Pennsylvania Avenue seem immobilized by a politics of avoidance, where poll takers and advertising producers are more influential than economists or engineers. (Oreskes 1990, 22)

Where is the ethical issue? Officeholders have always wanted to please their constituents. It is their nature to do so, and it has been their custom to keep an eye on the next campaign. How have things become different, and where have these practices begun to raise eyebrows about moral principles of government?

The question is one of process and degree. Few would question the use of polls to monitor the pulse of public attitudes. Concerns arise, however, over the dominance of public opinion in the formulation of public policy. This democracy does not submit every public issue for popular vote because we expect elected officials to research the details of complex matters and to act on our behalf. We pay them to study the options and to use their judgments in making decisions that best advance the public interest. Public opinion should be only one of the considered factors. The U.S. system of government was configured to allow elected representatives to be the surrogates of the people on matters not best resolved through public vote. When officials substitute public opinion for their own judgment, they abrogate their responsibilities and dodge their constitutional obligations.

Senate majority leader George J. Mitchell has expressed his "frustration over what he calls the new breed of 'wet-finger politicians,' who he said spend more time sampling the political winds than reading policy papers" (cited in Oreskes 1990, 22). In answer to our earlier question, ethical issues arise when the public good is not well served by the political system.

Besides displacing more reasoned judgment, advice from the polls often is not very good. The public nearly always takes the easy way out. Survey respondents typically express personal preferences for utopian conditions without a sense of obligation to the system or accountability for the outcomes. People answering a pollster's questions one by one have no collective sense of responsibility. They also are unlikely to know much more about an issue than what they see in a few newscasts and, in a diminishing number of cases, read in a daily newspaper. Oreskes says, "We have public opinion now, which is people's private reflexes. But we don't have public judgment" (1990, 22). This is an understandable although undesirable condition. It is a matter of political fraud when elected officials allow the substitution of such expressions for their own judgment. The matter becomes even more intolerable when the process is adopted for political expedience.

Les AuCoin, a representative from Oregon, has been coached by political consultants to pay greater attention to public opinion. He finds little merit in the advice. "The science of public opinion measuring is being misused to lock you in where you are today rather than to lead society to where you think you ought to be" (quoted in Oreskes 1990, 22). Public opinion offers a helpful statement of general impressions and values, but it does not offer much vision. It does not project. It measures the present and the past but offers little guidance for the future. Senator James A. McClure of Idaho says the "polls are measuring emotional responses, not thought-out views" (Oreskes 1990, 22).

Polling data, the bedrock of a campaign, is quicksand for a government. Elected officials find themselves trapped by the technology that helped them achieve office. Their weak coalitions must be serviced. Voters have become increasingly unlikely to recognize the candidate's responsibility to sit in judgment on many issues. This weakness is fostered by the widespread adoption of campaign technologies that help cultivate such isolated coalitions. The trend is of some concern for campaigns; it is critical for the operation of the government.

Consider just one case in point. During the 1988 campaign no single issue dominated more than taxes. Candidate Bush's unequivocal "Read my lips, no new taxes" statement became the acid test for candidates of both parties. Political death would befall any candidate who uttered the "T" word. Since then, the class of 1988 has been facing a frightening conundrum. The polls continue to register widespread public rejection of taxes, and while the national deficit climbs out of sight, all the attending problems of a financially crippled nation are emerging. Loyalty to the polls and the conflicting recognition of their own irresponsibility are tormenting many elected officials. Fear of voter disappointment caused the deferral of many unpopular decisions during the 1980s, but the country's financial woes now demand action. The "T" word must be spoken. Public opinion says "no." All logic says "yes." On this issue the polls have paralyzed the government.

Like quitting a drug, it is not easy for a candidate to kick the habit of the new technologies. Candidates acquire a taste for the sense of control granted by voter information and targeted access. They have cultivated tenacious constituency groups who then cling to promises of specific action on narrow issues. Their indebtedness forces them to return to the polls for guidance. They must ask again and again what the voters think about the issues and about their performance. Modern campaigning techniques thus resonate beyond the campaign. Much of our government's current immobility is due in large part to an unyielding reliance on the polls and attendant technologies.

SUMMARY

New York Times writer Robin Toner summarizes the condition faced in modern campaigning.

Today's campaigns have become a kind of harrowing arms race, fueled by ever more sophisticated technologies, waged with ever more brutal and efficient techniques, covering more and more personal political terrain. . . . The toll is not simply on the quality of government but on the political culture at large. (1990, A1)

Not that it matters much, now that the genie is out of the bottle, but it is instructive to ask how we have reached such a condition: Did technologies impose themselves on political campaigns or did campaigns seek out the technologies? Likely it was a bit of each. Certainly computer and polling technologies evolved to serve needs larger than those of a campaign. Once available, however, they quickly found a natural home in political camps. Given a demonstration of what they could achieve, political candidates encouraged additional applications, and the process developed its own inertia.

The problem is what to do. As we noted at the beginning of this chapter, there is little sense of personal liability for a process that exhibits effects only from aggregate involvement. A diffusion of responsibility ensures that no candidate bears guilt for a condition resulting from everyone's actions.

Moreover, there is nothing inherently corrupt or sinister about the process itself. Candidates collect data and send out messages. They tell the people what they want to hear. No one's motivations are anything but noble. They may even be commendable. The goal of our political system is to have elected officials represent the will of the people. How better to determine the public will than by polls? How better to assure the public that its will is done than through an efficient communication strategy? The argument is neat and clean. Candidates hear the voters. Voters hear the candidates. There is feedback and reciprocity. Political campaigns are communication campaigns. Effective communication translates into effective politics.

Maybe not. Hidden problems challenge such a conclusion. With all the good intentions we see the dangers of single-issue politics. Voters lose perspective. They fix their sights on one or two issues that absorb their attention and blunt their concern for other matters. Targeted strategies elevate the significance of many issues and diminish the importance of other matters more deserving of public concern. Flag burning has taken the spotlight from the deficit. Willie Horton[4] stole public attention from problems in the nation's cities, the environment, the developing savings and loan scandal, and a host of matters begging for notice. Political campaigns manipulated groups of voters with emotional hot-button issues that, on balance, have little substance.

Lone Ranger campaigns, now skillfully managed with computer technologies, no longer require the input of political parties. Party power has obvious problems, but it also imposes perspective and restraint on a campaign. It discourages mavericks who exploit a sensational issue or promote a radical ideology. There is evidence of an increasing number of successful candidates wading out of mainstream waters with masses of followers, persuaded one by one.

As we have seen, the effects of campaign practices follow candidates into government service. Candidates have divided and conquered. They have made promises on many issues to different groups whose members will not forget. The groups have seen not the panorama but only small portions of the landscape, and so they fix on the details. This keeps officials looking over their shoulders and reading the polls to be sure they govern to the satisfaction of each group to which they have become beholden.

In the process of running such a campaign, candidates amass an enormous amount of personal data on voters. Towering lists of information serve the needs of targeting strategies that use such facts to form incisive appeals. A gain for the campaign, though, may be a loss for the voter: a loss of privacy and of the prerogative to keep personal matters personal, a loss of anonymity as a natural defense against persuasion and persistent campaign appeals.

While these technologies affect the well-being of voters, the political system, and the operation of government, there is a frightening absence of public discussion. None of this is heard in campaign reform talks, political strategy debates, and other forums. Voters generally are unaware that powerful persuasion techniques are being used to win them over. Few people know the extent of data bases that stockpile their personal secrets, or the level of familiarity campaigns have of them. This is a risky topic. The public may object to the techniques. Which candidate will be first to limit use of the methods, or to abandon them? Who will suffer through the discussions about disclosure or limits on the use of technology, the data, or the targeting strategies?

One can find little comfort in the recognition that computer campaign technologies are in their infancy. In the 1980s concatenation was nothing more than a difficult word to spell. Today it describes the fundamental process whereby campaigns build operational intelligence files. Mapping, regression weightings, and other refinements on the use of growing data bases are just the beginning. Technology spreads its influence exponentially. What of the next decade?

NOTES

1. State and national press associations have survey reporting guidelines that many news organizations choose to ignore.

2. Availability of data bases is described in Frenkel 1989a.

3. A CD-ROM disk is a high-density storage medium that contains information read by lasers. A single disk can hold huge amounts of data. In appearance and operation, it resembles a stereo compact disk.

4. Willie Horton was a convicted murderer in Massachusetts who was let out on a prison furlough program. While on release he committed another murder. The Bush campaign used this incident to argue that the Democratic opponent, Michael Dukakis, governor of Massachusetts, was soft on crime. Television commercials depicting Willie Horton and constant reference by the Bush campaign were seen by many as an easy dodge of more difficult political issues.

REFERENCES

Balz, D. 1990. "President mixing business, pleasure with a vengeance." *The Washington Post*, August 20, p. A15.

Berkman, R., and L. W. Kitch. 1985. *Politics in the media age*. New York: McGraw-Hill.

Brower, B. 1988. "The pernicious power of the polls." *Money* (March): 144–58.

Edsall, T. B. 1990. "GOP leaders tap frustration over local election support." *The Washington Post*, August 11, p. 2.

Frenkel, K. 1989a. "Computing as a political force." *Personal Computing* (October): 99–106.

———. 1989b. "The new breed of campaign manager." *Personal Computing* (October): 198–210.

Greenfield, Meg. 1989. "Thinking small." *The Washington Post*, April 19, p. A13.

Newsweek. "David Duke: A racist turns populist." August 13, p. 37.

Oreskes, M. 1990. "American politics loses way as polls displace leadership." *New York Times*, March 18, pp. 1, 22.

Rand, A. 1943. *The Fountainhead*. New York: Macmillan.

Toner, R. 1990. " 'Wars' wound candidates and the process." *New York Times*, March 19, pp. A1, B6.

Chapter Ten

Political News: Narrative Form and the Ethics of Denial

Gary C. Woodward

Objectivity is a myth, but it is a myth with consequences.
—Gross 1988, 189

Among the rush of news stories that unfolded during the December 1989 U.S. invasion of Panama, perhaps nothing was more unusual or revealing than a brief moment in a presidential news conference. On December 21, President Bush decided to hold a briefing to discuss his administration's bold decision to capture and prosecute Panama's leader, Manuel Noriega. The military ruler had once been on the Central Intelligence Agency's payroll, but his indictment as the recipient of Latin American drug money made him an embarrassment to the United States. Noriega soon surrendered, but not before the fighting of the initial invasion claimed the lives of 25 U.S. soldiers and hundreds of Panamanians. Through a fluke of timing Bush began his meeting with the press at the same time that the remains of the Americans who had died were scheduled to arrive at Dover Air Force Base in Delaware.

All of the major television news services interrupted their regular programming to carry the president's remarks. In addition, most had the capability of going live with the solemn ritual of removing the caskets of the deceased soldiers from returning military cargo planes. Similar ceremonies at the flag-draped Dover receiving center had been etched in the minds of Americans over the last four decades, the inevitable consequence of military actions ranging from Vietnam to Lebanon. But on this day the simultaneous unfolding of the press conference and the ritual of the military honor guard required quick editorial decisions. CBS,

CNN, and ABC decided to present portions of both events by using a split screen. For several minutes the president's conference could be seen next to a picture showing the caskets as they were silently taken from the bellies of the arriving Air Force C–141s. CNN Vice President Ed Turner later noted that he "supported the technique because oddly, you had a confluence of events" (Gerard 1990, 11). On one side of the screen Bush continued to answer general questions from the press, in some cases offering lighthearted and casual responses to political queries. On the other side, pictures from the stark white Dover hangar were shown continuously and without comment.

Bush did not know what many of the nation's television viewers were seeing. Nor did he have any idea that the sum of these two parts created a third unintentional message that was badly out of sync with the first two. In the context of his own briefing he alternately expressed sadness over the loss of American lives in Panama and commented in a more jocular style on less lethal political aspects of the invasion. ABC's Roone Arledge was among the first to catch the fact that the melding of Bush's characteristically informal briefing with the solemn pictures from Dover was creating an unintentional commentary. He quickly called the network's broadcast control room, ordering an end to the live coverage from Delaware. Peter Jennings later apologized on the air to ABC's viewers, explaining that Bush did not know that the network had used the split-screen technique (Gerard 1990, 11). But the damage was already done. As the president noted in a subsequent meeting with the press, "I got a lot of mail after the last press conference . . . because when I was speaking here in this room, juxtaposed against my frivolous comments at the time" a split television screen also showed caskets "of dead soldiers coming home." He asked the networks to notify him if they again intended to use this technique. "I could understand why the viewers were concerned about this. They thought their president, at a solemn moment like that, didn't give a damn. And I do. I do" (Bush 1990, A10).

The fallout from this incident was minimal, and Bush's request for advance notice was made more in a conciliatory than in a critical tone. The deeper significance of this small moment lies in what it reaffirms about the news industry, especially that portion of the national press devoted to the reporting of politics. The Dover-Washington hookup was driven by the familiar urge to be immediate, and by a planning process that involved varied amounts of intention and accident. What was instantaneously created was something different from what observers in both locations would understand: a synthetic reality transcending the normal limitations of a specific context. The jarring mismatch between Bush's informal amiability and Dover's ritual of mourning was a uniquely journalistic creation, notable for the ironic fact that it was available only to Americans who were *not* at either scene.

The key elements of this exchange point to several assertions about political reporting that are at the heart of the issues raised in this chapter: that any full discussion of political ethics would be incomplete without including the political media; that the burden of shaping and communicating the nation's civil life is borne by news producers and editors as well as by the subjects of their reports; and that members of the news media are not just passive observers but—in ways that many still deny—are important *participants* in the process of formulating news narratives.

JOURNALISTS AS RHETORICAL AGENTS

In a landmark study social scientist Andrew Weigert described what he called the "immoral rhetoric" of those forms of sociology which attempt to bring the appearance of neutral science—if not the science itself—to the study of human affairs. "If a sociologist practices rhetoric, but identifies himself (to self and/or others) as a scientist," he wrote, "he renders his rhetoric immoral, the immoral rhetoric of identity deception" (Weigert 1970, 111). Communicators who pass themselves off as the providers of neutral descriptions and straightforward "facts" are always suspect. It is not that we should hold journalism to the standards of science and the search for immutable truth; rather, Weigert's caution carries an important warning for any profession that embraces an ethic of impartiality and accuracy.

Political reporting is increasingly mired in the moral dilemma of accepting an ethic that it cannot fulfill. By retaining its doctrines of neutral reporting and objectivity, much political journalism clings to a kind of semiofficial agnosticism that it cannot sustain. It presumes to exist outside of the political convictions of the people and events it surveys—a stance that no longer carries much force with the general public or comports with our increasingly thorough knowledge of the contingent and perspective nature of most versions of news. Beginning with Walter Lippman (1965) and continuing with influential studies by Gaye Tuchman (1978), Herbert Gans (1980), Edward Epstein (1974), and others (Graber 1989; Altheide 1976; Fishman 1980, Nimmo and Combs 1985; Smith 1977; Hackett 1984), a significant body of thoughtful press criticism and analysis has outlined how the routines of news work cannot help but impose their own rhetorical emphases.

The problem with an ethic of objectivity is also compounded by the artificial impression that journalism is an institution which exists apart from its commercial roots. Formal standards for judging the minimal responsibilities of journalists still imply that no marriage between the political and commercial worlds has taken place.[1] But it has, and the relationships it has created are increasingly recognized by news consumers and subjects alike.[2] Most political reporters have an acute sense of their own limitations, but they may be the last to concede that they are no longer the political virgins their professional codes of ethics imply.

The objective of this chapter is thus to show that political journalism is—against its own high standards—a flawed enterprise: that its inherent limitations cannot fulfill its frequently stated public service objectives. The elements of this ethical quandary can be suggested only in very broad strokes. We begin by briefly describing what is *not* a part of our criticism. Then two different lines of analysis follow. One explores how the standard vehicle for the presentation of events, the story format, carries its own rhetorical obligations, obligations that are intensified by commercial pressures and the constraints of space and time. The second considers issues of fairness that grow out of the special visual and narrative biases of television reporting.

CAVEATS

In many obvious ways the American public is well served by the large and varied institution of American journalism. The sheer amount of time and space devoted to national politics is often impressive. While there are significant lapses in coverage—especially in the reporting of actions in Congress and the executive agencies—there is little doubt that major events benefit from extensive if not always thoughtful reporting. In 1988, for example, an attentive news consumer had ample opportunities at least to hear *about* (if not always hear) the major party contenders for the presidency. Even before the summer conventions, the three major networks' nightly news broadcasts devoted more than 20 hours to the campaign in nearly 1,500 separate reports (Nimmo 1989, 466). In addition, the national newsweeklies, the wire services, and additional broadcasts devoted to the campaign (including ABC's *Nightline*, assorted Sunday talk shows, and reports on CNN) guaranteed many opportunities to see and read about the candidates. The campaign predictably became the object of sometimes brilliant reporting in major dailies such as the *New York Times* and *Los Angeles Times*, and weeklies as diverse as the *New Yorker* and the *Washington Monthly*. On many major political issues an impressive pluralism contributes to the expression of opinions and facts.

Moreover, as these cases suggest, the press is not a monolith. Although major outlets such as daily papers and television stations are owned by fewer corporations than in the recent past (Bagdikian 1990, 3–26), political reporting is still spread over a number of diverse entities. On a major story in the United States, the average household can easily gain access to the reporting of eight or nine separate sources.[3] Even though the brief narratives of the three networks still dominate most Americans' exposure to news,[4] there are many alternatives to their highly compressed versions of events. Political coverage in the United States is especially enriched by the more analytical "long-form" journalism that characterizes much of the reporting in outlets like the *New Yorker*, the *New York Times*, the *Washington Post*, and cable television's C-SPAN.

Finally, the press functions with an understandable realism that is hard to quarrel with. Stories must be developed on short notice by reporters who have inherited rather than created many of the constraints they must live with. It is easy to dismiss what can seem like the airy assertions of press critics who point out the shortcomings of the working press but have never had to construct a story under the pressure of a deadline. This gap between the day-to-day realities of news reporting and its lofty public service ideals is probably why even so distinguished an observer as the *Washington Post's* David Broder has noted that "it is difficult to write about 'journalism ethics' without sounding like a jerk" (Klaidman and Beauchamp 1987, 3). It is part of the popular mythology of reporting to revel in the anarchy of the "real" world. Over the years we have romanticized journalism that flouts conventional rules affecting the reporting of crime (*The Front Page*), political scandals (*All the President's Men*), Asian wars (*The Killing Fields*), and foreign intrigue (*The Year of Living Dangerously*). Narrow ethical issues seem pale in comparison with the events that may require all of a reporter's ingenuity simply to cover. Even so, it is hard to overlook the unique constitutional protections of the press, and the special role we have given it as a semiofficial characterizer of the motives and actions of others. The old cliché is still true: the press is our window on the world. Its unmatched position in every advanced society puts it at the center of enormous expectations about its accountability. As press critic Jeff Greenfield has noted, "I don't think that the free press can assert the privileges of the divinely protected priesthood" (1986, 53), and not take seriously those ethical issues which are raised about its conduct.

FEEDING THE NARRATIVE BEAST: THE RHETORICAL PRESS

Imagine for a moment that you are a senior news producer for one of the network evening news programs. In the conference that is held every morning to determine stories that will be featured in the day's newscast, a reporter notes that there has been unusual activity at the White House and State Department. Yesterday several cars with diplomatic license plates delivered Syrian and other Middle Eastern members of the diplomatic corps to the more private driveway between the Old Executive Office Building and the western side of the White House. Reporters at the State Department have also noted a similar flurry of unannounced arrivals and departures at the department's secluded basement entrance off of Washington's C Street. All of this has occurred within one day of an announcement by the relative of an American hostage that she saw "some progress" toward the release of a group of long-detained Americans and Europeans kidnapped in and around Beirut by Islamic conservatives. Publicly, administration members indicate that nothing unusual seems to be happening, and refuse to disclose the names of visitors at these two locations. Correspondents on Capitol Hill and in Cyprus have reported that they have heard about the sudden "flurry" of diplomatic activity in Washington, but can offer little hard evidence to suggest that anything has changed in Syria and Iran, two countries U.S. officials believe could arrange for the freedom of the hostages.

Is there a story in these facts? If so, what is it? Should the network's White House correspondent relay these events in a "stand-upper" from the front lawn, or should the telling of these events be part of a larger "package" featuring file footage of the hostages, the arrival and departure of the diplomatic cars, and the denials by U.S. officials of any "breakthrough"? On a light news day the package could be expanded even more by including the responses of several members of the Senate known to have different views on how best to secure the return of the hostages.

This is a story that could easily consume 4 of the total 22 minutes of the newscast, or it could be scrapped entirely. The dilemma posed here is not unusual in the range of options it presents to those responsible for structuring versions of the day's events. The sketchy and selective events offered here provide what may be only a series of discontinuous and idiosyncratic circumstances. If they are to become a "story," they will have to be worked into a continuous thread of narration that will explain their possible significance. The decision to commit airtime to these events will probably involve the anchorperson, who will have to put them in a context, perhaps by referring to the president's long-standing public assurances that he will pursue "high-level" diplomatic efforts to secure the release of the hostages. The narration that continues over photos of the captives and the arrival and departure of cars will make a further effort to give these specific actions a unifying motive and a possible outcome.

Such is the nature of narrative as an organizing device that even a short segment can be completed along formulaic lines, supplied in part by viewers' previous beliefs and expectations about the Middle East, and filled in with a running account of plausible relationships that will give the event significance in relationship to the others around it. Narratives usually perform such an organizing function. In Sharon Lynn Sperry's words, they transform the "chaos of reality" into some sort of understandable coherence. "Man is," she notes, "a shape maker, a metaphorist, an incorrigible imagist. To know and give order to the world he lives in, man has always devised and shared stories" (Sperry 1981, 297–98). The process of narration blends what we know with what we think, imposing on moments of time a self-contained sequence with a dominant theme. It benefits from our ability to give significance to facts beyond what the facts by themselves may justify. Press critic Tom Wicker recalls satirist Russell Baker's more prosaic description of this impulse to give form to human events. The "ideal" journalism school, Baker noted, would need only one exercise. It would simply require a student "to stand in front of a closed door for six hours, at the end of which the door would open, an official spokesman would look out, and speak two words—'No Comment.' Whereupon the door would close and the student would be required to go to the typewriter and turn out six hundred words against a deadline" (Wicker 1978, 176).

The Rhetorical Attributes of Narration

What are the elements of narration? An internal memo quoted in Edward Epstein's News from Nowhere sums up well how literal the story form may be to practicing television journalists. Its writer, NBC News President Reuven Frank, advised staffers that "every news story should, without any sacrifice of probity or responsibility, display the attributes of fiction, of drama" (Epstein 1974, 241). These attributes should include "conflict, problem and denouement" in the context of "a beginning, middle and end." Similarly, law reporter Fred Graham complained that during his long stint at CBS News nearly every event had to fit the same fundamental mold. Stories on the CBS Evening News "tended to become two-minute morality plays with heroes or villains and a tidy moral, to be summed up at the end. Unfortunately, many important events did not present clearcut heroes, villains or morals, but some CBS correspondents became expert at finding them nevertheless" (Graham 1990, 215).

The same pattern has long been evident in the self-contained stories used in popular newsweeklies. Articles in Time and Newsweek, for example, share with most forms of fiction the careful evocation of settings, characters, and action. Like the concise short story form that they frequently duplicate, they typically define scenes by the characters who populate them, assigning to various characters attributes that have the effect of moving the narrative along. Conflict arises from relationships between these agents and others, or between these agents and even larger forces.[5]

Such a structure for framing human events serves at least three rhetorical purposes. First, it provides a context for our urge to find closure to serious conflicts. That is, it sets in motion a series of events that implicitly play to our need to see some final resolution to a problem. Second, it serves the obvious function of clearing away a good deal of ambiguity about the complex relationships that naturally exist between institutions and people. The narrative helps to construct order out of the natural disorder of everyday life. David Paletz and Robert Entman (1981, 151–58) make a compelling case that the routines of reporting can make political groups seem more organized and purposeful than they really are. While the actions of agencies or city councils may take place amid a variety of cross-purposes and misunderstood information, the reporting on such groups often imposes a coherence that nonjournalist observers do not see. Third and most important, both fictional and factual narratives play to a basic human impulse to judge the actions and motives of others. The story format in all of its manifestations holds the promise of the archetypal biblical parable, inviting us to assess and comment on the choices and options exercised by specific individuals. Walter Fisher has described man as *homo narrans*, the only creature who naturally constructs "advisory discourse" with the purpose of "reconstructing and accounting for" the specific choices and actions of ourselves and others (Fisher 1987, 62). Narration offers cautionary lessons about the moral or immoral nature of the society we inhabit. Whether a president *should* be negotiating with Syrian or Iranian "extremists," for example, is one clear issue that a report constructed about negotiations to free hostages would pose.

News narratives have at least one other important function that turns out to add significantly to the commercial value of news. In ways that are both obvious and mysterious, any information that is conveyed in a narrative context can usually be made to fit into a number of preexisting and comfortable habits of thought. As a way of organizing events for others, narratives provide socially useful ways to impose old myths and stereotypes onto new events. While good reporters are rightfully fearful of playing to gross stereotypes and prejudices, it is far less likely that any storyteller will be able to completely escape the repertory of cultural commonplaces, myths, and shared fantasies that exist in part to give meaning to new information. As Robert Darnton has noted, press "stories must fit cultural preconceptions of news" (1975, 192). News is part of the flow of shared experiences that identify a culture. The writer who ignores cultural norms by constructing narratives that challenge them jeopardizes his outlet's connections to its audience as well as his own career. After working at a New Jersey newspaper, Darnton concluded that journalism often involves finding a delicate balance between telling a compelling story with some surprises and actually issuing challenges that would test the basic beliefs of readers:

A clever writer imposes an old form on a new matter in a way that creates some tension—will the subject fit the predicate?—and then resolves it by falling back on the familiar. . . . The trick will not work if the writer deviates too far from the conceptual repertory that he shares with his public and from the techniques of tapping it that he has learned from his predecessors. (1975, 192)[6]

News, Walter Lippmann (1965) noted, uses a generally limited set of stereotypes and plot lines as suitable angles for most stories. In the context of the 1990s, for example, an American reporter who wanted to venture the observation that the much-despised Iranian government was taking the initiative to find a way to free American hostages would probably have a "tough sell" to his or her producer, whatever the circumstantial evidence indicated. A combination of comfortable stereotypes, old facts, and a sense of shared victimization would restrict how such dissonant information could be offered. What defines an important story is primarily that it is *shared*, not that it is verifiable with some more enduring notion of the Truth (Bormann 1972; Tuchman 1978, 82–132). Narratives proceed from a variety of cultural and personal sources, of which "the facts" are only a part.

Alternatives to the Narrative Style

As pervasive as the narrative impulse is, it is not strictly a requirement for communicating information. Viewers of television's C-SPAN, for example, get unnarrated coverage of the floor action in the House and Senate, along with hearings, panels, and other legislative action. The same may be said for viewers of presidential press conferences, readers of the full text of a presidential message, or observers of unreconstructed political debates. As Hayden White (1981) has noted, narration is not the only way to organize and restate past events. Chronological lists and scientific annals that focus on single dimensions (e.g., events without actors) are different from narration, as are accounts that leave actions literally to speak for themselves, and artifacts such as records of executions, contracts, and bills. There may be times, he notes, when "real events should simply be; they can perfectly well serve as the referents of a discourse, can be spoken about, but they should not pose as the tellers of a narrative" (White 1981, 4).

Yet the impulse to understand events in the framework of storytelling is very strong. When a commercial airliner crashes, for instance, it is not usually defined as an "accident" for very long—at least in the most basic sense of that term. Even when the primary cause stems from natural rather than human agents (such as sudden changes in weather or an encounter with a flock of airborne birds), the narrative soon takes over, and with it, the search for human accountability. A failure of the plane's machinery or a fluke of bad weather leaves us only with a few unsettling facts, without a context for making those facts "mean" something. The resulting stories may serve to transform what are sometimes chance events into human dramas about heroes, victims, and possible villains who contributed to the loss of life. In the process, interestingly, the story will often shift subtly from a retelling of the facts of the crash to a narrative about political and moral culpability. Was the Federal Aviation Administration lax in checking on safety procedures? Did the president give the FAA the money it requested? Was the airline's management too concerned with profits to provide adequate pilot training? To be sure, such questions may be justified by solid evidence. What is important to note here is that narration carries its own requirement to frame events in the context of purposive agents engaged in conflict or conciliation.[7]

THE RITUALS OF NARRATION: SUBTLE ISSUES OF FAIRNESS

Most discussions of journalistic ethics deal with what are now reasonably clear standards of conduct involving possible conflicts of interest, violations of privacy, questionable assertions, and balance (Christians, Rotzoll, and Fackler 1987; Goldstein 1985; Gomber and Moyne 1986). But beyond these fundamental concerns about intellectual honesty and accuracy remains a less obvious range of issues that arise from the narrative model. Challenges to journalistic fairness, note Steven Klaidman and Tom Beauchamp, "encompass impartial treatment, bias, incompleteness, imbalance, and numerous similar subjects" (1987, 21). In the context of this limited study we turn to specific patterns of reporting that raise questions about the structural requirements of narration which would seem to make fairness an unattainable goal. They include the tendency to let narrators dominate stories, the tendency to equalize opposing views, and a bias that leads to the personalization rather than the bureaucratization of ideas. Our objective here is not to settle on a comprehensive definition of journalistic fairness but to explore whether the neutrality that it implies obscures the inherently rhetorical nature of storytelling.

Whose Story Is It?

The issue of *whose* point of view gets expressed in a particular instance of political reporting is obviously at the core of any discussion of accuracy. In a sense, the question answers itself. While a reporter in any medium negotiates a variety of perspectives in the process of putting together a story, in the end he/she or his/her surrogates will control the outcome of the news-gathering act. The rhetorical skills of most newsmakers are largely secondary to the near-total control of form and substance that reporting often permits. Journalism is but another form of portraiture. It requires the selective reconstruction of a reality from a broad palette of materials.

Consider the following summary of a story by ABC's Brit Hume several days before the 1988 presidential election:

We see a police car skidding dramatically in a demonstration of high-speed-chase training. Cut to a watchful [George] Bush. We see patrol cars driving in formation. Cut to Bush. Cut to a new scene of candidate surrounded by cheering uniformed cops, receiving plaque from beefy officer. Officer: "America's number one crimefighter award!" Finally, we hear Bush's attack line: "The [Democratic] leadership, much of it, is a remnant of the sixties, the New Left, those campus radicals. . . . "

Meanwhile, in his voice over, Hume all but mocks the contrived proceedings: "Bush didn't get to go to Disneyland today, but given the enthusiasm he's shown for law enforcement in this campaign, he probably thought the place he did go was even better. . . . Bush didn't go on the rides they have here, but watched with obvious interest and later he got some prizes—a jacket and a cap. (Boot 1989, 26)

The rituals and formulas of the news narrative are intact in this piece. Editing links the prime figure of the story—candidate George Bush—to an interesting and photogenic locale. A small amount of time is reserved for a brief sample of what Bush said, and the piece predictably closes with the reporter telling us what it all means, with the strong suggestion that the event was contrived as an opportunity to generate good pictures and to support a noncontroversial cause. Most campaign and political reporting follows this format, with differences of depth rather than of kind as we move from television to extended forms of print.

If we think about who fundamentally *owns* this story, the answer must be that it is—in large part—ABC's. This is not to suggest that the network falsified what happened. Bush was surely intent on creating the event that would provide the raw materials for the coverage, but the actual presentation of the narrative belongs to ABC's field producer for the piece, his editor, and Hume, who constructed a frame of reference for understanding the Bush visit. Commercial television especially makes the reporter the key presence in most stories, and requires a point of view that can establish significance and meaning in a short period of time. Indeed, in a typical 45- or 90-second story the reporter will probably be on camera longer than any of the subjects that the piece is ostensibly about. Such is the bias of the narrative form that it encourages distanced reporting *about* events rather than coverage *of* events.

This last point brings us face to face with a very practical prescription about fairness that deserves more attention. Serious news reporting of political leaders and those affected by their decisions should include substantial segments of their own rhetoric. There is something fundamentally wrong with reporting that has the effect of making the subject of a story subordinate to the twin exigencies of narration and celebrity journalism. The ostensible objects of reporting should not be reduced to actors in dramas created by others. They ought to have the opportunity to communicate their own agenda in their own way. In Larry Gross's words, "groups should be allowed to speak for themselves" (1988, 191). Gross analyzed network coverage of homosexual issues in several CBS news documentaries, noting that the producers rarely yielded their firm grasp of the flow and pacing of their programs to the ostensible subjects. In one *CBS Reports* program entitled "The Homosexual," for example, narrator and co-writer Mike Wallace rarely allowed his subjects the luxury of developing their own thoughts. Psychiatric experts were interviewed to comment on the mental and physical health of gay men, and confirmed homosexuals were queried on their fate as "displaced" and "anonymous" outsiders. Gross's point was not just that this approach was ideologically biased against its subjects—the traditional complaint made against much reporting—but also that it held to an unyielding formula which allowed the narrator to completely frame the context in which the subjects of news stories were portrayed.

Had Gross searched for a different model, he probably could have done no better than to contrast the structure of CBS's coverage with Robert Epstein's 1985 documentary, *The Times of Harvey Milk.* Epstein's Oscar-winning study is openly sympathetic to the gay San Francisco politician who was murdered, along with Mayor George Moscone, by a member of the city's Board of Supervisors. It has clear political points to make on behalf of the gay movement. But neutrality or the lack of it is not the issue here. What is fundamentally different about Epstein's film is its willingness to allow its subjects relatively extended moments of discussion on camera. Its narrator, Harvey Fierstein, remains off-camera, and his sparse narration is secondary to footage of a wide range of friends and colleagues who are allowed to have their say about their experiences and contacts with Milk.

When politicians make complaints similar to Gross's about heavy-handed editing, we tend to dismiss their objections as the laments of people who would turn news stories into extended commercials. But many of these criticisms have a substantive point. In 1984, for example, Democratic presidential candidate George McGovern noted that his announcement to enter the race rated little more than a "put-down" from CBS. His statement was minimized in favor of a colorful "tell" story about the leader who had been the Democratic Party's nominee in 1972.

Dan Rather and Bruce Morton of CBS gave a brief scoffing account of my September 13 announcement on the news that evening which included the information that "when he ran in 1972, junior staff members called him 'McGoo.' " After the barest possible reference to my differences on the issues with the other candidates, Morton devoted the balance of his brief commentary to my wife's reservations about another campaign. (McGovern 1984, 29)

Admittedly, television has a restricted news agenda created by very limited time. And certainly there is an obvious need for reporting the evaluations and comments on the claims of public officials. Even so, McGovern and the CBS viewers probably would have been better served by replacing correspondent Morton's observations with more precious seconds devoted to the candidate's stated reasons for seeking the presidency. We have less to fear from politicians who would use their rhetoric to mislead the public than from popular versions of news that no longer treat substantive public discourse as the centerpiece of reporting.

It is instructive to observe how much time is actually spent on the ideas and remarks of major news sources. In 1980 Michael Robinson and Margaret Sheehan identified a pattern of compressed reporting of actual messages that has since made the "sound bite" a notorious villain of most presidential campaigns. Their exhaustive analysis of the coverage of CBS and United Press International over five days in September reveals that incumbent Jimmy Carter gave 8 public speeches and interviews, for a total 1,135 sentences that could have been reported. From all of this material CBS actually quoted only 16 sentences, less than 2 percent of the public remarks available to them. Such "heavy editing," they wrote, "renders hollow the year-long editorial complaint that Carter was hiding and not giving the press a chance to get at him . . ." (Robinson and Sheehan 1983, 59). A comparative study of the 1968 and 1988 campaigns by Harvard sociologist Kiku Adatto found a similar pattern. Considering all of the networks in those years, Adatto discovered that the average length of a quote from George Bush or Michael Dukakis in 1988 was only 9.8 seconds, down from an average of 42.3 seconds in the 1968 campaign that pitted Hubert Humphrey against Richard Nixon. He also found that the total length of time devoted to quotes dropped significantly between 1968 and 1988 (Rothenberg 1990, E4). It seems that television campaign reporting uses direct quotes from the campaign trail largely as decoration, something added to lend at least a veneer of authenticity to the reporter's story.

This problem of limited coverage and enormous compression of what is covered is even more apparent when journalistic accounts of the actions of Congress are studied. In spite of the fact that video coverage has been permitted in the House of Representatives since 1979, a Vanderbilt News Archives analysis notes that congressional stories have actually been on the decrease. The number of segments about Congress offered by the three television networks dropped by 50 percent between the late 1970s and 1984 (Schneiders 1985, 44). The reason is hardly a mystery. Most correspondents covering Capitol Hill know that legislative stories amounting to more than brief headlines are a "hard sell" to their program's producers. Networks would rather show almost anything than several minutes of congressional debate. One of the few exceptions in broadcast television is PBS's *MacNeil/Lehrer Newshour*, which routinely explores major policy debates by inviting leaders to discuss their differences in 15- or 20-minute segments.

In his analysis of Gary Hart's 1984 race for the presidency, Mark Crispin Miller identified a similar pattern of substituting narration *about* events for coverage *of* them. In Miller's view, the video press in particular used its well-cultivated "pretense of uninvolvement" to work harder on a narrative angle for the Colorado Democrat than on the more straightforward task of relaying his substantive messages. That Hart had something to say, Miller notes, was evident to any reader of a comprehensive newspaper. But he was the victim of a "schizophrenic" pose by television journalists who "played deaf to his positions, while writing stories on his muteness":

For instance, just after his first successes, the newsmen began to peg their stories on this burning rhetorical question: "Will Hart be able to get his message across?" The answer was implicit in the question, and the answer was "no." So long as TV newsmen are wondering aloud about any candidate's so called "message," that message isn't going to come across, since it's up to them to find it out and tell us about it. . . . Through that dishonest question, the newsmen managed, in one deft stroke, both to withhold his "message" and to blame Hart for their silence. (Miller 1988, 103)

The common reply which television executives make to complaints that they emphasize events over substance is that all forms of popular media need variety and pacing. Audiences, they note, will not tolerate patterns of presentation that diverge significantly from the commercial and entertainment environment that makes up most of television's content. In Robert MacNeil's words, network news has "not escaped the tyranny of show business ideas of pacing. To be dull is worse than being informative" (1968, 36). But it is not always necessary to make stories longer or uninteresting in order to be faithful to the ideas of those whom journalists seek to represent. Sometimes the simple substitution of a sustained quote of an advocate's message for the time-consuming ritual of storytelling can be helpful. Such substitutions are hardly new to television or other media. They exist in forms as complex as Fredrick Wiseman's award-winning no-narration documentaries (Wilkes 1988), or as simple as the decision of a newspaper to publish the complete transcript of an interview.

Presumably, political journalism is fundamentally about ideas more than about the strategic maneuvering that is plotted in such detail by many contemporary reporters. It may well be that fear of being "taken in" by a political agent carries its own antidote which triggers an intentionally distanced narrative. Political journalists are now extremely sensitive to charges that have been made by press critics Tim Crouse (1972), Mark Hertsgaard (1989), and Edward Herman and Noam Chomsky (1988) that they are the tools of political elites: hapless accomplices of "spin doctors" and media specialists who know how to manage the news. Their defense is to lay down limits that restrict the possibilities for presenting and amplifying anyone's political position. In the process they claim at least an ersatz kind of objectivity; they "own" their stories and they carefully signal it to their wary viewers and readers. A defiant refusal to extensively report what a leader says, along with commentary or visual imagery that undercuts what is reported, produces a superficial form of political journalism. But there is no doubt that it often plays well to the general antipolitical bias that dominates the views of Americans who buy newspapers and consume the products that television wants to sell.

On the Outside Looking in

Too much can be made of the value of objectivity. All observation carries the bias of some perspective. Taken from its literal visual roots, a "perspective" requires someone to be in a particular place: if not in a physical sense, then at least in temporal or ideological terms. The very term is a useful reminder that we are always somewhere—not everywhere—and that narration involves observation from a position that is often on the outside looking in. Hence, the idea of "point of view" ought to be a given in discussions of reporting; it should not be the defining characteristic of a suspicious form of journalism.

Too often the "problem" of perspective is solved with an operational approach to objectivity that involves the portrayal of equal but opposite adversaries. An adversarial framework makes it possible to report by using a safe kind of neutrality, a neutrality that functions on a sort of "zero-sum" formula. In this pattern the viewpoints of opposing sides are offered, both are suggested to have some merit, and the narrator closes with a well-framed description of a standoff that suggests his or her impartiality. An important rhetorical consequence of this common pattern is the implicit suggestion of equivalency. The subtext of such reporting frequently leaves the impression that various factions in a controversy have claims that are more or less equal in their merits and limitations. Thus the "zero-sum" formula implies that there are at least two sides to an issue and that each side can claim only partial validity.

Thus, when political advertising scholar Kathleen Jamieson appeared on talk programs to discuss distorted television ads in the 1988 campaign, inevitably the networks included an equal number of examples from the Dukakis and Bush campaigns. This enforced balance, Jamieson noted, gave the false impression that the commercials from both sides were "equally sleazy and unfair." The truth was more complex. "It was difficult . . . to make the point that Bush's ads were, one, effective and, two, lies, and that Dukakis's ads were, one, ineffective, and two, truthful" (Boot 1989, 28).

It is an undeniable fact of open societies that the presentation of countervailing views is important. The dialectic of campaigns and policy debates is enriched when a number of views are offered. But rarely are events or different positions so neat as the zero-sum formula for reporting would suggest, a fact that frequently explains why television portrayals of domestic political crises—Watergate and Iran-Contra, to name two—have been so slow to communicate the accumulated evidence against the operatives involved.[8]

The Personalistic Presumption

Between the early months of 1988 and the spring of 1990, Americans saw a trickle of reports about bank failures in the Southwest suddenly turn into a torrent of stories about greed, theft, and financial mismanagement. What had been a crisis in the making for nearly ten years was belatedly the subject of widespread news coverage, and the facts were numbing. Hundreds of savings banks had gone broke and were taken over by the government. A confluence of causes played roles in this collapse. The economy was not as robust as managers of thrift institutions had hoped, but many had sown the seeds of their own destruction through a combination of bad loans, fraud, and gross incompetence. An industry that had been designed primarily to hold federally insured deposits and issue home mortgages had instead gone on a binge of risky ventures in office buildings, junk bonds, and corporate spending. By May of 1990, the General Accounting Office estimated a cost to taxpayers of between $325 and $500 billion, or about $5,000 for every household (Rosenbaum 1990, D4).

Americans expressed shock and surprise at the scandal, wondering how it was allowed to happen. More than a few asked where the press had been. Why hadn't the bad loans been discovered sooner? Why was there little discussion of congressional inaction or the regulators who had been charged with keeping tabs on the financial health of the banks? As Harvard's Ellen Hume (1990) asked, why was the press that was able to report on presidential candidate Gary Hart's sexual infidelities or Vice President Dan Quayle's modest academic record not able to see the coming of this enormous debacle? Part of the answer, Hume noted, was in the nature of this crisis. It was not easily portrayed in the familiar framework of network news, which routinely uses the dramatic actions of people as windows on most events.

It was a numbers story, not a "people" story. While the trade press . . . reported important developments in the scandal years ago, it was all too complicated and boring to interest many mainstream journalists. . . . Financial stories are particularly hard for television. A reporter or candidate competing to create the most memorable sound bite wasn't about to get one with the thrift question. When asked why TV hadn't covered the crisis much even after it made headlines in 1988, the President of NBC News, Michael Gartner, observed that the story didn't lend itself to images, and without such images, "television can't do facts." (Hume 1990, A25)

Television journalism is—in Richard Sennett's fitting phrase—" 'compulsively' personalistic, always making the private life of the politician the center of interest" (1978, 284). It is the natural bias of the medium to place people in the middle of events, not on the periphery. Television finds it difficult to amplify complex ideas without anchoring them in specific events or personalities. Like drama in general, the medium usually considers abstract ideas as expressions coming through a specific persona. Print may handle concepts in their own terms: as abstractions sustained through the complementary abstraction that is language itself. On television, however, ideas typically emerge only as factors that motivate specific agents. For instance, a print journalist may feel comfortable discussing a Supreme Court decision on an individual state's capital punishment statute largely in terms of the principles involved. The details of the specific criminal case that triggered the ruling may be secondary to the article's description of the Court's reasoning. The video counterpart of such a story, however, is more likely to overlay any discussion of those principles with graphic pictures that take viewers back to the horror of the crime which initiated the Court's deliberations, with all of its attendant anger and grief. Every broadcast needs such "moments," CBS's Van Gordon Sauter once preached to his news staff (Boyer 1988, 139). Large audiences could be gained only if news stories touched people at a visceral level. As Peter Boyer described the former CBS News chief's doctrine,

There were no *moments* to be found in a minute-fifteen report on unemployment told by a CBS News correspondent standing outside the Department of Labor in Washington, D.C. There was, however, a moment of the highest sort as the CBS News camera studied the strained and expectant face of a young Pittsburgh mother as she stood (babe in arms) beside an employment line as her husband asked for a job. (Boyer 1988, 139)

As the formulas of television news have been defined since the 1950s, news content is routinely focused more on presentational rather than on discursive communication (Meyrowitz 1985, 94–95). Television *shows* rather than *explains*, shunning general descriptions of anything in favor of the riveting specifics of an event and someone's response to it. It favors dwelling on the faces of grieving crime victims over the summation of crime statistics, on moments of interpersonal conflict rather than on sustained portrayals of consensus building, and on defining aspects of a specific personality over generalizations about groups. Television gives us vivid pictorial referents to events that require no specialized knowledge or abstract reasoning, a fact that is reflected in the language of video production. "Reaction shots," "two-shots," and "close-ups" explicitly invite viewers to consider the expressive aspects of an individual's persona. In a Mike Wallace interview, for example, we may be more impressed by his guest's anger than by the substantive reasons provided for it. In ways that are sometimes quite subtle, we believe that the cues we observe can act as a window on the soul, revealing far more than the disembodied words of the printed page. It is little wonder that the major networks continue to assign more reporters and air time to the presidency than to the Congress or the Supreme Court (Broder 1987, 202), or that popular news programs (*60 Minutes, Barbara Walters Specials, 20/20*) emphasize extended interrogatories taken in tight close-up. As many analysts of political news have noted, a story organized around a single figure is much easier to construct than one that attempts to shed light on institutions or ideas (Minow, Martin, and Mitchell 1973; Grossman and Kumar 1981).

Even television journalism's fascination with the results of political polls has some of its roots in this pattern. Rather than amplifying ideas, the presence of poll results often has the effect of providing conclusions without reasons: declarations about "winning" and "losing" candidates, descriptions of causes that are now in or out of favor, and lists of issues that have the support of specific types of people (Kalb 1988). Polls commissioned by news organizations do a better job of communicating attitudes about issues than the underlying rationales for those attitudes. Their appeal is partly the appeal of narratives in general. While they are represented in numbers that have the aura of hard fact, they also provide a kind of contingent closure that all narratives need. If a campaign is not completely over until Election Day, it can at least be written as a drama of several acts as new polls track the rise and fall of major figures.

All of this would seem to suggest that we are vainly attempting to hold broadcast journalism to standards about completeness of policy discussion that better apply to print. If this is the case, a reasonable question arises. Is it fair or profitable to hold journalists in one medium to criteria that are largely derived from another medium? The answer must be "yes," for two reasons.

First, television may add new kinds of personalistic information to what was once a subject dominated by discursive media, but that does not excuse its ignoring the enduring responsibilities that come with the task of representing events and ideas. Some standards for what constitutes substantive and worthwhile reporting are rightly independent of specific media (Christians, Rotzoll, and Fackler 1987, 1–22; Broder 1987, 306–67). In addition, too many successful examples of idea-centered coverage exist in the video format to dismiss television as incapable of dealing with public policy issues.[9] It is not unreasonable or hopelessly romantic to expect that the requirements of responsible political journalism should come first, prior to the natural tendencies of a medium. That "form should follow function" is a principle of undeniable utility in a wide range of endeavors, but it has its limits. In the 1930s a similar dictum led to the modernist impulse in architecture, and eventually to scores of austere commercial skyscrapers that now tower like massive undecorated tombstones over their urban surroundings. The analogous pattern in commercial television—where the function of entertainment undeniably dictates its form—has much the same effect. What may distract us or demand our attention may finally be very different from what we actually need as members of political and social communities. If the special status given the Fourth Estate means anything, it defines what amounts to a special franchise—with an important constitutional protection—to provide information and ideas that contribute to the public and civil life of the nation. Presenting difficult choices, communicating the substance of political debate, and exploring the social origins of problems should remain the goals of political journalism. Because it is a linchpin of a functioning representative democracy, political intelligence has an educative function that justifiably includes providing citizens with what they *need* to know, not just what they *want* to know.

Second, television journalism is dogged by the unwarranted insistence that its success should be measured in largely commercial terms. It is an old but valid observation that ratings lie at the heart of this problem, arguably playing a larger role in affecting television content than circulation figures play in altering the news agendas of daily newspapers.[10] Ratings have always been a notorious addiction of those responsible for producing popular entertainment; but they have a far more questionable role when they begin to affect what will be offered to the public as issues of public policy they need to consider. The prospect that many readers will not look at an article about an experimental public housing program in Boston may not stop an editor from including it in a major newspaper. But such a story is an unusual exception if it surfaces as a feature in a network newscast. The commercial logic of television news is now virtually the same as that in prime time, dominated by a concern to keep the viewer's hand away from the channel selector. It is hardly surprising that what now frequently passes for news at the local level closely approximates the content and narrative form of the evening entertainment schedule: "police blotter journalism," dramatic confrontations, and disasters (Westin 1982, 208–9). Fires, accidents, murders, and grisly descriptions of sexual assaults act as a sponge on most available news time, leading CBS's Charles Kuralt to observe that "television news, as it is practiced in most places, is not the field in which a serious journalist would wish to live" (Wright n.d.).

There is an obvious validity to expressions of concern about holding audiences, attracting advertisers, and engaging in thoughtful reporting. But it still surprises many inside and outside the news industry that broadcast journalism should *have* to function as a profit source within the industry. Most networks and stations have a long broadcast day and an ample supply of entertainment programs to improve their profit margins. In addition, it is worth remembering that unacceptably low viewer ratings for serious news programs still represent huge audiences. Their ratings are frequently "low" only in comparison with the escapist fare that other broadcasters program against them. A "dismal" national rating of 2, for example, means that 2 percent of the approximately 85 million "TV households" in the United States are estimated to have tuned in to a particular program. At the current average of 2.3 viewers per household, such a figure translates into an audience of almost 4 million people. Only in the peculiar environment of U.S. television would this be considered a negligible audience. There was a time at both CBS and NBC when serious news shows were largely exempted from the requirement to match the audiences that readily exist for entertainment programming (Graham 1990, 206–8). Edward R. Murrow's warning to news directors in 1958 is a still a sobering jeremiad about incompatible journalistic allegiances:

One of the basic troubles with radio and television news is that both instruments have grown up as an incompatible combination of show business, advertising, and news. Each of the three is a rather bizarre and demanding profession. And when you get all three under one roof, the dust never settles. The top management of the networks, with a few notable exceptions, has been trained in advertising, research, sales, or show business. But by the nature of the corporate structure, they also make the final and crucial decisions having to do with news and public affairs. (Murrow 1958, 34)

SUMMARY

Journalists are peculiarly a part of the political process: at once independent of the individuals and institutions they cover, and equally tied to an expectant and overlapping constituency of consumers. Recognizing that most political information comes through someone's journalistic gate, this chapter has explored several issues raised by the conventions and commercial needs of political news gatherers. It has argued in part that members of the press have overlooked the need to recognize their own rhetorical and political roots.

In many ways, the central dilemma of political journalism is how to meet requirements for completeness against huge and often unreasonable limits on time and space. The problem is compounded by the narrative form, which serves as the archetype for most kinds of reporting. Narration carries a number of requirements that are also limitations, including:

- an emphasis on reporting *about* agents and events rather than the ideas of political argument
- a pattern of framing public policy issues through the narrowing context of advocates, and real or potential victims
- a tendency to find protection against charges of bias by making issue advocacy appear to involve participants with more or less equally valid positions
- in the case of television, a nearly crippling fascination with the expressive content of nearly all human interaction.

In many ways this last problem is representative of the issues raised here. A commercially driven incentive to frame political ideas largely through the perspective of the traumas and triumphs of individual agents unmistakably plays to a lucrative form of mass voyeurism, but sometimes at the expense of sustained discussion of important issues.

ACKNOWLEDGMENTS

Gary Woodward wishes to thank Karen Greenberg and Robert Cole for their suggestions on an early draft of this chapter, and the Trenton State College Faculty and Institutional Research Committee for research support.

NOTES

1. Many codes of ethics exist. See, for example, Klaidman and Beauchamp (1987, 59–75) and the codes of ethics cited by Swain (1978, 111–34).

2. For example, in her popular guide to the realpolitik of modern television news, *And So It Goes*, Linda Ellerbee made it clear that what she did at NBC and elsewhere made her very much a part of the marketing function of television.

Please remember that in television the product is not the program; the product is the audience and the consumer of that product is the advertiser. The advertiser does not "buy" a news program. He buys an audience. The manufacturer (network) that gets the highest price for the product is the one that produces the most product (audience). It might be said that the value of any news program is measured by whether it increases productivity; the best news program, therefore, is the one watched by the greatest number of people. (Ellerbee 1987, 101)

3. It would be an unusual household that did not have easy access to all or most of the following news outlets: CBS, NBC, ABC, CNN, PBS, National Public Radio, a local paper carrying UPI or AP wire service reports, and one national newsmagazine. Beyond these, a second tier of periodicals of opinion and analysis exists in great number, ranging from *The Atlantic* to *Commonweal*.

4. Although cable television's CNN has made some inroads into the major networks' news audiences, network television news remains a major source of national news for most Americans. See, for example, Roper polls summarized in Denton and Woodward (1990, 163).

5. Consider the scene-setting short-story form built into the first sentences of *Time* and *Newsweek* articles dealing with controversial television programs: "The taping was only 20 minutes old, and Phil Donahue was agitated. Not because of a raging controversy over abortion or the death penalty; the trouble with this particular show, featuring a studio audience of Moscow teenagers, was the absence of any controversy at all" (Zoglin 1987, 79); "It was Halloween week, and the electronic jack-o'lantern was casting a decidedly weird spell. On NBC, the mini-series "Favorite Son" showed sadomasochistic bondage, near explicit masturbation and a dog lapping up the blood of a murder victim. On ABC, a made-for-TV movie focused on a psychotic father setting fire to his sleeping son" (Waters 1988, 72). For background on the writing style of the newsweeklies, see Friedrich (1964), Newman (1966), and Carmody (1990).

6. Darnton's perspective also points out the inadequacy of simple ideas about fact and fiction in reporting. For example, in his thoughtful analysis of the modern press, David Broder notes that "the most flagrant category of professional sins" involves "passing off fiction for fact" (1987, 309). He obviously means that falsehoods should not be presented as facts. And yet the very term "fiction" subtly deflects attention away from what has been described here as a common part of the journalist's enterprise. Just as it is self-evident that the facts must be selected prior to being reported, so it also follows that the *form* of fiction will have some effect on the substance of reporting.

7. The importance we normally attach to purposive action in place of "sheer motion" is explained by Kenneth Burke (1968) as part of a general theory of dramatism.

8. For a general discussion on the rhetorical uses of objectivity, see Bennett (1988, 118–23).

9. PBS's *MacNeil/Lehrer Newshour*, ABC's *Nightline*, and CNN's coverage of major political stories have been widely—if not universally—lauded. Also, every year many winners of Alfred I. DuPont/Columbia University Awards in broadcast journalism serve as reminders that many local and national broadcasters have pushed past the bounds of formulaic television news to cover topics with depth and sensitivity. For a representative listing of such programs see Barrett (1982, 156–59).

10. Consider the 1961 remarks of former FCC Chairman Newton Minow to a group of broadcast executives:

You know, newspaper publishers take popularity ratings too. The answers are pretty clear: it is almost always the comics, followed by the advice to the lovelorn columns. But, ladies and gentlemen, the news is still on the front page of all newspapers, the editorials are not replaced by more comics, the newspapers have not become one long collection of advice to the lovelorn. (Minow 1964, 276)

REFERENCES

Altheide, David L. 1976. *Creating Reality: How TV News Distorts Events*. Beverly Hills, CA: Sage.

Bagdikian, Ben H. 1990. *The Media Monopoly*, 3rd ed. Boston: Beacon Press.

Barrett, Marvin. 1982. *Broadcast Journalism, 1979–1981*. New York: Everest.

Bennett, W. Lance. 1988. *News: The Politics of Illusion*, 2nd ed. New York: Longman.

Boot, William. 1989. Campaign 88: TV Overdoses on the Inside Dope. *Columbia Journalism Review* 27 (January/February): 23–29.

Bormann, Ernest G. 1972. Fantasy and Rhetorical Vision: The Rhetorical Criticism of Social Reality. *Quarterly Journal of Speech* 58:396–407.

Boyer, Peter J. 1988. *Who Killed CBS?* New York: Random House.

Broder, David. 1987. *Beyond the Front Page*. New York: Simon and Schuster.

Burke, Kenneth. 1968. Dramatism. In *International Encyclopedia of the Social Sciences*, vol. 7, pp. 445–52. New York: Free Press.

Bush, George. 1990. Transcript of Bush News Conference on Noriega and Panama. *New York Times*, January 6, p. A10.

Carmody, Deirdre. 1990. Time Speaking with New Voice. *New York Times*, June 4, pp. C1, C7.

Christians, Clifford G., Kim B. Rotzoll, and Mark Fackler. 1987. *Media Ethics: Cases in Moral Reasoning*, 2nd ed. New York: Longman.

Crouse, Timothy. 1972. *The Boys on the Bus*. New York: Ballantine.

Darnton, Robert. 1975. Writing News and Telling Stories. *Daedalus* 104:175–94.

Denton, Robert E., Jr., and Gary C. Woodward. 1990. *Political Communication in America*, 2nd ed. New York: Praeger.

Ellerbee, Linda. 1987. *And So It Goes: Adventures in Television*. New York: Berkley Books.

Epstein, Edward Jay. 1974. *News from Nowhere*. New York: Vintage.

Fisher, Walter R. 1987. *Human Communication as Narration: Toward a Philosophy of Reason, Value and Action*. Columbia: University of South Carolina Press.

Fishman, Mark. 1980. *Manufacturing the News*. Austin: University of Texas Press.

Friedrich, Otto. 1964. There Are 00 Trees in Russia: The Function of Facts in Newsmagazines. *Harpers* (October): 59–65.

Gans, Herbert J. 1980. *Deciding What's News: A Study of CBS Evening News, NBC Nightly News, Newsweek and Time*. New York: Vintage.

Gerard, Jeremy. 1990. President Complains About TV's Use of Split Images. *New York Times*, January 6, p. 11.

Goldstein, Tom. 1985. *The News at Any Cost*. New York: Simon and Schuster.

Gomber, Mary Anne, and Robert S. Moyne. 1986. *The Newsmongers: How the Media Distort Political News*. Toronto: McClelland and Stewart.

Graber, Doris. 1989. *Mass Media and American Politics*, 3rd ed. Washington: Congressional Quarterly Press.

Graham, Fred. 1990. *Happy Talk: Confessions of a TV Newsman*. New York: W. W. Norton.

Greenfield, Jeff. 1986. Ethics: For Wimps Only? In Doug Ramsey and Dale Ellen Shaps, eds., *Journalism Ethics: Why Change?*, pp. 48–53. Los Angeles: Foundation for American Communication.

Gross, Larry. 1988. The Ethics of (Mis)representation. In Larry Gross, John Stuart Katz, and Jay Ruby, eds., *Image Ethics: The Moral Rights of Subjects in Photographs, Film and Television*, pp. 188–202. New York: Oxford University Press.

Grossman, Michael Baruch, and Martha Joynt Kumar. 1981. *Portraying the President: The White House and the News Media*. Baltimore: Johns Hopkins University Press.

Hackett, Robert A. 1984. Decline of a Paradigm?: Bias and Objectivity in News Media Studies. *Critical Studies in Mass Communication* 1:229–59.

Herman, Edward S., and Noam Chomsky. 1988. *Manufacturing Consent: The Political Economy of the Mass Media*. New York: Pantheon.

Hertsgaard, Mark. 1989. *On Bended Knee: The Press and the Reagan Presidency*. New York: Schocken.

Hume, Ellen. 1990. Why the Press Blew the S & L Scandal. *New York Times*, May 24, p. A25.

Kalb, Marvin. 1988. Looking for Better Ways to Run Elections. *New York Times*, November 13, p. 3.

Klaidman, Steven, and Tom L. Beauchamp. 1987. *The Virtuous Journalist*. New York: Oxford University Press.

Lippmann, Walter. 1965. *Public Opinion*. New York: Free Press.

MacNeil, Robert. 1968. *The People Machine: The Influence of Television on American Politics*. New York: Harper & Row.

McGovern, George. 1984. George McGovern: The Target Talks Back. *Columbia Journalism Review* 22 (July–August): 27–31.

Meyrowitz, Joshua. 1985. *No Sense of Place*. New York: Oxford University Press.

Miller, Mark Crispin. 1988. *Boxed in: The Culture of TV*. Evanston, IL: Northwestern University Press.

Minow, Newton. 1964. The Vast Wasteland. In Glen E. Mills, ed., *Reason in Controversy*, pp. 27–82. Boston: Allyn and Bacon.

Minow, Newton N., John Bartlow Martin, and Lee M. Mitchell. 1973. *Presidential Television*. New York: Basic Books.

Murrow, Edward R. 1958. A Broadcaster Talks to His Colleagues. *The Reporter*, November 13, pp. 32–36.

Newman, Robert P. 1966. The Weekly Fiction Magazines. *Central States Speech Journal* 17:118–24.

Nimmo, Dan. 1989. Episodes, Incidents, and Eruptions. *American Behavioral Scientist* 32:464–78.

Nimmo, Dan, and James E. Combs. 1985. *Nightly Horrors: Crisis Coverage in Television Network News*. Knoxville: University of Tennessee Press.

Paletz, David L., and Robert M. Entman. 1981. *Media Power Politics*. New York: Free Press.

Robinson, Michael J., and Margaret A. Sheehan. 1983. *Over the Wire and on TV*. New York: Russell Sage Foundation.

Rosenbaum, David E. 1990. A Financial Disaster with Many Culprits. *New York Times*, June 6, p. D4.

Rothenberg, Randall. 1990. Politics on TV: Too Fast, Too Loose? *New York Times*, July 15, p. E4.

Schneiders, Greg. 1985. The 90 Second Handicap: Why TV Coverage of Legislation Falls Short. *Washington Journalism Review* 7:44–46.

Sennett, Richard. 1978. *The Fall of Public Man*. New York: Vintage.

Smith, Craig R. 1977. Television News as Rhetoric. *Western Journal of Speech Communication* 41:147–59.

Sperry, Sharon Lynn. 1981. Television News as Narrative. In Richard P. Adler, ed., *Understanding Television: Essays on Television as a Cultural Force*, pp. 295–312. New York: Praeger.

Swain, Bruce M. 1978. *Reporters' Ethics*. Ames: Iowa State University Press.

Tuchman, Gaye. 1978. *Making News: A Study in the Construction of Reality*. New York: Free Press.

Waters, Harry. 1988. Trash TV. *Newsweek*, November 14, p. 72.

Weigert, Andrew J. 1970. The Immoral Rhetoric of Scientific Sociology. *The American Sociologist* 5:111–19.

Westin, Av. 1982. *News-Watch: How TV Decides the News*. New York: Simon and Schuster.

White, Hayden. 1981. The Value of Narrativity in the Representation of Reality. In W. J. T. Mitchell, ed., *On Narrative*, pp. 1–24. Chicago: University of Chicago Press.

Wicker, Tom. 1978. *On Press*. New York: Viking Press.

Wilkes, Paul. 1988. Documentarian Offers Viewers a Challenge. *New York Times*, June 19, Sec. 2, p. 31.

Wright, William F. n.d. TV Newsman Dumps on TV News. In Don Fry, ed., *Believing the News*, pp. 223–25. St. Petersburg, FL: Poynter Institute for Media Studies.

Zoglin, Richard. 1987. Stirring up the Comrades. *Time*, February 16, p. 79.

Selected Bibliography

Abramson, Jeffrey, F. Christopher Arterton, and Gary Orren. 1988. *The Electronic Commonwealth*. New York: Basic Books.

Adler, Mortimer J. 1970. *The Time of Our Lives: The Ethics of Common Sense*. New York: Holt, Rinehart and Winston.

———. 1988. *Reforming Education: The Opening of the American Mind*. New York: Holt, Rinehart and Winston.

Albert, J. A. 1986. The Remedies Available to Candidates Who Are Defamed by Television or Radio Commercials of Opponents. *Vermont Law Review* 11:33–73.

Alderman, Harold. 1982. By Virtue of a Virtue. *Review of Metaphysics* 36 (September): 127–53.

Altheide, David L. 1976. *Creating Reality: How TV News Distorts Events*. Beverly Hills, CA: Sage.

Altheide, David, and Robert Snow. 1979. *Media Logic*. Beverly Hills, CA: Sage.

American Association of Political Consultants. 1990. *Code of Professional Ethics*. Washington, DC: AAPC.

Andersen, K. E. 1984. Communication Ethics: The Non-participant's Role. *Southern Speech Communication Journal* 49:219–28.

———. 1989. The Politics of Ethics and the Ethics of Politics. *American Behavioral Scientist* 32:479–92.

Archibald, S. J., ed. 1971. *The Pollution of Politics*. Washington, DC: Public Affairs Press.

Arendt, Hannah. 1958. *The Human Condition*. Chicago: University of Chicago Press.

Aristotle. 1943. *Politics*. Trans. Benjamin Jowett. New York: Modern Library.

———. 1954. *Rhetoric*. Trans. W. Rhys Roberts. New York: Modern Library.

Armstrong, Richard. 1988. *The Next Hurrah: The Communications Revolution in American Politics*. New York: Beech Tree Books.

Arnowitz, Stanley. 1987. Postmodernism and Politics. *Social Text* 18:99–115.

Arterton, Christopher. 1984. *Media Politics*. Lexington, MA: Lexington Books.

Bailey, F. G. 1988. *Humbuggery and Manipulation: The Art of Leadership*. Ithaca, NY: Cornell University Press.

Bagdikian, Ben H. 1990. *The Media Monopoly*. Third edition. Boston: Beacon Press.

Barber, B. J. 1984. *Strong Democracy: Participating Politics for a New Age*. Berkeley: University of California Press.

Barber, James David. 1972. *The Presidential Character: Predicting Performance in the White House*. Englewood Cliffs, NJ: Prentice-Hall. Third edition, 1985.

Barrett, Marvin. 1982. *Broadcast Journalism, 1979–1981*. New York: Everest.

Baudrillard, Jean. 1983. *In the Shadow of the Silent Majorities*. New York: Semiotext.

Baukus, R. A., J. G. Payne, and M. S. Reisler. 1985. Negative Polispots. In *Argument and Social Practice: Proceedings of the Fourth SCA/AFA Conference on Argumentation*, J. R. Cox, M. O. Sillars, and G. B. Walker, eds., 236–52. Annandale, VA: SCA.

Beckelhymer, Hunter. 1974. No Posturing in Borrowed Plumes. *Christian Century* 6 (February): 138–42.

Becker, Lawrence C. 1975. The Neglect of Virtue. *Ethics* 85 (January): 110–22.

———. 1986. *Reciprocity*. London: Routledge and Kegan Paul.

Becker, Samuel L. 1971. Rhetorical Studies for the Contemporary World. In *The Prospect of Rhetoric*, Lloyd Bitzer and Edwin Black, eds., 21–43. Englewood Cliffs, NJ: Prentice-Hall.

Beiner, Ronald. 1983. *Political Judgment*. Chicago: University of Chicago Press.

Bennett, W. Lance. 1977. The Ritualistic and Pragmatic Bases of Political Campaign Discourse. *Quarterly Journal of Speech* 63:219–38.

———. 1988. *News: The Politics of Illusion*. Second edition. New York: Longman.

———. 1989. Where Have All the Issues Gone? Explaining the Rhetorical Limits in American Elections. In *Spheres of Argument*, Bruce E. Gronbeck, ed., 128–35. Annandale, VA: Speech Communication Association.

Berkman, R., and L. W. Kitch. 1985. *Politics in the Media Age*. New York: McGraw-Hill.

Biagi, Shirley. 1990. *Media/Impact*. Belmont, CA: Wadsworth.

Bigsby, C. W., ed. 1984. *Approaches to Popular Culture*. Bowling Green, IN: Popular Press.

Birkhead, Douglas. 1989. An Ethics of Vision for Journalism. *Critical Studies in Mass Communication* 6 (September): 283–94.

Bittner, John. 1986. *Mass Communication*. Fourth edition. Englewood Cliffs, NJ: Prentice-Hall.

Bitzer, Lloyd F. 1981. Political Rhetoric. In *Handbook of Political Communication*, Dan D. Nimmo and Keith R. Sanders, eds., 225–48. Beverly Hills, CA: Sage.

Blumenthal, Sidney. 1980. *The Permanent Campaign: Inside the World of Elite Political Operatives*. Boston: Beacon Press.

Boot, William. 1989. Campaign 88: TV Overdoses on the Inside Dope. *Columbia Journalism Review*. 27 (January/February): 23–29.

Booth, Wayne C. 1988. *The Company We Keep: An Ethics of Fiction*. Berkeley: University of California Press.

Bormann, Ernest G. 1960. Ghostwriting and the Rhetorical Critic. *Quarterly Journal of Speech* 46:287–88.

———. 1961a. Ethics of Ghostwritten Speeches. *Quarterly Journal of Speech* 47:262–67.

———. 1961b. Ghostwriting Speeches—A Reply. *Quarterly Journal of Speech* 47:420–21.

———. 1972. Fantasy and Rhetorical Vision: The Rhetorical Criticism of Social Reality. *Quarterly Journal of Speech* 58:396–407.

Boyer, Peter J. 1988. *Who Killed CBS?* New York: Random House.

Boyne, Roy, and Scott Lash. 1984. Communicative Rationality and Desire. *Telos* 61:152–58.

Brandt, R. B. 1981. W. K. Frankena and the Ethics of Virtue. *Monist* 64 (July): 271–92.

Brigance, W. Norwood. 1956. Ghostwriting before Franklin D. Roosevelt and the Radio. *Today's Speech* 4:10–12.

Broder, David S. 1987. *Beyond the Front Page*. New York: Simon and Schuster.

Browne, Ray B. 1990. *Against Academia*. Bowling Green, IN: Popular Press.

Burke, Kenneth. 1968. Dramatism. In *International Encyclopedia of the Social Sciences*, vol. 7, 445–52. New York: Free Press.

Burke, Peter. 1978. *Popular Culture in Early Modern Europe*. New York: Harper & Row.

Cathcart, Robert S. 1978. Confrontation as a Rhetorical Form. *Southern Speech Communication Journal* 43:233–47.

———. 1980. Defining Social Movements by Their Rhetorical Form. *Central States Speech Journal* 31:267–73.

Caywood, C. L., and G. R. Laczniak. 1985. Unethical Political Advertising: Decision Considerations for Policy and Evaluation. In *Marketing Communications—Theory and Research*, M. J. Houston and R. J. Lutz, eds., 37–41. Chicago: American Marketing Association.

Chagall, David. 1981. *The New Kingmakers*. San Francisco: Harcourt Brace Jovanovich.

Charland, Maurice. 1990. Rehabilitating Rhetoric: Confronting Blindspots in Discourse and Social Theory. *Communication* 11:253–64.

Chesebro, James W. 1976. Political Communication. *Quarterly Journal of Speech* 62:289–300.

Christians, Clifford, Kim Rotzell, and Mark Fackler. 1987. *Media Ethics: Cases in Moral Reasonings*. Second edition. New York: Longman.

Clinger, J. H. 1987. The Clean Campaign Act of 1985: A Rational Solution to Negative Campaign Advertising Which the One Hundredth Congress Should Reconsider. *Journal of Law and Politics* 3, 4 (Spring, 1987): 727–48.

Cobb, Roger W., and Charles D. Elder. 1981. Communication and Public Policy. In *Handbook of Political Communication*, Dan D. Nimmo and Keith R. Sanders, eds., 391–416. Beverly Hills, CA: Sage.

Cochran, Clarke E. 1982. *Character, Community, and Politics*. University: University of Alabama Press.

Code, Lorraine. 1987. *Epistemic Responsibility*. Hanover, NH: University Press of New England.

Combs, James E. 1980. *Dimensions of Political Drama*. Santa Monica, CA: Good-year.

Condit, Celeste Michelle. 1987. Crafting Virtue: The Rhetorical Construction of Public Morality. *Quarterly Journal of Speech* 73:79–97.

Crichton, J. 1980. Morals and Ethics in Advertising. In *Ethics, Morality, and the Media*, L. Thayer, ed., 105–15. New York: Hastings House.

Crouse, Timothy. 1972. *The Boys on the Bus*. New York: Ballantine Books.

Cunningham, Stanley B. 1970. Does "Does Moral Philosophy Rest upon a Mistake?" Make an Even Greater Mistake? *The Monist* 54 (January): 86–99.

Cushman, Donald C., and David Dietrich. 1979. A Critical Reconstruction of Jurgen Habermas' Holistic Approach to Rhetoric as Social Philosophy. *Journal of the American Forensic Association* 16:128–37.

Dance, Frank E. X. 1973. Speech Communication: The Revealing Echo. In *Communication: Ethical and Moral Issues*, Lee Thayer, ed., 277–86. New York: Gordon and Breach.

Darnton, Robert. 1975. Writing News and Telling Stories. *Daedalus* 104:175–94.

Day, Dennis G. 1966. The Ethics of Democratic Debate. *Central States Speech Journal* 17:5–14.

DeGeorge, Richard T. 1986. *Business Ethics*. Second edition. New York: Macmillan.

Denton, Robert E., Jr., 1988. *The Primetime Presidency of Ronald Reagan*. New York: Praeger.

Denton, Robert E., Jr., and Gary C. Woodward. 1990. *Political Communication in America*. Second edition. New York: Praeger.

Devlin, L. Patrick. 1974. The Influences of Ghostwriting on Rhetorical Criticism. *Today's Speech* 22:7–12.

———. 1989. Contrasts in Presidential Campaign Commercials of 1988. *American Behavioral Scientist* 32:389–414.

Dewey, John. 1916. *Democracy and Education*. New York: Free Press.

———. 1954. *The Public and Its Problems*. Chicago: Swallow Press. Reprint of 1927 ed.

Diamond, E., and S. Bates. 1984. *The Spot*. Cambridge, MA: MIT Press.

Diamond, E., and A. Marin. 1989. Spots. *American Behavioral Scientist* 32:382–88.

Dionisopoulos, G. 1986. Corporate Advocacy Advertising. In *New Perspectives on Political Advertising*, L. Kaid, D. Nimmo, and K. R. Sanders, eds., 82–106. Carbondale: Southern Illinois University Press.

Druker, Peter. 1979. *Adventures of a Bystander*. New York: Harper & Row.

Duffy, Bernard K., and Mark Royden Winchell. 1989. "Speak the Speech I Pray You": The Practice and Perils of Literary and Oratorical Ghostwriting. *Southern Speech Communication Journal* 55:102–15.

Dundes, Alan. 1965. *The Story of Folklore*. Englewood Cliffs, NJ: Prentice-Hall.

Einhorn, Lois J. 1982. The Ghosts Unmasked: A Review of Literature on Speechwriting. *Communication Quarterly* 30:41–47.

———. 1988. The Ghosts Talk: Personal Interviews with Three Former Speechwriters. *Communication Quarterly* 36:94–108.

Ellerbee, Linda. 1987. *And So It Goes: Adventures in Television*. New York: Berkley Books.

Elstain, Jean. 1981. Democracy and the Qube Tube. *The Nation*, August 7, 108–10.

Entman, Robert. 1988. *Democracy Without Citizens*. New York: Oxford University Press.

Epstein, Edward Jay. 1974. *News from Nowhere*. New York: Vintage Books.

Erickson, Paul. 1985. *Reagan Speaks*. New York: New York University Press.

Farrell, Thomas B. 1986. Rhetorical Resemblance: Paradoxes of a Practical Art. *Quarterly Journal of Speech* 72:1–19.

Felknor, B. 1966. *Dirty Politics*. New York: W. W. Norton.

Ferrara, Alessandro. 1990. A Critique of Habermas' *Discursethik*. In *The Interpretation of Dialogue*, Tuillo Maranhao, ed., 303–37. Chicago: University of Chicago Press.

Fish, Duane R. 1989. Image and Issue in the Second Bush-Dukakis Debate: The Mediating Role of Values. In *Sphere of Argument*, Bruce E. Gronbeck, ed., 151–57. Annandale, VA: Speech Communication Association.

Fisher, Walter R. 1984. Narration as a Human Communication Paradigm: The Case of Public Moral Argument. *Communication Monographs* 51:1–22.

———. 1987. *Human Communication as Narration: Toward a Philosophy of Reason, Value, and Action*. Columbia: University of South Carolina Press.

Fishman, Mark. 1980. *Manufacturing the News*. Austin: University of Texas Press.

Fishwick, Marshall W. 1977. *Parameters of Popular Culture*. Bowling Green, IN: Popular Press.

———. 1985. *Seven Pillars of Popular Culture*. Westport, CT: Greenwood Press.

Foot, Phillipa. 1978. *Virtues and Vices and Other Essays in Moral Philosophy*. Oxford: Basil Blackwell.

Frankena, William K. 1970. Pritchard and the Ethics of Virtue. *Monist* 54 (January): 1–17.

Fraser, Nancy. 1986. Toward a Discourse Ethic of Solidarity. *Praxis International* 5:425–29.

———. 1989. *Unruly Practices: Power, Discourse and Gender in Contemporary Social Theory*. Minneapolis: University of Minnesota Press.

French, Peter A., Theodore Uehling, Jr., and Howard K. Wettstein, eds., 1988. *Midwest Studies in Philosophy*, vol. 13, *Ethical Theory—Character and Virtue*. Notre Dame, IN: University of Notre Dame Press.

Frenkel, K. 1989a. Computing as a Political Force. *Personal Computing*, October, 99–106.

———. 1989b. The New Breed of Campaign Manager. *Personal Computing*, October, 198–210.

Frentz, Thomas S. 1985. Rhetorical Conversation, Time, and Moral Action. *Quarterly Journal of Speech* 71:1–18.

Gans, Herbert J. 1980. *Deciding What's News: A Study of CBS Evening News, NBC Nightly News, Newsweek and Time*. New York: Vintage Books.

Garramone, G. M. 1984. Voter Responses to Negative Political Advertising. *Journalism Quarterly* 61:250–59.

Garramone, G. M., C. K. Atkin, B. Pinkleton, and R. T. Cole. 1990. Effects of Negative Political Advertising on the Political Process. *Journal of Broadcasting and Electronic Media* 34:299–311.

Garver, Peter. 1977. *The Virtues*. Cambridge: Cambridge University Press.

Goldstein, Tom. 1985. *The News at Any Cost*. New York: Simon and Schuster.

Gomber, Mary Anne, and Robert S. Moyne. 1986. *The Newsmongers: How the Media Distort Political News*. Toronto: McClelland and Stewart.

Gonchar, Ruth, and Dan Hahn. 1973. Rhetorical Biography: A Methodology for the Citizen-Critic. *Speech Teacher* 22 (January): 48–53.

Goodin, R. E. 1980. *Manipulatory Politics*. New Haven: Yale University Press.

Graber, Doris. 1989. *Mass Media and American Politics*. Third edition. Washington, DC: Congressional Quarterly Press.

Graham, Fred. 1990. *Happy Talk: Confessions of a TV Newsman*. New York: W. W. Norton.

Green, Mark, and Gail MacColl. 1987. *Reagan's Reign of Error*. Revised and enlarged edition. New York: Pantheon Books.

Greenfield, Jeff. 1986. Ethics: For Wimps Only? In *Journalism Ethics: Why Change?*, Doug Ramsey and Dale Shaps, eds., 48–53. Los Angeles: Foundation for American Communication.

Gregg, Richard B. 1989. The Rhetoric of Denial and Alternity. In *American Rhetoric: Context and Criticism*, Thomas W. Benson, ed., 385–417. Carbondale: Southern Illinois University Press.

Gronbeck, Bruce E. 1985. The Presidential Campaign Dramas of 1984. *Presidential Studies Quarterly* 15:386–93.

———. 1987. Functions of Campaigns. In *Political Persuasion in Presidential Campaigns*, L. Patrick Devlin, ed., 137–58. New Brunswick, NJ: Transaction Books.

———. 1989a. Mythic Portraiture in the 1988 Iowa Presidential Caucus Bio-Ads. *American Behavioral Scientist* 32:351–64.

———. 1989b. Electric Rhetoric: The Remaking of American Presidential Campaigns. In *Conference in Rhetorical Criticism 1989*, John Hammerback and Karen L. Fritts, eds. Hayward: Department of Speech Communication, California State University, Hayward.

Gross, Larry. 1988. The Ethics of (Mis)representation. In *Image Ethics: The Moral Rights of Subjects in Photographs, Film and Television*, Larry Gross, John Stuart Katz, and Jay Ruby, eds., 188–202. New York: Oxford University Press.

Grossman, Michael Baruch, and Martha Joynt Kumar. 1981. *Portraying the President: The White House and the News Media*. Baltimore: Johns Hopkins University Press.

Habermas, Jurgen. 1970. Towards a Theory of Communicative Competence. In *Recent Sociology #2*, Hans Peter Dreitzel, ed., 114–48. London: Collier Macmillan.

———. 1971. *Knowledge and Human Interest*. Trans. Jeremy Shapiro. Boston: Beacon Press.

———. 1975. *Legitimation Crisis*. Trans. Thomas McCarthy. Boston: Beacon Press.

———. 1976. Some Distinctions in Universal Pragmatics. *Theory and Society* 3:155–67.

———. 1979. *Communication and the Evolution of Society*. Trans. Thomas McCarthy. Boston: Beacon Press.

———. 1981. Modernity Versus Postmodernity. *New German Critique* 22:3–14.

————. 1985. Questions and Counterquestions. In *Habermas and Modernity*, R. J. Bernstein, ed. Cambridge, MA: MIT Press.

Hackett, Robert A. 1984. Decline of a Paradigm?: Bias and Objectivity in News Media Studies. *Critical Studies in Mass Communication* 1:229–59.

Hahn, Dan, and Ruth Gonchar. 1972. Political Myth: The Image and the Issue. *Today's Speech* 20 (Summer): 57–65.

Haiman, Franklyn S. 1958. Democratic Ethics and the Hidden Persuaders. *Quarterly Journal of Speech* 44:385–92.

Hannaford, I. 1972. Machiavelli's Concept of Virtù in *The Prince* and *The Discourses* Reconsidered. *Political Studies* 20 (June): 185–89.

Hariman, Robert. 1989. Before Prudence: Strategy and the Rhetorical Tradition. In *Spheres of Argument*, Bruce E. Gronbeck, ed., 108–16. Annandale, VA: Speech Communication Association.

Hart, Roderick. 1984. *Verbal Style and the Presidency*. Orlando, FL: Academic Press.

————. 1987. *The Sound of Leadership*. Chicago: University of Chicago Press.

Hauerwas, Stanley. 1977. *Truthfulness and Tragedy*. Notre Dame, IN: University of Notre Dame Press.

————. 1981a. *A Community of Character: Toward a Constructive Christian Social Ethic*. Notre Dame, IN: University of Notre Dame Press.

————. 1981b. *Vision and Virtue*. Notre Dame, IN: University of Notre Dame Press.

Hauser, Gerard A. 1989. Administrative Rhetoric and Public Opinion: Discussing the Iranian Hostages in the Public Sphere. In *American Rhetoric: Context and Criticism*, Thomas W. Benson, ed., 323–84. Carbondale: Southern Illinois University Press.

Herman, Edward S., and Noam Chomsky. 1988. *Manufacturing Consent: The Political Economy of the Mass Media*. New York: Pantheon.

Hertsgaard, Mark. 1989. *On Bended Knee: The Press and the Reagan Presidency*. New York: Schocken.

Hiebert, Ray, Donald Ungurait, and Thomas Bohn. 1988. *Mass Media V*. New York: Longman.

Hill, R. P. 1989. An Exploration of Voter Responses to Political Advertisements. *Journal of Advertising* 18(4):14–22.

Hirschfield, Charles. 1980. *The Modern World*. New York: Harcourt Brace Jovanovich.

Hoff, Paul S., and K. Bernstein. 1988. *Congress and the Media: Beyond the 30-Second Spot*. Washington, DC: Center for Responsive Politics.

Holsinger, Ralph L. 1987. *Media Law*. New York: Random House.

Homer, Frederic D. 1983. *Character: An Individualistic Theory of Politics*. Lanham, MD: University Press of America.

Hulteng, John. 1985. *The Messenger's Motives: Ethical Problems of the News Media*. Englewood Cliffs, NJ: Prentice-Hall.

Ingram, David. 1982. The Possibility of a Communication Ethic Reconsidered. *Man and the World* 15:149–61.

Innis, Harold. 1964. *The Bias of Communication*. Revised edition. Toronto: University of Toronto Press.

————. 1972. *Empire and Communication*. Revised edition. Toronto: University of Toronto Press.

Iyengar, Shanto, and Donald Kinder. 1987. *News That Matters*. Chicago: University of Chicago Press.

Jamieson, Kathleen Hall. 1984. *Packaging the Presidency: A History and Criticism of Presidential Campaign Advertising*. New York: Oxford University Press.

———. 1988. *Eloquence in an Electronic Age: The Transformation of Political Speechmaking*. New York: Oxford University Press.

Jeffres, Leo. 1986. *Mass Media*. Prospect Heights, IL: Waveland Press.

Jensen, J. Vernon. 1990. Directions to Consider in Communication Ethics. In *Proceedings of the First National Communication Ethics Conference*, 1–16. Hickory Corners, MI: Kellogg Biological Station Educational Center on Gull Lake.

Johannesen, Richard L. 1985. An Ethical Assessment of Reagan Rhetoric: 1981–1982. In *Political Communication Yearbook, 1984*, Keith R. Sanders, Lynda Lee Kaid, and Dan Nimmo, eds., 226–41. Carbondale: Southern Illinois University Press.

———. 1990. *Ethics in Human Communication*. Third edition. Prospect Heights, IL: Waveland Press.

Jonas, F. H., ed. 1970. *Political Dynamiting*. Salt Lake City: University of Utah Press.

Jonsen, Albert R., and Stephen Toulmin. 1988. *The Abuse of Casuistry: A History of Moral Reasoning*. Berkeley: University of California Press.

Joslyn, Richard A. 1980. The Content of Political Spot Ads. *Journalism Quarterly* 57:92–98.

———. 1986a. Keeping Politics in the Study of Political Discourse. In *Form, Genre, and the Study of Political Discourse*, Herbert W. Simons and Aram A. Aghazarian, eds., 301–38. Columbia: University of South Carolina Press.

———. 1986b. Political Advertising and the Meaning of Elections. In *New Perspectives on Political Advertising*, Lynda Kaid, Dan Nimmo, and Keith Sanders, eds., 139–83. Carbondale: Southern Illinois University Press.

Kaid, Lynda, and Dorothy Davidson. 1986. Elements of Videostyle. In *New Perspectives on Political Advertising*, Lynda Kaid, Dan Nimmo, and Keith Sanders, eds., 184–209. Carbondale: Southern Illinois University Press.

Kaid, Lynda, and Keith Sanders. 1978. Political Television Commercials: An Experimental Study of Type and Length. *Communication Research* 5:57–70.

Kellner, Douglas. 1988. Postmodernism as Social Theory: Some Challenges and Problems. *Theory, Culture, and Society* 5:239–69.

Kern, Montague. 1989. *30-Second Politics*. New York: Praeger.

Kernell, Samuel. 1986. *Going Public*. Washington, DC: Congressional Quarterly Press.

Klaidman, Stephen, and Tom L. Beauchamp. 1987. *The Virtuous Journalist*. New York: Oxford University Press.

Kolenda, Konstantin, ed. 1988. *Organizations and Ethical Individualism*. New York: Praeger.

Kruger, Arthur N. 1967. The Ethics of Persuasion: A Re-examination. *The Speech Teacher* 16:295–305.

Kupfer, Joseph. 1982. The Moral Presumption Against Lying. *Review of Metaphysics* 36 (September): 103–26.

Kupperman, Joel. 1988. Character and Ethical Theory. In *Midwest Studies in*

Philosophy, vol. 13, *Ethical Theory: Character and Virtue*, Peter French, Theodore Uehling, Jr., and Howard K. Wettstein, eds., 115–25. Notre Dame, IN: University of Notre Dame Press.

Lanigan, Richard L., and Rudolf L. Strobl. 1981. A Critical Theory Approach. In *Handbook of Political Communication*, Dan D. Nimmo and Keith R. Sanders, eds., 141–68. Beverly Hills, CA: Sage.

Lasch, Christopher, 1979. *The Cult of Narcissism: American Life in an Age of Diminishing Expectations*. New York: W. W. Norton.

Lebacqz, Karen. 1985. *Professional Ethics*. Nashville, TN: Abingdon Press.

Levin, Martin. 1980. A Call for a Politics of Institutions, Not Men. In *The Post-Imperial Presidency*, Vincent Davis, ed. New York: Praeger.

Lichter, S. Robert, Daniel Amundson, and Richard Noyes. 1988. *The Video Campaign: Network Coverage of the 1988 Primaries*. Washington, DC: American Enterprise Institute.

Lilla, Mark T. 1981. Ethos, "Ethics," and Public Service. *The Public Interest* 63(Spring): 3–17.

Lippmann, Walter. 1965. *Public Opinion*. New York: Free Press.

Lowi, Theodore. 1985. *The Personal President*. Ithaca, NY: Cornell University Press.

Lucaites, John Louis. 1990. A Rhetorical Response: Or Towards a Rhetorical Consciousness of "Politics" in the Realms of Culture and the Public. *Communication* 12:49–64.

Lyotard, Jean-Francois. 1984. *The Postmodern Condition: A Report on Knowledge*. Trans. Geoff Bennington and Brian Massami. Minneapolis: University of Minnesota Press.

MacIntyre, Alasdair. 1984. *After Virtue*. Second edition. Notre Dame, IN: University of Notre Dame Press.

MacNeil, Robert. 1968. *The People Machine: The Influence of Television on American Politics*. New York: Harper & Row.

Manheim, Jorol. 1984. Can Democracy Survive Television? In *Media Power in Politics*, Doris Graber, ed. Washington, DC: Congressional Quarterly Press.

Marchand, Philip. 1989. *Marshall McLuhan: The Medium and the Messenger*. New York: Knopf.

Mayo, Bernard. 1958. *Ethics and the Moral Life*. London: Macmillan.

McGee, Michael. 1978. "Not Men, but Measures": The Origins and Import of an Ideological Principle. *Quarterly Journal of Speech* 64 (April):141–54.

———. 1985. 1984: Some Issues in the Rhetorical Study of Political Communication. In *Political Communication Yearbook 1984*, Keith R. Sanders, Lynda Lee Kaid, and Dan Nimmo, eds., 155–82. Carbondale: Southern Illinois University Press.

McGlon, Charles A. 1954. How I Prepare My Sermons: A Symposium. *Quarterly Journal of Speech* 40:49–62.

McGovern, George. 1984. George McGovern: The Target Talks Back. *Columbia Journalism Review* 22 (July–August):27–31.

McLuhan, Marshall. 1964. *Understanding Media*. New York: New American Library.

———. 1967. *The Medium Is the Message*. New York: Bantam Books.

Medhurst, Martin J. 1987. Ghostwritten Speeches: Ethics Isn't the Only Lesson. *Communication Education* 36:241–49.

Meilaender, Gilbert C. 1984. *The Theory and Practice of Virtue*. Notre Dame, IN: University of Notre Dame Press.

Merritt, S. 1984. Negative Political Advertising: Some Empirical Findings. *Journal of Advertising* 13:27–38.

Meyrowitz, Joshua. 1985. *No Sense of Place*. New York: Oxford University Press.

Michell, Gillian. 1984. Women and Lying: A Pragmatic and Semantic Analysis of "Telling It Slant." *Women's Studies International Forum* 7:375–83.

Mickelson, Sig. 1989. *From Whistle Stop to Sound Bite: Four Decades of Politics and Television*. New York: Praeger.

Miller, Arthur H., Martin P. Wattenberg, and Oksana Malanchuk. 1985. Cognitive Representations of Candidate Assessments. In *Political Communication Yearbook 1984*, Keith R. Sanders, Lynda Lee Kaid, and Dan Nimmo, eds., 183–210. Carbondale: Southern Illinois University Press.

Miller, Mark Crispin. 1988. *Boxed in: The Culture of TV*. Evanston, IL: Northwestern University Press.

Minnick, Elizabeth. 1985. Why Not Lie? *Soundings* 68 (Winter):493–509.

Minow, Newton. 1964. The Vast Wasteland. In *Reason in Controversy*, Glen E. Mills, ed., 271–82. Boston: Allyn and Bacon.

Minow, Newton, John Bartlow Martin, and Lee M. Mitchell. 1973. *Presidential Television*. New York: Basic Books.

Mitroff, I., and W. Bennis. 1989. *The Unreality Industry*. New York: Carol Publishing Group.

Murphy, John, and Karen Callaghan. 1988. Postmodernism and Social Research: An Application. *Social Epistemology* 2:83–91.

Naisbitt, John. 1982. *Megatrends*. New York: Warner Books.

Newman, Robert P. 1966. The Weekly Fiction Magazines. *Central States Speech Journal* 17:118–24.

Nilsen, Thomas R. 1974. *Ethics of Speech Communication*. Second edition. Indianapolis: Bobbs-Merrill.

Nimmo, Dan. 1989. Episodes, Incidents, and Eruptions. *American Behavioral Scientist* 32:464–78.

Nimmo, Dan, and James E. Combs. 1980. *Subliminal Politics: Myths & Mythmakers in America*. Englewood Cliffs, NJ: Prentice-Hall.

———. 1983. *Mediated Political Realities*. New York: Longman.

———. 1985. *Nightly Horrors: Crisis Coverage in Television Network News*. Knoxville: University of Tennessee Press.

Noddings, Nel. 1984. *Caring: A Feminine Approach to Ethics and Moral Education*. Berkeley: University of California Press.

Noonan, Peggy. 1990. *What I Saw at the Revolution: A Political Life in the Reagan Era*. New York: Random House.

O'Leary, Stephen D. 1989. Machiavelli and the Paradox of Political Hypocrisy: The Fragmentation of Virtue in the Public and Private Spheres. In *Spheres of Argument*, Bruce E. Gronbeck, ed., 117–27. Annandale, VA: Speech Communication Association.

Oliver, Robert T. 1962. Syngman Rhee: A Case Study in Transnational Oratory. *Quarterly Journal of Speech* 48:115–27.

Paletz, David L., and Robert M. Entman. 1981. *Media Power Politics*. New York: Free Press.

Palmour, Jody. 1987. *On Moral Character: A Practical Guide to Aristotle's Virtues and Vices*. Washington, DC: Archon Institution for Leadership Development.

Pinckaers, Servais. 1962. Virtue Is Not a Habit. *Cross Currents* 12(Winter): 65–81.

Pincoffs, Edmund L. 1986. *Quandaries and Virtues: Against Reductivism in Ethics*. Lawrence: University of Kansas Press.

Pomper, Gerald, Ross Baker, Charles Jacob, Scott Keeter, Wilson McWilliams, and Henry Plotkins. 1985. *The Election of 1984*. Chatham, NJ: Chatham House.

Rabinow, Paul, ed. 1984. *The Foucault Reader*. New York: Pantheon Books.

Rajchman, John. 1986. Ethics After Foucault. *Social Text* 13/14:165–83.

Reagan, Ronald, and Richard Huber. 1981. *Where's the Rest of Me?* New York: Dell.

Reedy, George. 1970. *The Twilight of the Presidency*. New York: World Publishing.

Reeves, Richard. 1985. *The Reagan Detour*. New York: Simon and Schuster.

Regan, R. J., Jr. 1986. *The Moral Dimensions of Politics*. New York: Oxford University Press.

Reid, Herbert G., and Ernest J. Yanarella. 1974. Toward a Postmodern Theory of American Political Science and Culture: Perspectives from Critical Marxism and Phenomenology. *Cultural Hermeneutics* 2:91–166.

Richters, Annemeik. 1988. Modernity-Postmodernity Controversies: Habermas and Foucault. *Theory, Culture, and Society* 5:611–43.

Robinson, Michael, and A. Ranney, eds. 1985. *The Mass Media in Campaign '84*. Washington, DC: American Enterprise Institute for Public Policy Research.

Robinson, Michael, and Margaret Sheehan. 1983. *Over the Wire and on TV*. New York: Russell Sage Foundation.

Rockman, Bert. 1984. *The Leadership Question*. New York: Praeger.

Roddy, B. L., and G. M. Garramone. 1988. Appeals and Strategies of Negative Political Advertising. *Journal of Broadcasting and Electronic Media* 32:415–27.

Rogge, Edward. 1959. Evaluating the Ethics of a Speaker in a Democracy. *Quarterly Journal of Speech* 45:419–25.

Rogin, Michael. 1987. *Ronald Reagan, the Movie*. Berkeley: University of California Press.

Rogin, Michael Paul. 1967. *The Intellectuals and McCarthy: The Radical Spectre*. Cambridge, MA: MIT Press.

Rooney, Andy. 1984. The Journalist's Code of Ethics. In *Pieces of My Mind*. New York: Atheneum.

Rorty, Amelie Oksenberg, ed. 1980. *Essays on Aristotle's Ethics*. Berkeley: University of California Press.

Rotzell, Kim, James Haefner, and Charles Sandage. 1986. *Advertising in Contemporary Society*. Cincinnati: South-Western.

Sabato, Larry J. 1981. *The Rise of Political Consultants*. New York: Basic Books.

———. 1984. *PAC Power*. New York: W. W. Norton.

Safire, William. 1968. *The New Language of Politics*. New York: Random House.

Sanford, Terry. 1981. *A Danger of Democracy*. Boulder, CO: Westview Press.

Schaeffer, John D. 1990. *Sensus Communis: Vico, Rhetoric, and the Limits of Relativism*. Durham, NC: Duke University Press.

Schlesinger, Arthur. 1973. *The Imperial Presidency*. Boston: Houghton Mifflin.

Schneiders, Greg. 1985. The 90 Second Handicap: Why TV Coverage of Legislation Falls Short. *Washington Journalism Review* 7:44–46.

Schram, Martin. 1987. *The Great American Video Game*. New York: William Morrow.

Schwartz, Tony. 1973. *The Responsive Chord*. New York: Anchor Books/Doubleday.

———. 1983. *Media: The Second God*. New York: Anchor Books/Doubleday.

Scott, William G., and Terence R. Mitchell. 1988. The Problem or Mystery of Evil and Virtue in Organizations. In *Organizations and Ethical Individualism*, Konstantin Kolenda, ed., 47–72. New York: Praeger.

Segar, Matthew W. 1985. Ghostbusting: Exorcising the Great Man Spirit from the Speechwriting Debate. *Communication Education* 34:353–58.

Sennett, Richard. 1977. *The Fall of Public Man*. New York: Knopf.

Sheehy, Gail. 1988. *Character: America's Search for Leadership*. New York: William Morrow.

Shusterman, Richard. 1988. Postmodernist Aestheticism: A New Moral Philosophy? *Theory, Culture, and Society* 5:337–55.

Sichel, Betty A. 1988. *Moral Education: Character, Community, and Ideals*. Philadelphia: Temple University Press.

Simon, Yves R. 1986. *The Definition of Moral Virtue*. New York: Fordham University Press.

Slote, Michael. 1983. *Goods and Virtues*. New York: Oxford University Press.

Smith, Anthony. 1980. *Goodbye Gutenberg*. New York: Oxford University Press.

Smith, Craig R. 1976. Contemporary Political Speech Writing. *Southern Speech Communication Journal* 42:52–67.

———. 1977a. Appendum to "Contemporary Political Speech Writing." *Southern Speech Communication Journal* 42:191–94.

———. 1977b. Television News as Rhetoric. *Western Journal of Speech Communication* 41:147–59.

———. 1989. *Freedom of Expression and Partisan Politics*. Columbia: University of South Carolina Press.

Smith, Donald K. 1961. Ghostwritten Speech. *Quarterly Journal of Speech* 47:416–20.

Smith, Hedrick. 1988. *The Power Game*. New York: Ballantine Books.

Sommers, Christina Hoff. 1984. Ethics Without Virtue. *The American Scholar* 53(Summer):381–89.

———. ed. 1985. *Vice and Virtue in Everyday Life*. New York: Harcourt Brace Jovanovich.

Spero, R. 1980. *The Duping of the American Voter*. New York: Lippincott & Crowell.

Sperry, Sharon Lynn. 1981. Television News as Narrative. In *Understanding Television: Essays on Television as a Cultural Force*, Richard P. Adler, ed., 295–312. New York: Praeger.

Streitmatter, Rodger. 1985. The Impact of Presidential Personality on News Coverage in Major Newspapers. *Journalism Quarterly* 62, 1(Spring):66–73.

Stuckey, Mary. 1990. *Playing the Game: The Presidential Rhetoric of Ronald Reagan*. New York: Praeger.

Surlin, S., and T. Gordon. 1976. Selective Exposure and Retention of Political Advertising. *Journal of Advertising Research* 5:32–44.

Susman, Warren I. 1984. *Culture as History*. New York: Pantheon Books.

Swain, Bruce. 1978. *Reporters' Ethics*. Ames: Iowa State University Press.

Tarrance, V. L. 1980. *Negative Campaigns and Negative Votes*. Washington, DC: Free Congress Research and Education Foundation.

Tarver, Jerry. 1982. *Professional Speech Writing*. Richmond, VA: The Effective Speech Writing Institute.

Thompson, Dennis F. 1987. *Political Ethics and Public Office*. Cambridge, MA: Harvard University Press.

Toffler, Alvin. 1980. *The Third Wave*. New York: Bantam Books.

Trent, Judith S., and Robert V. Friedenberg. 1983. *Political Campaign Communication: Principles and Practices*. New York: Praeger.

Tuchman, Gaye. 1978. *Making News: A Study in the Construction of Reality*. New York: Free Press.

Tulis, Jeffrey. 1987. *The Rhetorical Presidency*. Princeton, NJ: Princeton University Press.

Van Hooft, Stan. 1976. Habermas' Communicative Ethics. *Social Praxis* 4:147–75.

Wallace, James D. 1978. *Virtues and Vices*. Ithaca, NY: Cornell University Press.

Wallace, Karl R. 1955. An Ethical Basis of Communication. *The Speech Teacher* 6:1–9.

Walton, Clarence C. 1988. *The Moral Manager*. Cambridge, MA: Ballinger.

Wander, Philip. 1981. Cultural Criticism. In *Handbook of Political Communication*, Dan Nimmo and Keith R. Sanders, eds., 497–528. Beverly Hills, CA: Sage.

———. 1984. The Ideological Turn in Modern Criticism. *Central States Speech Journal* 34:1–18.

———. 1990. The Politics of Despair. *Communication* 11:227–90.

Wayne, Stephan. 1984. *The Road to the White House*, Second edition. New York: St. Martin's Press.

Weigert, Andrew J. 1970. The Immoral Rhetoric of Scientific Sociology. *The American Sociologist* 5:111–19.

Weiner, Norbert. 1960. *The Human Use of Human Beings*. New York: Doubleday.

Westin, Av. 1982. *News-Watch: How TV Decides the News*. New York: Simon and Schuster.

White, Hayden. 1981. The Value of Narrativity in the Representation of Reality. In *On Narrative*, W. J. T. Mitchell, ed., 1–24. Chicago: University of Chicago Press.

Wicker, Tom. 1978. *On Press*. New York: Viking Press.

Williams, Bernard. 1981. *Moral Luck*. Cambridge: Cambridge University Press.

Wills, Garry. 1987. *Reagan's America*. New York: Doubleday.

Winsbro, J. 1987. Misrepresentation in Political Advertising: The Role of Legal Sanctions. *Emory Law Journal* 36:853–916.

Wood, Neil. 1967. Machiavelli's Concept of Virtù Reconsidered. *Political Studies* 15(June):159–72.

Index

About the Contributors

MARTHA COOPER is Associate Professor and Director of Graduate Studies in the Department of Communication Studies at Northern Illinois University. She is author of *Analyzing Public Discourse* and has published essays relating to contemporary rhetorical theory, rhetorical criticism, and political communication.

ROBERT E. DENTON, JR., is Head of the Department of Communication Studies at Virginia Polytechnic Institute and State University. He is author of several books, including *The Primetime Presidency of Ronald Reagan*, *Political Communication in America*, second edition (with Gary Woodward), and *Presidential Communication* (with Dan Hahn). Denton serves as associate editor of *Presidential Studies Quarterly* and as editor for the Praeger Series in Political Communication.

LOIS EINHORN is Associate Professor in the Department of English, General Literature, and Rhetoric at the State University of New York at Binghamton. She has published numerous articles in a variety of communication journals.

MARSHALL W. FISHWICK is Professor of Communication Studies and Humanities at Virginia Polytechnic Institute and State University. He is the author of over twenty books, including *Common Culture and the Great Tradition; Symbolism; Symbiosis; The Hero in Tradition;* and *The Hero: American Style*. He also serves as editor of *International Popular Culture* and as advisory editor for the *Journal of Popular Culture* and the *Journal of Amer-*

ican Culture. He is currently completing a book entitled *Go and Watch a Falling Star: The Puzzle of Popularity.*

BRUCE E. GRONBECK is Professor and Chair of the Department of Communication Studies at the University of Iowa. He teaches and writes in the areas of presidential rhetoric, television, popular culture, and rhetorical criticism. In addition to numerous articles and book chapters, Gronbeck is author of *Writing Television Criticism,* coauthor of *Principles of Speech Communication* and *Principles and Types of Speech Communication,* and editor of *The Spheres of Argument* and the forthcoming *Media, Consciousness, and Culture.*

RICHARD L. JOHANNESEN is Chair and Professor in the Department of Communication Studies at Northern Illinois University. In addition to numerous articles and book chapters, he is author of *Ethics in Human Communication,* third edition, editor of *Ethics and Persuasion,* and coeditor of *Contemporary American Speeches,* sixth edition. His essay assessing the ethicality of President Reagan's rhetoric appeared in *Political Communication Yearbook 1984.*

LYNDA LEE KAID is Professor of Communication at the University of Oklahoma. She is founder of the University of Oklahoma Political Communication Center and directs the Cataloging Project for the Political Commercial Archive. She is coauthor of *Political Campaign Communication: A Bibliography and Guide to the Literature* and coeditor of *New Perspectives on Political Advertising, Political Communication Yearbook 1984,* and *Mediated Politics in Two Cultures.*

GARY W. SELNOW is a consultant with the National Academy of Sciences. In addition to numerous articles and book chapters, he is author of *Planning, Implementing, and Evaluating Specialized Communication Programs: A Manual for Business Communicators* (with William Crano) and *Television Content: Processes and Analyses.*

GARY C. WOODWARD is Associate Professor in the Department of Speech, Communication and Theatre Arts at Trenton State College in New Jersey. In addition to numerous articles in the areas of communication and rhetorical theory, he is the author of *Persuasive Encounters: Case Studies in Constructive Confrontation* and coauthor (with Robert E. Denton, Jr.) of *Political Communication in America* and of *Persuasion and Influence in American Life.*